our COMMUNITIES, *our* HOMES

Pathways to Housing and Homeownership in America's Cities and States

HENRY G. CISNEROS   JACK F. KEMP

NICOLAS P. RETSINAS   KENT W. COLTON

Library of Congress Control Number: 2007933540

ISBN 0-9761481-1-0

CONTENTS

PREFACE

Home defines who we are and prepares us for all we can be.

Home should be a source of joy. But for too many people, poor living conditions or the loss of a home engender sorrow.

Home should provide a respite from life's hardships. But for too many households, crushing housing costs leave little for other necessities, heightening stress and magnifying problems.

Home should lay the platform for meeting life's challenges. But for too many children, economic isolation or unstable housing stunts achievement and breeds despair.

Home should furnish the stage for a rich family life and strong communities. But for too many parents, multiple jobs or long commutes consume time and energy, leaving little for helping children with homework or cheering on the youth soccer league.

Home at the very least should be shelter from cold and protection from predation. But for the least among us, home is a heating grate or a tarp in the park.

It should not be this way.

Our firm, shared belief in the potential to better the lives of American families by improving the nation's housing policies first brought us together several years ago. We sought to push housing higher on the national agenda so that more people could experience the hope and vitality conferred by stable, safe homes. In 2004, we published *Opportunity and Progress: A Bipartisan Platform for National Housing Policy.* With its emphasis on affordable housing as a critical American value shared across the political spectrum, the book struck a chord and attracted significant interest.

Our bipartisan national housing agenda won the 2005 Common Ground Award from Search for Common Ground, the world's largest nongovernmental organization dedicated to conflict resolution. National policymakers have taken some steps toward addressing our 12 recommendations to preserve, expand, or reform housing programs. Federal policy advances include legislation to sustain homelessness funding, proposals to bring more stability to voucher funding and curb predatory lending, progress toward reforming congressionally chartered home mortgage investors, and keeping alive the HOPE VI program that supports the transformation of distressed public housing sites.

But the affordable housing crisis continues to escalate. The urgency of the problem calls for immediate action by local and state leaders. Indeed, much of the success in addressing housing challenges must come at the local government level, supported and inspired by state action and resources. This guide to state and local housing strategies is meant for those leaders who are serious about preserving the vitality of their economies, communities, and families.

ACKNOWLEDGMENTS

The blending of diverse perspectives and so many examples into a cohesive action plan benefited greatly from the exceptional talents of Lora Engdahl. Her full partnership in this endeavor proved invaluable, as she brought to the project a refreshing inquisitiveness, keen judgment, and special ability to see the "trees" as well as the "forest."

We would also like to thank Freddie Mac, Kimball Hill Homes, and the National Housing Endowment—the sponsors without whom this project would not have been possible. We also acknowledge the support of CityView and the Federal Home Loan Bank of New York in disseminating our work. Although the authors take full responsibility for content, our sponsors provided critical resources to research and publish this guidebook.

Assembling information on successful housing strategies in communities across the country also required the cooperation of hundreds of individuals who provided information on their programs and research and then helped us review our facts prior to publication. While it would be impossible to cite all of our sources, we are pleased to be able to spread the word about their work and we thank them for their assistance.

We do want to recognize by name the following individuals who generously shared their time and expertise to help us flesh out our recommendations and provided thoughtful feedback on particular sections of the book:

Michael Allen	Deb Gross	Nan Roman
Peter Beard	Kathleen Keest	Barbara Sard
Tom Bledsoe	Heidi Li	Debra Schwartz
Michael Bodaken	Jeffrey Lubell	Robin Snyderman
Paul Bradley	Beth Marcus	Rod Solomon
Mary E. Brooks	Zixta Q. Martinez	Deidre Swesnik
Sheila Crowley	Chris Nelson	Steve Tuminaro
Mary Cunningham	Craig Nickerson	Margery Austin Turner
Doug Dylla	Matt Perrenod	Chuck Wehrwein
Conrad Egan	Sara Pratt	Jim Wheaton
David Engel	Elizabeth A. Renuart	Carol Wilkins
Rick Gentry	Garth B. Rieman	Sunia Zaterman

At the Joint Center for Housing Studies, Elizabeth England, Angela Flynn, Meg Nipson, Laurel Trayes and Abbe Will deserve special thanks for their hard work and dedication to the project. In addition, we acknowledge with appreciation the incisive and insightful contributions of our editor/designer team Marcia Fernald and John Skurchak.

INTRODUCTION

Housing Matters

Housing is essential to solid families, good neighborhoods, and strong cities and states. It is a critical element of the local infrastructure, along with roads, schools, and courts.

Stable, affordable housing improves educational outcomes for children and helps adults get and keep jobs. Attainable housing near employment reduces traffic and increases family time. Affordable homeownership provides one of the most effective means for building assets, helping to create and sustain the middle classes that are the bedrock of communities.

Housing is also the most durable form of economic development. Housing can support rebirth in cities once steeped in industrial uses that are looking for a new future. Affordable housing shelters the workers essential to a community's hospitals, schools, retail establishments, public and nonprofit agencies, and businesses.

In some ways, Americans today are better housed than ever before, with higher rates of homeownership and less overt discrimination. But in other ways, housing conditions for many Americans are much worse.

About 17 million low- and middle-income households are straining under the weight of severe housing cost burdens. An estimated 744,000 people are homeless at any given time. Low-income older Americans who are able to get on waiting lists for a limited supply of subsidized senior housing must wait more than a year to move in.[1]

Housing costs are not just a problem for poor and nonworking Americans. Labor shortages and long commutes caused in part by a lack of workforce housing are hurting economic growth in our cities and our states.

Although the surge in home sale prices of the last few years has abated, homeownership and rental housing is still out of reach for many average working people. In many communities across the country, the wage a household must earn to afford rental housing is two, three, and even four times the minimum wage. That means people in lower-paid occupations, from nursing aides to janitors to retail salespeople, are unable to find decent apartments that they can afford.[2]

Families once considered solidly in the middle class and thus within reach of homeownership are also struggling. A January 2007 study by the Center for Housing Policy found that teachers, police officers, and licensed practical nurses do not earn nearly enough to afford a median-priced home in more than 150 of over 200 metropolitan areas surveyed. Even higher-paid registered nurses are priced out of homeownership in 115 areas.

More and more homebuyers are bridging the gap between their incomes and escalating home prices with risky mortgage products that may preclude building home equity or, worse, lead to foreclosure. In 2006, more than 1.2 million foreclosure filings were reported nationwide, equivalent to one for every 92 households.[3]

THE GROWING CHALLENGE OF UNAFFORDABILITY

From West to East coasts and points in between, leaders are starting to refer to the confluence of the problems relating to the unaffordability of housing.

In his inaugural address, New York Governor Eliot Spitzer talked about the "perfect storm of unaffordability" threatening New York's competitiveness. It costs businesses and people too much to live and work in the state, he asserted. He committed to revitalizing the state's economy in part through investing in infrastructure, which he said means housing.

In Massachusetts, where the labor force has been shrinking in part because of unaffordability, housing has been elevated to a cabinet-level position in state government. The state's new secretary of housing and economic development, Daniel O'Connell, noted that keeping the "best and brightest" in the state requires housing that is affordable to its workforce.

In California, jobs have shifted inland since 1990, following workers who left the pricey coast for more affordable housing in the interior.[4]

It's not just a coastal or urban issue. Wyoming legislators meeting in Cheyenne are talking about workforce housing shortages in their communities and the need to boost state support for affordable housing development.

Big city mayors are taking the lead because they are the ones feeling the brunt of the housing challenge. More suburban and county leaders are also heeding the call because their constituencies demand it.

Business leaders care about housing because they fear for their livelihood. In many communities, employers are increasingly worried about their ability to attract and retain lower-paid workers, such as waiters, retail clerks, bus drivers, and entry-level professionals. In some areas, the lack of housing is dissuading even moderate-income professionals such as college professors from accepting job offers.

Civic leaders care about housing because they fear losing the mix of jobs that ensures a well-rounded and therefore stable economy. Businesses will leave, or choose not to locate in, places where there is no housing for their workers. In some areas of the country, such as Los Angeles, there are concerns about losing the entire middle class.

Public administrators care about housing because they know that many of the social ills that generate costs for jails, courts, police, and family services arise in the absence of quality affordable housing. Foreclosures also consume city dollars and hurt property values, deflating local tax coffers.

Ordinary Americans care about housing because they are unhappy about having to live beyond their means to pay the rent or mortgage or to commute ever longer distances, spending less time with children and friends. They are uneasy about having the nurses, firefighters and police officers they rely upon living one or two towns away because they cannot afford homes in the community. Parents are upset that their adult children must either live at home or move far away. Elderly people on fixed incomes worry that they will be unable to remain in the communities where they have spent their lives.

People from all walks of life who subscribe to American ideals of equality and opportunity care about housing. They are disappointed to learn that the gap in homeownership rates between whites and minorities persists, retaining with it a disturbing disparity between the wealth of white and minority families. They do not consider it "progress" when our communities have become so out of reach for average workers that the only opportunity for interaction across social strata is over the service counter.

In November 2006, more than 4.8 million Californians approved state spending of about $6.1 billion on housing for lower-income residents and development in urban areas near public transportation. Proposition 1C, a $2.85 billion statewide housing bond, passed with nearly 58 percent of the vote. Interest on the bond is expected to cost $3.3 billion over 30 years.

At the same time, more than 400,000 Los Angelenos—nearly 63 percent of those who went to the polls—voted for higher property taxes so that the city could issue $1 billion in bonds to finance more affordable housing. Though the measure failed to win the two-thirds of the vote needed to pass, many viewed the extent of support as confirmation that the electorate cares about housing.

A CALL TO ACTION

The nation's housing affordability challenges will persist and grow in the years ahead as the economy continues to generate low-wage jobs and as the aging baby boomers swell the ranks of seniors on fixed incomes, increasing demand for low-cost housing. Over the next decade, the number of US households is expected to grow by 14.6 million. Without a commensurate expansion in supply at the lower end of the spectrum, communities may be faced with a "Sophie's Choice" between providing homes for low-income working families or for vulnerable seniors.

Leaders must expand affordable housing opportunities in their communities and states. The challenge requires patience and concerted leadership. Housing development is complex and takes time. It offers more incremental success and fewer "photo ops" than building a new plant and holding a ribbon-cutting ceremony. It requires pushing back hard against old, outdated notions.

Recently, the *San Francisco Chronicle* reported that Habitat for Humanity was planning to build four three-bedroom homes in an affluent Bay area community. The project has the backing of county officials, who say teachers and other low-wage workers are being priced out of the area. The county has been largely unable to site needed lower-cost homes anywhere but in minority communities, officials said. Habitat is widely respected for its model of housing development, which requires hard-working homebuyers to invest "sweat equity" in their homes, and for its commitment to helping homeowners maintain their homes. But some residents of the $1 million and $2 million properties near the proposed Habitat site have raised $100,000 to fight the project, saying the homes won't "fit in." "Do you know how many nails that could buy?" the local Habitat director asked the Chronicle reporter.

In some cases, neighborhood opposition arises when people mistakenly associate affordable housing with the fortress-like "projects" of old. Thoughtful design and better communication can go far to chip away at such ideas. Today's affordable housing complexes are in fact winning awards locally and nationally for design, community-building amenities, and environmentally friendly features. In many of the new mixed-income communities, it's impossible to tell whose rent or mortgage is subsidized and whose is not.

MOVING FORWARD

This guide is intended to spur more local government officials to action by presenting a set of recommendations that reflect both bipartisan values and what can be done. These strategies aim to create stronger families and healthier communities. Although the bulk of the recommendations speak directly to local officials, each chapter also addresses how states can ensure that their policies and programs support local housing efforts.

Many of the strategies in this guide are already gaining some traction and producing results on the ground. While some of these ideas are not new, there is value in presenting them in one coherent action plan that recognizes the connections between policy areas that too often operate in isolation.

Every community will approach its housing challenges in its own way. What works in one market won't work in another. Our guide provides a range of examples—in essence, it is a workbook of best practices—to assist local leaders, recognizing that there is no master template. But there is a growing shared urgency to act. As communities tailor their local strategies, they must not forget that, often, the most valuable thing that local leaders can provide is "moral suasion." Some of the programs that have worked so well are not necessarily unique. But they had a powerful champion in a mayor, governor, or other local leader. Leadership can see communities through difficult situations to a more opportunity-filled future.

ENDNOTES INTRODUCTION

1. "Developing Appropriate Rental Housing for Low-Income Older Persons: A Survey of Section 202 and LIHTC Property Managers," AARP Policy Institute, January 2007.

2. National Low Income Housing Coalition, "Out of Reach 2006," **www.nlihc.org**. The study calculates the amount of money a household must earn to afford a rental unit in a range of sizes at the area's Fair Market Rent, based on the generally accepted affordability standard of paying no more than 30 percent of income for housing.

3. RealtyTrac, Inc., "More Than 1.2 Million Foreclosures Reported in 2006," press release, January 25, 2007.

4. California Budget Project, "California Jobs Have Shifted Inland," *Policy Points,* January 2007, **www.cbp.org/pdfs/2007/0701_pp_inlandcoastal.pdf**.

New York Tackles the High Cost Of Letting Homelessness Be

Until recently, New York City was spending about $40,500 a year to do nothing about Will Culper. Will is a middle-aged veteran with bipolar disorder who, after years of self-medication, also suffers from alcoholism. Will had been homeless almost continuously for 15 years, sleeping in parks or doorways or on the subway. He would stay a few nights in a shelter or be brought by the police to the psychiatric emergency room where he was well-known and occasionally admitted for several weeks. He also spent time locked up at Riker's Island and Bedford Hills.

The best efforts of these costly services, rendered without Will's asking, never provided what he most needed—a place of his own. When people like Will are placed in permanent supportive housing, they use public services at a much lower rate. In fact, the public savings from the decline in service use covers nearly the entire cost of providing the housing.[1] "Supportive housing costs no more than the homeless shelters, emergency rooms, and prison cells that for too long have been the refuges of last resort for too many homeless men and women," according to Mayor Michael R. Bloomberg. And the outcomes—"the improved quality of life"—are much better.

As part of a city initiative to end chronic homelessness, Will got a private apartment and access to services through a program called Pathways to Housing. Will is for the first time collecting disability benefits, which pay part of his rent. He meets regularly with a caseworker who helps him maintain medical treatments and medication schedules for various ailments and ensures that he is receiving the services to which he is entitled. Will has reconnected with other veterans and his sister, with whom he had been out of touch for more than six years. Will now has a home base from which to rebuild his life.

HOME FROM THE STREETS

Putting an End to Chronic Homelessness

The chronically homeless are those 150,000 to 200,000 or so members of our society who have fallen through the cracks.[2] They spend years or even decades on the streets, moving in and out of shelters, treatment programs, and jails. Many have confounding factors such as drug addiction, mental illness, HIV/AIDS, or other disabilities that leave them homeless for long periods or cause them to become homeless repeatedly. As a result, their mental and physical health conditions worsen and become more expensive to treat. After their hard lives exposed to the elements, they die at a much younger age than the general population.[3]

Local officials must lead efforts to end chronic homelessness in their communities using a research-driven approach incorporating the "housing first" model. The model focuses on quickly placing people in permanent supportive housing—subsidized units accompanied by on- or off-site services to help people succeed in that housing. This approach departs from longstanding practices of requiring chronically homeless people with mental health and substance abuse issues to clean up their acts before qualifying for housing. Unable or unwilling to meet these rules, many individuals remain on the street, where they become more ill and remain a visible problem.

It is more humane and more cost-effective to get chronically homeless people into housing than it is to let them cycle endlessly through the emergency medical care, mental health, and corrections systems. While making up roughly ten percent of all homeless people, chronically homeless single adults use about half of the emergency shelter system's resources,[4] limiting the ability of communities to serve people who are temporarily homeless because of an economic or other crisis. These households enter the homeless system, receive help, and exit the system relatively quickly.

This is not to suggest that communities should overlook temporarily homeless individuals or families. Instead, the initial attack on chronic homelessness should rally the troops around clear, achievable outcomes that can lead to system changes, which in turn can serve temporarily homeless adults, youth, and families. In fact, many of the innovations for addressing long-term homeless families (who share with chronically homeless individuals similar barriers to sustained housing) and the temporarily homeless are being piloted in communities that are successfully tackling the chronic homelessness problem.

In their efforts to end homelessness, local governments should take advantage of the resources provided by organizations tackling this issue to produce an emerging set of best practices. For example, the National Alliance to End Homelessness helped to set in motion a ten-year planning process that is currently sweeping the country. NAEH offers numerous guides and publications, including a January 2007 report counting the number of homeless by community, state, and nation. The US Department of Housing and Urban Development, the Corporation for Supportive Housing, the Partnership to End Long-Term Homelessness, and many other entities are addressing this issue.

Of special note is the US Interagency Council on Homelessness, an independent federal entity charged with coordinating 20 federal agencies' responses to homelessness that publishes research on best practices and innovative approaches. The council also helps localities and states study the costs of homelessness, draft and adopt ten-year plans, and create state interagency councils.[5] Though specific plans vary based on local needs, most share the goal of redirecting resources away from temporary solutions to prevention and permanent supportive housing. They also bring health, corrections, and other agencies to the table—a recognition of the often overlooked linkages between housing and these critical systems.

The plans are showing success. The number of individuals living on New York City streets dropped 13 percent in just one year, from 2005 to 2006. San Francisco saw a 28 percent decrease in overall homelessness and a 41 percent decline in chronic street homelessness from late 2002 to early 2005. Chronic street homelessness in Portland, Oregon also fell by 20 percent from 2004 to 2005.[6] These are just a few of the cities redirecting resources to reduce their street homeless populations.

Although there is no cookie cutter approach to ending chronic homelessness, the following recommendations highlight some of the key strategies that should serve as the cornerstone of local plans.

RECOMMENDATIONS FOR LOCAL ACTION

1 Streamline the Financing System for Permanent Supportive Housing

Studies have demonstrated that formerly homeless people in supportive housing experience a 56 percent decline in emergency room visits, an 89 percent decline in use of emergency detoxification services, and a 74 percent decline in incarceration rates. More than 80 percent remain housed for at least one year.[7] Despite this strong return on investment, there is no national funding system specifically for supportive housing development. (There are, however, federal grant programs that primarily provide rental subsidies for supportive housing projects that serve homeless people with disabilities.)

Supportive housing needs capital, rental subsidy, and services funding. Any given development project will likely use multiple sources of capital for construction or rehabilitation of housing units;[8] numerous grants from foundations and government agencies to fund program administration, case management, mental health treatment and other services;[9] and rent or operating subsidy programs as well as tenant incomes from work and/or public benefits.

According to a July 2005 report by the Corporation for Supportive Housing, projects surveyed cited 34 sources of capital and 20 sources of operating funds. This ad hoc approach will not produce sufficient supportive housing on the scale called for by local efforts to end homelessness. Generating sufficient funds for new housing units requires public and private agencies to combine their purchasing power more effectively to drive the system toward a shared set of priorities. To streamline the financing system, public leaders must break down the institutional divide between housing and service funding by setting clear production goals to which agencies are held accountable. In addition to creating a reliable and adequate flow of money to meet development goals, communities must strengthen developer capacity to build the units.

▼ CASES IN POINT

City/State Partnership Boosts Supportive Housing Production In New York City

Since 1990, New York City and New York State have produced many thousands of supportive housing units under a series of "New York/New York" agreements. The agreements commit the city and state to share capital costs through such funding sources as tax levy dollars, tax credits, commercial financing, and federal pass-through funds. The first and second agreements, in 1990 and 1999, used state mental health service dollars to fund services and produce 5,300 units targeted exclusively to people with serious mental illness and some history of homelessness.

The agreements predate Mayor Bloomberg's June 2004 plan to reduce homelessness by two-thirds by 2009, in part by creating 12,000 new units of permanent supportive housing. The New York/New York III agreement was shaped by that plan and will provide $1 billion in capital and $157 million in annual operating and service funding to add 9,000 new units of supportive housing over 10 years. About 6,000 of these units will be newly constructed apartment buildings, with the rest scattered-site units in existing complexes.[10]

Although 3,950 units are specifically for chronically homeless and mentally ill single adults, a broader set of city and state partner agencies[11] will allow the initiative to extend the target market to other groups of homeless or vulnerable populations.[12] The program has mechanisms to give priority to people who have been homeless for a while, use several Medicaid-funded and other publicly funded services, and/or live in neighborhoods with a rising incidence of shelter use. The initiative also includes a $200 million capital fund for nonprofit developers to use as bridge funding to secure and retain sites.

Reforms Redirect Funds to Supportive Housing in San Francisco

San Francisco's Ten-Year Plan calls for a massive 3,000-unit expansion of supportive housing, created in large part by redirecting funds from shelters, transitional housing, and other sources. A welfare reform initiative called "Care Not Cash," launched in 2004, cut welfare checks to homeless people from as much as $410 a month to as little as $59. Care Not Cash promises housing to any homeless person whose check was cut and wants a place to live.[13] The city used the approximately $14 million in annual savings under the reform to help fund 1,483 supportive housing units—bringing the total to 1,912 units as of November 2006.[14] The city redevelopment agency, which uses tax increment funding to build affordable housing, is also setting aside some units for formerly homeless people.

New Rental Subsidies Encourage Developers to Commit Units to Homeless

Implementing a housing first philosophy in the San Francisco Bay Area is especially challenging because of the high housing costs and the very low incomes of homeless and marginally housed people. Part of the solution is the creation of shallow rental subsidies, flexibly allocated. In 2006, San Francisco created a new program to provide housing subsidies and rental assistance to families using a general fund allocation. The city will pledge the local rent subsidy to nonprofit housing developers that commit units to the formerly homeless. In this way, the local subsidy operates much like project-based Section 8 subsidies.

"Funnel" Mechanisms Simplify the Funding Process

As part of their Ten-Year Plan to End Homelessness, the City of Portland and Multnomah County, Oregon are creating 1,600 new housing units for the chronically homeless and 600 new units for homeless families. The housing includes a mix of new construction, existing nonprofit units reconfigured for the target market, and private rental units. The development program blends funding from county human services resources, city capital resources, Temporary Assistance for Needy Families (TANF) funding, 300 project-based Section 8 vouchers, and $12 million in city bond funds. In addition, the US Departments of Housing and Urban Development, Health and Human Services, and the Veterans Administration provided $9.2 million in special chronic homelessness initiative grants to subsidize rentals in the private market and in supportive housing developments.[15] To make it easier for developers to access the funding, the city and county are moving toward a unified RFP process that offers blended funding from partner agencies. Portland is also establishing an operating subsidy fund which, when coupled with debt-free housing, will enable the city to serve people with no income.

Seven States Pilot Coordinated Funding Systems

Through its Taking Health Care Home Initiative, the Corporation for Supportive Housing works with government leaders and nonprofits to create more coordinated systems for producing supportive housing. As of April 2006, the initiative operated in seven states— California (focusing on the Los Angeles region), Connecticut, Kentucky, Maine, Oregon (focusing on Portland and Multnomah County), Rhode Island, and Washington (focusing on Seattle and King Counties).

2 Create New Funding Streams for Supportive Housing And Other Homeless Programs

Many communities will likely need new funding streams to meet development goals. Local governments have devised a number of innovative funding sources or have tapped some new resources for this effort.

Local Gas, Restaurant, and Property Taxes Fund Homeless Housing

In Broward County, Florida, a gas tax enacted in 1999 provides $7.5 million annually to support programs for homeless people. These funds are augmented by general revenue, bringing the county homeless services budget to more than $10 million annually. Since the one-cent per gallon fuel tax must be used for transit-related services, the county redirected the equivalent amount of general revenue devoted to transit and dedicated it to homeless services. The county recently renewed the gas tax and the homeless general revenue set-aside through 2029.

Miami's special tax on restaurant services collects close to $13 million annually, roughly 85 percent of which goes to homeless services. Most of the balance is allotted to domestic violence programs, with a small percentage going to the tax collector. Since enactment in 1994, the tax has generated more than $100 million for programs serving homeless people and domestic violence victims.

In 2005, King County, Washington voters approved a ballot measure expected to generate $13.3 million annually for six years to help veterans and others in need, including helping to reduce homelessness. The Veterans and Human Services Levy lasts six years and adds five cents per $1,000 of assessed value to property taxes. The implementation plan for the levy targets a large share for permanent supportive housing. In Seattle and Columbus, voter-approved property tax levies also provide funds for supportive housing.

Cities Tap TIFs, Bonds, Private Investors for Housing Support

A recent report for HUD's Office of Policy Development and Research identifies other innovative funding sources for supportive housing.[16] These sources include tax increment financing in San Diego and redevelopment bonds in Philadelphia. The report also includes a list of more than 25 potentially underused resources—from Federal Home Loan Bank grants to HUD Housing Opportunities for People with AIDS funds to Medicaid and Medicaid Waiver programs. Atlanta, San Francisco, and Minnesota have also created special funds to collect contributions from the business community for their efforts to end homelessness, usually to support housing production.

National Funds for Supportive Housing Leverage Local Contributions

The Partnership to End Long-Term Homelessness is a collaboration of national foundations and financial institutions, with the Corporation for Supportive Housing (CSH) and the National Alliance to End Homelessness (NAEH) as the implementing partners. The partnership seeks to create 150,000 units of permanent supportive housing by 2014. As part of this effort, the funders initially committed more than $37 million in grants and loans to CSH, NAEH, and other groups. They hope to leverage another $100 million from other local and national foundations, financial institutions, businesses, and other resources. CSH and NAEH are also providing development expertise as well as grants and loans to supportive housing sponsors, and helping reform public policy to make it easier to create and operate supportive housing.

Under its Homelessness Initiative, Fannie Mae is committing $10 million in corporate matching grants to CSH and NAEH. Fannie Mae is also providing at least $25 million in low-cost predevelopment and acquisition financing for permanent supportive housing. In addition, it is partnering with Enterprise Community Investment, Inc. and the National Equity Fund to create two $100 million Low-Income Housing Tax Credit funds for financing permanent supportive housing development.

3 Seek Out New Supportive Housing Production Partners

To foster development of supportive housing, local government leaders must nurture community partnerships, including with entities that may be new to supportive housing construction. Efforts to end chronic homelessness provide housing authority directors, nonprofit leaders, and others with the opportunity to demonstrate their capabilities as community partners with the energy and resources to help solve problems. Other potential partners include housing finance agencies, national intermediaries such as Enterprise Community Partners, and community development corporations.

▼ CASES IN POINT

Public Housing Authorities Back Supportive Housing

With their new flexibility to target (using project-based certificates) up to 20 percent of their Section 8 vouchers, local housing authorities have an emerging part to play in supportive housing. Project-based vouchers, although historically difficult to use for supportive housing populations, can be a key piece of the funding package. New regulations issued in October 2005 clear many of the hurdles.[17] Housing authorities can also use their tenant-based Section 8 vouchers, land, and available vacant units to further homelessness initiatives.

In 2007, the Los Angeles Housing Department and agency partners will commit $100 million in capital and operating funds to projects creating 600 permanent supportive housing units.[18] Homeless people living on Skid Row will receive priority as part of a city effort to eliminate the criminal element that preys on the homeless who congregate there. Every unit financed will have a Section 8 voucher attached, funded by a $29 million expansion of the Section 8 rental subsidy program.

Chicago Partners with Faith Group, State Child Welfare Office

With strong support from the mayor's office, the Interfaith Housing Development Corporation of Chicago and its partners are developing three permanent supportive housing complexes with 164 units. The projects will serve young adults aging out of foster care—a population at high risk of long-term homelessness—and families who are homeless and disabled or have extremely low incomes. The city issued a low-income housing bond in the amount of $26 million that will generate $16 million in equity. The Illinois Housing Development authority is providing $8.5 million in HOME funds, state trust monies, and state tax credits. Some units will receive project-based rental subsidies, including a new type of subsidy from the Department of Children and Family Services for wards of the state aging out of foster care.[19] On all three projects, the sponsor is partnering with a service provider that is new to permanent supportive housing.

Boston Provides Predevelopment Grants to Help Nonprofit Providers Get in the Game

Boston developers receiving linkage fees and CDBG, HOME, and project-based Section 8 support must make some of their units available to very low- and extremely low-income households. The city provides predevelopment grants to help nonprofit homeless services gain experience in building supportive housing. The goal is to integrate housing for the homeless into communities rather than isolate formerly homeless people with special needs.

---

4 Use Vacant Rental Properties to House The Homeless

Given the relatively high cost of creating new units, efforts to end long-term homelessness must take advantage of the existing private rental stock. Grants from foundations and government agencies are also needed to help fund program administration and services. Program caseworkers are needed to help clients access the federal and state benefits offered to the disabled and the poor, including Supplemental Security Income (SSI) and Section 8 vouchers.

Accessing the private market early in a ten-year plan to end homelessness allows progress to be made while the production pipeline is filling up. In fact, most of the local efforts profiled in the previous section are meeting their supportive housing goals with a mix of new development and subsidies for existing private and nonprofit rental housing.

CASES IN POINT

Pathways to Housing Clients Become Part of NYC Neighborhoods

Pathways to Housing in New York City places its clients in scattered-site permanent housing, encouraging landlord participation by guaranteeing to pay rent. Given its emphasis on integrating clients into the neighborhood, the program does not rent more than 10–20 percent of units in any one building. Like any tenant, clients can be evicted for not paying their bills, breaking the law, causing disturbances, or violating other terms of their leases. In contrast, they cannot be evicted for such things as failing to take their medication or drinking. More than 200 landlords participate in the program.[20] The New York program serves about 450 homeless individuals with psychiatric disabilities and addictions. Pathways to Housing has also created a Washington, DC program that will serve about 150 people, with rents to be subsidized by Section 8 vouchers.

Streamlined Rent Assistance, Other Incentives Lure Portland Landlords

The Portland/Multnomah County, Oregon plan to end long-term homelessness, launched in 2005, aims to place chronically homeless individuals and families into permanent housing. As of October 2006, 937 chronically homeless people had moved into housing, almost half of them from the streets. In addition, 641 homeless families with children were placed in permanent housing. Roughly half of these families were "high resource users," facing such barriers to housing as foster care involvement, corrections systems involvement, and physical or behavioral disability. Many of the individual and family placements were in private rental apartments or nonprofit complexes. New city funds for rental assistance,[21] a streamlined rent assistance program, and support of the housing first philosophy from service providers helped produce the success.

Moving forward, the City of Portland has created an $800,000 risk mitigation pool to address the needs of landlords who rent to the chronically homeless or formerly homeless. Such tenants often have spotty rent histories or poor credit ratings. The pool seeks to encourage quality property managers in the mainstream affordable housing community to consider renting to these families and individuals by guaranteeing reimbursement for any excessive expenses incurred.

---

5 Offer "No Strings Attached" Housing For the Hardest to Serve

Comprehensive plans to end chronic homelessness should ensure that at least some of the housing created is "low-demand housing." This specialized housing carries fewer restrictions on eligibility, recognizing that some chronically homeless people are unwilling or unable to satisfy requirements for sobriety, abstinence, or mental health treatment as a condition of entry. Low-demand housing offers a way to treat the least functional of the chronically homeless by helping to arrest the mental and physical deterioration that comes from living on the streets. In turn, stable housing can serve as a foundation for the recovery process.

Through its Supportive Housing Program, HUD funds Safe Havens—low-demand housing and supportive services for hard-to-serve homeless people with serious mental illness.[22] Philadelphia is aiming for a Safe Haven approach by not requiring abstinence as a condition of entry, but setting clear expectations that residents will use treatment and other services offered.

6 Establish and Strengthen Outreach Efforts

A coordinated outreach and engagement system that encourages homeless people to access services and permanent housing is an important tool in ending homelessness. Data-driven outreach programs can also get some of the top users of emergency or other services out of the repeat cycle and into treatment and housing. Effective outreach requires the collaboration of shelters, mental health agencies, faith-based nonprofits, law enforcement, and other service providers.

▼ CASES IN POINT

Philadelphia Lauded for Coordinated Outreach, Centralized Intake

Between 1997 and 2003, Philadelphia reduced its center city homeless population by some 60 percent, from a high of 500 to a low of 203.[23] Experts credit much of the drop to a combination of aggressive outreach and access to transitional and permanent housing and services. While the number of street homeless did creep back up to 365 in 2006, Philadelphia's strategies are still considered a national model for outreach that has been adopted by other cities seeking to end long-term homelessness.

A linchpin of the city's approach is the Outreach Coordination Center (OCC) run by Project H.O.M.E., with significant city funding. The center operates a 24-hour homeless hotline, maintains updated lists of program availability, and coordinates five teams of outreach workers. When businesses, citizens, or others call the center, a team is dispatched to help homeless people access basics such as food or clothing, public benefits, healthcare, medication, detoxification, mental health counseling, substance abuse treatment, safe havens, and other low-demand housing. The OCC attempts to get chronically homeless street people directly into housing rather than send them to shelters first. Most are currently sent to safe havens or other low-demand residential or transitional settings. As the city ramps up availability of units, homeless people will increasingly go to permanent supportive housing.

The city Office of Supportive Housing (OSH) does central intake for all of the shelters and transitional programs that it funds. This approach has helped to increase the efficiency of shelter use, with occupancy rates rising from 80 percent to 97 percent.[24] The OSH also operates a database tracking emergency shelter and some transitional housing stays. By linking it to the OCC database of persons contacted, officials are able to identify which individuals are chronic users of emergency services.

Housing Access Plays Critical Role in San Francisco's Outreach Success

In 2004, the city Public Health and Human Services Departments partnered with the nonprofit Community Awareness and Treatment Services, Inc. to launch a San Francisco Homeless Outreach team charged with connecting the street homeless to housing and services. In addition to targeting neighborhoods with the most homeless people, the team of outreach and treatment workers responds to incidents reported by health professionals and the public through a centralized dispatch system. Working with their clients, outreach workers develop "street-to-home" plans that include housing, primary care, behavioral health treatment, and SSI benefits. The team has access to available shelter, treatment, and detox beds, along with crisis slots, urgent care, and housing. Critical to the program's success has been an increase in the number of "stabilization rooms" in hotels and detox slots where clients can be placed before accessing permanent supportive housing. The city is beginning to replace some shelter and transitional housing beds with 24-hour crisis clinics and sobering centers in an effort to get homeless people into permanent housing more quickly. The city is also building 3,000 new supportive housing units.

For their part, the City and County of San Francisco Fire Departments and Health Departments spun off a special outreach team charged with getting homeless individuals who frequently use ambulance services (primarily chronic inebriates) into city-funded case management programs, treatment beds, supportive housing, SSI benefit programs, and other health services. Team members from both departments track and rank the highest-cost and highest health-risk users by mapping 911 calls. The maps show where the ambulance pickups usually occur and which emergency departments are frequented. Program officials have also hammered out an agreement between emergency medical services, police, and hospitals so that paramedics can take patients to an authorized sobering center without fear of legal reprisal.

7 Prevent Healthcare, Public Safety and Other Systems From Discharging People into Homelessness

Local systems must reform their discharge practices to ensure that people have a place to live and a means to retain their housing. Communities that are taking this challenge seriously have formed discharge planning task forces that work across administrative silos. Data collection has played a key role in this area, providing officials with information on the extent and nature of the problem and allowing them to target services to frequent users. Of course, availability of permanent supportive housing is crucial.

▼ CASES IN POINT

NYC Program Breaks the Jail-Homelessness Cycle

New York City's Frequent Users Service Enhancement (FUSE) program finds permanent housing for people who continually cycle from jails to homelessness because of chronic health conditions such as substance abuse. The program is administered by the Departments of Corrections and Homeless Services, in collaboration with the Corporation for Supportive Housing, under the leadership of the city's Discharge Planning Collaboration partners.

Using data from various sources, program administrators compile a list of frequent users of jails, shelters, and other emergency systems. Selected nonprofit service providers find and engage those on the lists in housing and services. As of November 2006, nine service providers were working to place 100 individuals into supportive housing through a mix of project-based Section 8, New York/New York, and other Department of Homeless Services subsidies. Early retention statistics show that 92 percent of clients remained housed. Program officials hope to demonstrate cost savings from reduced jail and shelter use to persuade the city to fund the program going forward.

On a broader scale, New York City is reprioritizing its existing supportive housing stock to provide access to people coming out of detox facilities and other homeless feeder systems. In the near future, the city will require detox facilities to provide access to rehabilitation programs that in turn have access to housing. Since most services are funded by the state or Medicaid as inpatient care, the city is working with state agencies to require grantees to demonstrate linkage.

Los Angeles and San Francisco Curb Medical Discharges into Homelessness

The Los Angeles city attorney and police department are cracking down on the "dumping" of homeless hospital patients onto Skid Row. In San Francisco, the Department of Public Health is placing frequent users of its medical and shelter services directly into permanent supportive housing bought or leased by the agency. The city's sobering centers will soon expand to include medical respite for indigent people released from hospitals but still needing care before being placed in permanent housing. The Department of Public Health's web-based case management system covers the 400 top users of emergency medical services and the more than 4,000 individuals exiting sobering centers or contacted by outreach and intensive case management teams. The database allows public health agencies or private hospitals to coordinate treatment so that patients do not continue to cycle through the system.

Portland Reforms Corrections and Medical Discharge Systems

At the behest of the Oregon Discharge Planning Committee of Portland/Multnomah County, many institutional partners in the plan to end homelessness are reforming their discharge systems. The city hired a discharge planner to find housing for people who would otherwise be homeless when they leave jail. Between January and October 2006, 45 percent of the homeless people assigned to the planner were placed in housing. The county sheriff's office is creating a guide for other discharge planners and forging relations between jails and housing planners.

Under the Housing Rapid Response program, Portland's Police Bureau and Office of Neighborhood Involvement are working with a downtown business group and the nonprofit Central City Concern (CCC) to offer permanent housing to nearly 50 chronically homeless people who are often cited for low-level street crimes such as aggressive panhandling or illegal camping. Portland's primary shelter provider, Transition Project Inc., has hired a case manager to move people on the shelter waiting list directly into permanent or transitional housing.

Two Portland institutions—Providence Health System and Oregon Health and Science University Hospitals—have contracted with CCC to provide housing and services to frequent emergency room users. This allows the hospital to save on expensive hospital days because of a lack of discharge options. Kaiser Permanente has also hired CCC to provide housing and services to uninsured homeless individuals. CCC has consolidated the awards ($150,000 total from the two hospitals and $450,000 from Kaiser) into a single "recuperative care" program.

The Multnomah County Department of Community Justice operates the Joint Access to Benefits Program, which connects disabled ex-offenders with Social Security benefits and Medicaid four months prior to release. (Such benefits are stopped during incarceration.) In the past, disabled former inmates might cycle through the shelter system for up to two years while they waited to have their benefits restored.

8 Address the Needs of Both Chronically And Temporarily Homeless Families

A small but significant portion of homeless families are chronically homeless. In many cases, these families are headed by a parent with some of the same substance abuse or mental illness challenges as chronically homeless individuals. Communities should look for savings from reductions in chronic homelessness to fund homeless prevention and services for families that are homeless for a relatively short time.

Homeless families, too, can pose significant costs to public services, notes the National Alliance to End Homelessness in its report on tackling family homelessness. The annual cost of an emergency shelter bed is about $8,087, more than the average annual cost of a federal housing voucher. In addition, family homelessness further burdens the child welfare system, particularly when children in homeless families end up in foster care.

The National Alliance to End Homelessness recommends taking a rapid re-housing approach with temporarily homeless families. Similar to the housing first philosophy, rapid re-housing emphasizes quickly getting families back into homes and linking them with jobs and appropriate mainstream services. These programs help families clear barriers such as poor tenant history and poor credit, negotiate with landlords, ensure that households receive the public benefits for which they are eligible, and follow up to avert crises that threaten housing stability. To help families afford the rent on their new housing, it is important to connect them with mainstream benefits and job search and employment advancement assistance.

▼ CASES IN POINT

New York Uses Shelter Data to Target At-Risk Neighborhoods

HomeBase, a $12 million homelessness prevention pilot program in New York City, targets six at-risk neighborhoods. The Department of Homeless Services chose the communities that were sending the most families to shelters. Through an RFP process, nonprofit agencies received $2 million to operate community-based interventions to prevent families from becoming homeless due to economic hardship. Services include job training and search assistance, housing search assistance, security deposits, and advocating for access to entitlement programs. In a July 2006 speech to the National

Alliance to End Homelessness, Mayor Michael Bloomberg reported that the program had helped almost 4,000 men, women, and children stay in their homes, at an average cost of $4,000 per client, compared with the $35,000 it takes to shelter a family for a year. At the same time, the mayor stated that the share of shelter entrants coming from the targeted neighborhoods fell from 25 percent to 20 percent.

Portland Takes Prevention Through Rental Assistance to Scale

Between 2001 and 2005, Portland's Transitions to Housing program helped 1,749 households avoid homelessness or move into permanent housing with a shallow, short-term rent subsidy. Roughly $420,000 in Portland City General Fund monies enabled 10 nonprofits to provide the service. Over the course of the program, 12-month retention rates were 73 percent. To take the program to scale, the city, Multnomah County, and the Housing Authority consolidated Transitions to Housing with other funding sources into a Short-Term Rent Assistance program. The new program, administered by the housing authority, had $1.6 million in funding as of fall 2006.

Hennepin County, MN Rapid Exit Program Works with Landlords

Under the Hennepin County Rapid Exit Program, families and individuals entering shelters are screened for barriers to tenancy and paired with caseworkers who help them address the obstacles. Caseworkers have strong relationships with private sector landlords to create openings for program participants and provide intensive follow-up services for six months to prevent a relapse. In fiscal 2005, the program placed 564 families and 165 single adults in homes. A year later, 95 percent of the families and 94 percent of the individuals were still housed. The county has also expanded prevention efforts, such as providing financial assistance and working with landlords to resolve issues before they lead to eviction.[25]

Los Angeles Program Helps Families Overcome Barriers to Housing

Beyond Shelter, Inc. of Los Angeles has been the national leader in rapidly re-housing homeless families. Families are referred to the service from more than 50 agencies throughout the LA area, including shelters, residential drug treatment programs, and domestic violence programs. Most of the families have had unstable living situations or episodic homelessness, in some cases because of domestic violence or substance abuse. Under Beyond Shelter's Housing First program, specialized housing staff help families negotiate leases, access move-in funds, and overcome such barriers to housing as poor credit or discrimination. About 75 percent of families receive a Section 8 rental subsidy and all receive six months of home-based case management, with a focus on linking families to mainstream programs and resources to address their special needs. One study found that almost 90 percent of participants maintained housing stability two to seven years after completing the program.[26] Beyond Shelter receives funding from the City of Los Angeles for several of its programs.

1 Target Existing Funds to Supportive Housing Development

Since they control many of the service dollars, states play a key role in efforts to reduce chronic homelessness through supportive housing development. States should follow the lead of their peers and bring mental health, addiction services, and corrections dollars to the table as part of multi-agency funding plans and/or as new revenue sources for homelessness reduction efforts.

Minnesota's ten-year plan to end homelessness by 2010 calls for spending $540 million to create 4,000 new supportive housing units statewide. The plan is funding a mix of rehabilitated units, subsidized private rental units, and newly constructed units—including some integrated into new mixed-income housing developments. The work is contracted out under a joint RFP process administered by the Minnesota Housing Finance Agency (MHFA). The financing package includes $50 million in MHFA earnings and other grants to fund rental assistance, another $40 million in funds from state-appropriated MHFA programs, and $60 million in Low-Income Housing Tax Credit equity.

The Department of Human Services expects to provide $120 million from such funding streams as medical assistance, TANF funds, welfare assistance, group residential housing, and a newly state-appropriated $10 million fund for the services component. State general obligation bonds will provide $90 million. An additional $180 million is expected from other sources, including the federal Section 8 and Shelter Plus Care programs, local governments, foundations and private businesses, and other state agencies. To generate as much new housing as possible from the resources at hand, the plan emphasizes maximizing the use of the private rental market and carefully targeting support service levels, so that families with less need for support aren't consuming more resources than necessary.

Connecticut's Supportive Housing Pilots Initiative aims to create 650 supportive housing units statewide over four years.[27] The program targets households headed by individuals with mental illness or chemical dependency who are homeless, at risk of homelessness, or earn up to 50 percent of the area median income. The Department of Mental Health and Addiction Services provided $5 million for support services and the Housing Finance Authority funded $23 million for capital costs. As of April 2006, about 350 newly constructed or rehabilitated units were in the pipeline (including many in mixed-income developments) and 300 units were available through private landlords. With the success of the pilot, the state launched a Next Steps initiative in 2006 to create 1,000 supportive housing units for families over five years.

The National Council of State Housing Agencies and the National Association of State Mental Health Program Directors have established a partnership to facilitate provision of affordable permanent housing for low- and extremely low-income people with mental illness and disabilities. As of November 2006, the groups had produced a memorandum of understanding outlining an action plan that includes such tasks as sharing information on successful state housing and mental health agency collaborations and encouraging state agencies to work together to identify ways to combine resources.

2 Tap New Funding Streams to Reduce Homelessness

Producing sufficient permanent supportive housing at scale will require new funding streams. With their capacity to enact recording fee surcharges and other levies as well as tap the bonding capacity of housing finance agencies, states are well equipped for this challenge.

California is a leader in providing substantial state funding to alleviate homelessness. In addition to programs funded by two massive bond measures (Propositions 46 and 1C), the Mental Health Services Act (Proposition 63) provides funds through an additional one-percent tax on incomes above $1 million. Approved in 2004, the fund seeks to reduce the consequences of untreated mental illness, including homelessness and incarceration. In 2006, Governor Arnold Schwarzenegger announced that $75 million of Proposition 63 funds would be designated each year for construction of supportive housing for homeless people with mental illness. Over time, the allocation is expected to help generate up to $4.5 billion in state, federal, and private funds and create more than 10,000 units statewide.[28]

In 2005, New Jersey established a $200 million Special Needs Housing Trust Fund, charged with creating 10,000 affordable housing opportunities for people with mental illness or physical or developmental disabilities. The fund is administered by the New Jersey Housing Mortgage and Finance Agency and supported by bonds issued by the New Jersey Economic Development Authority using fines on motor vehicle violations. The program will help create new housing options for some of the state's 8,000 chronically homeless people, most of whom suffer from mental illness. As of October 2006, the New Jersey Housing Mortgage and Finance Agency had committed more than $41 million to 40 special needs projects providing 460 housing opportunities, with an additional $45 million for 500 beds/unit in the pipeline.

After heavy lobbying by the City of Chicago, Illinois lawmakers created the Illinois Rental Housing Support Program in 2005 using an additional $10 fee on the recording of real-estate documents. Administered by the Illinois Housing Development Authority, the program is expected to provide about $25 million annually in rental subsidies to about 5,500 households earning no more than 30 percent of the area median income. By requiring that half of the funds go to support individuals earning less than 15 percent of the area median income, the program will likely be a new tool for creating housing for low-income people with mental or physical disabilities who might otherwise be homeless. Chicago is using its anticipated $10 million annually from the state to increase the number of very low-income households served by a city rental subsidy program from more than 2,000 to 4,000 per year.

3 Use Tax Credits for Supportive Housing Development

State agencies that allocate the federal Low-Income Housing Tax Credit program are actively encouraging development of supportive housing.[29] State policies include setting aside a portion of available credits for supportive housing developments, as is done by Arizona, California, Connecticut, Illinois, Iowa, Maine, Michigan, New Jersey, and Ohio. States can also award points for supportive housing developments in the competitive scoring process or establish certain requirements. For example, North Carolina requires certain projects to set aside the greater of five units or 10 percent of total units for people with disabilities or the homeless.

4 Enhance State Discharge Systems

Some of the public systems and institutions that serve the homeless are under state control. States therefore have the responsibility to ensure that these systems, such as foster care, provide people with housing opportunities and the support they need to maintain their housing upon discharge.

Under New Jersey's Promise Initiative, case managers line up prescriptions, services, and housing for inmates with mental health disorders as they move into the parole system.[30] Through general revenues, the Parole Board Division created a rental subsidy program to enable clients to rent apartments in scattered sites within neighborhoods. The state housing finance authority and Department of Community Affairs are also providing funds to help build new units.

The Minnesota Department of Human Services (DHS) administers a $2 million program to provide housing and other assistance to youths at risk of homelessness as they age out of foster care. Under contract with DHS, community agencies assess what the youths need to live independently and develop plans for the transition to independence. Older youths are placed in supportive housing and receive ongoing training in money management and in finding employment or continuing education.

AIDS HOUSING OF WASHINGTON
www.aidshousing.org

Nonprofit based in Seattle whose mission is to increase and sustain housing and related services for people living with HIV/AIDS or experiencing homelessness. AHW has developed a training guide, "From Locked Up to Locked Out," for communities to create post-release supportive housing for ex-prisoners.

CORPORATION FOR SUPPORTIVE HOUSING
www.csh.org

Works with local government leaders to streamline supportive housing financing systems and pilot innovative programs. The organization focuses primarily on the states where it has local offices (California, Illinois, Michigan, Minnesota, New Jersey, New York, Ohio, and Southern New England). Among many helpful resources, the CSH website provides fact sheets on the FUSE initiative and on the Connecticut Supportive Housing Pilots Initiative, as well as a paper charting the "Costs of Serving Homeless Individuals in Nine Cities."

NATIONAL ALLIANCE TO END HOMELESSNESS
www.endhomelessness.org

Nonprofit, nonpartisan organization working to solve the problem of homelessness and prevent its continued growth. The NAEH website offers extensive resources, including the January 2007 report, "Homelessness Counts," which establishes baseline homeless counts by community, by state, and the nation as a whole. NAEH also provides tools to end homelessness in the form of best practice profiles, including Pathways to Housing in NYC, Beyond Shelter in LA, and the Rapid Exit Program in Hennepin County, MN.

PARTNERSHIP TO END LONG-TERM HOMELESSNESS
www.endlongtermhomelessness.org

Includes nine national philanthropic, nonprofit, and financial organizations dedicated to ending long-term homelessness in America. The website features key data, case studies, and practical tips and strategies. Although primarily targeting foundations and corporations interested in funding efforts to end long-term homelessness, the site also provides material for policymakers and others. The site will host an ongoing series of teleseminars and maintain blogs on such issues as advocacy strategies, legislative updates, and supportive housing do's and don'ts.

RESOURCES

RESOURCES

RE-ENTRY POLICY COUNCIL
www.reentrypolicy.org

The Re-Entry Policy Council is a working group convened by the Council of State Governments and funded in part by the US Departments of Justice, Labor, and Health and Human Services. The 2005 "Report of the Re-Entry Policy Council" conveys the results of a series of meetings among 100 workforce, health, housing, public safety, family, community, and victim experts nationwide and provides a comprehensive set of recommendations around prisoner re-entry policies and practices. Chapter 19 of the report focuses on housing.

US DEPARTMENT OF HOUSING AND URBAN DEVELOPMENT
Office of Policy Development and Research (PD&R)
www.huduser.org

Responsible for maintaining current information on housing needs, market conditions, and existing programs, as well as conducting research on priority housing and community development issues. PD&R has commissioned several studies on homelessness reduction and prevention efforts.

US INTERAGENCY COUNCIL ON HOMELESSNESS
www.ich.gov

Responsible for providing federal leadership for activities to assist homeless families and individuals. The council has published many helpful guides, including "Innovations in Ten-Year Plans to End Chronic Homelessness in Your Community" plus a companion toolkit. The website also posts a list of communities with Ten-Year Plans. The "Innovative Initiatives that are Preventing and Ending Homelessness" tab on the website links to replicable programs and strategies.

ENDNOTES CHAPTER 1

1. Dennis Culhane, Stephen Metraux, and Trevor Hadley, "Public Service Reductions Associated with Placement of Homeless Persons with Severe Mental Illness in Supportive Housing." *Housing Policy Debate 13:1,* 2002. The calculation is in 1999 dollars. According to the study, placement in supportive housing was directly responsible for a $16,281 annualized per-unit decrease in the costs of using shelter, hospital, emergency room, outpatient healthcare, prison, and jail services. This represents about 94 percent of the $17,277 annualized per-unit cost of permanent supportive housing.

2. The National Alliance to End Homelessness (NAEH) defines the chronically homeless as those who have multiple episodes of homelessness or are homeless over a long period of time and whose condition is complicated by a disabling physical or mental health issue. This figure, which refers to the estimated number of chronically homeless in January 2005, is derived from homeless assistance submitted by Continuums of Care nationwide (NAEH Chronic Homelessness Brief, August 2006, **www.endhomelessness.org/content/general/detail/1060**). NAEH's more recent "Homelessness Counts" report, published in January 2007, found an estimated 744,313 homeless people, 23 percent of whom were chronically homeless.

3. For example, a study by Jonathan R. Hibbs et al., "Mortality in Cohort of Homeless Adults in Philadelphia," *New England Journal of Medicine,* August 4, 1994, found that homeless adults had an age-adjusted mortality rate nearly four times that of the general population. At particularly high risk were with men and individuals with substance abuse problems.

4. Randall Kuhn and Dennis P. Culhane, "Applying Cluster Analysis to Test a Typology of Homelessness by Pattern of Shelter Utilization: Results from the Analysis of Administrative Data," *American Journal of Community Psychology* 26:2, 1998.

5. National Alliance to End Homelessness, "A New Vision: What is in Community Plans to End Homelessness?" November 2006, **www.endhomelessness.org/content/article/detail/1397**. As of July 2006, about 90 jurisdictions had completed plans, with another 130 in process.

6. New York numbers are from Mayor Michael Bloomberg's keynote address to the July 2006 annual conference of the National Alliance to End Homelessness, **www.nyc.gov/html/dhs/html/press/pr071706.shtml**. San Francisco numbers are from San Francisco Department of Human Services, "San Francisco Homeless Count 2005 Final Report," March 18, 2005. Portland numbers are from Heather Lyons, homeless program manager for the city's Bureau of Housing and Community Development.

7. Figures on emergency room use and length of housing are from Tia Martinez and Martha Burt, "Impact of Permanent Supportive Housing on the Use of Acute Care Health Services by Homeless Adults." *Psychiatric Services* 57:7 (2000), 992–9. Figures on emergency detox service are from Lisa Thornquist, "Anishinabe Wakiagun Residents' Use of Emergency Services in Hennepin County, Minnesota," Hennepin County Adult Services, Chemical Health Division, 2001. Figures on incarceration rates are from Mental Health Association, Los Angeles County, cumulative data on California's AB34 program through May 2006.

8. A few of the major sources are Low-Income Housing Tax Credits, Community Development Block Grant Funds, HOME funds, federal McKinney-Vento Supportive Housing Program capital funds, local redevelopment funds, and Federal Home Loan Bank funds. A rule of thumb is that developers must assemble a financing package that will be debt-free.

9. To fund operations, agencies can access per-unit rental subsidies through McKinney's Section 8 Mod SRO and Shelter Plus Care programs; lump-sum operating funds through the McKinney Supportive Housing Program; and local rent subsidies if available. Accompanying services may be funded by federal homeless assistance grants and Medicaid (often through benefits available for mental health services or through federally qualified health centers). Mental health, corrections, TANF dollars, and human services agencies are increasingly being tapped to fund the services accompanying supportive housing.

10. "State and City Officials Announce Plan for 9,000 Units of Supportive Housing," *Real Estate Weekly*, November 16, 2005. An additional 3,000 units of permanent supportive housing are being produced by the New York City Department of Housing Preservation and Development, and the state and federal governments.

11. Key partners include but are not limited to the city Housing Preservation and Development Department, which funnels the capital for bricks and mortar; the city Department of Health and Mental Hygiene, which procures and manages the contracts; and the state Department of Human Services, which has responsibility for Medicaid and public assistance and determines eligibility.

12. Units will also be offered to people with substance abuse disorders that prevent them from living independently, families headed by someone with a disabling physical or mental condition or substance abuse disorder, young adults who have aged out of the foster care system or could leave the mental health treatment system if provided with supportive housing, and other categories.

13. Kevin Fagan, "Newsom Praises Care Not Cash Effort," *San Francisco Chronicle,* May 5, 2006. When Care Not Cash was launched on May 4, 2004, there were 2,497 homeless people receiving monthly welfare checks. As of May 2006, all had left the welfare rolls, with 1,318 having moved into permanent supportive housing.

14. Kevin Fagan, "Shame of the City; A Daily Walk Finds Fewer Homeless," *San Francisco Chronicle,* October 30, 2006, A1.

15. In 2003 and 2004, under an unprecedented federal initiative led by the United States Interagency Council on Homelessness, 11 communities were awarded a total of $55 million to create permanent supportive housing for 635 persons experiencing chronic homelessness. The RFP included funding from the US Departments of Housing and Urban Development, Health and Human Services, and Veterans Affairs. The awardees were Chattanooga; Chicago; Columbus, OH; Denver; Fort Lauderdale; Los Angeles; Martinez, CA; New York; Philadelphia; Portland, OR; and San Francisco. A HUD-Department of Labor partnership, Ending Chronic Homelessness Through Employment and Housing, also awarded grants and technical assistance totaling $13.5 million to Boston, Indianapolis, Los Angeles, Portland, and San Francisco.

16. Martha R. Burt et al., "Strategies for Reducing Chronic Street Homelessness," report prepared for US Department of Housing and Urban Development Office of Policy Development and Research by the Urban Institute and Walter R. McDonald & Associates, Inc., January 2004, **www.urban.org/uploaded*PDF/1000775.pdf.** The report highlights homelessness initiatives in Birmingham, AL; Boston, MA; Columbus, OH; Los Angeles, CA; Philadelphia, PA; San Diego, CA; and Seattle, WA.

17. Corporation for Supportive Housing, "HUD Issues Long-Awaited Rules for Project-Based Vouchers," January 2006, **www.csh.org/index.cfm?fuseaction=Page.viewPage&pageID=3599& noheader=1**. The rule allows public housing authorities to give preference to individuals and families who need services to be able to maintain themselves in housing. It also gives PHAs authority to set their own requirements for poverty deconcentration and allows exemptions from rules limiting no more than a quarter of units in a building to recipients of project-based vouchers.

18. The funds are for fiscal 2005-06 and 2006-07. Funds for the Permanent Supportive Housing Program come from the Los Angeles Housing Department, the Community Redevelopment Agency, the Housing Authority of the City of Los Angeles, the Los Angeles Department of Water and Power, and the Los Angeles Department of Transportation.

19. One type of subsidy requires that the head of the household be both homeless and disabled (HUD Shelter Plus Care); another requires that residents be wards of the state aging out of foster care; the third targets families making below 50 percent of area median income. To make it work, the state Department of Children and Family Services is providing a new type of project-based rent subsidy.

20. Program officials help eligible participants apply for benefits (which may include veterans' benefits, disability benefits, Section 8 rent assistance, and food stamps) and use some of the benefits toward the rent. Tenants pay 30 percent of their income, with the rest covered by Section 8 if available. Tenants without Section 8 vouchers are subsidized by grants from the HUD Shelter Plus Care program and the New York State Office of Mental Health.

21. The new rental funds are in the form of a $1 million allocation from the city for the "Key Not a Card" program, which empowers outreach workers at four nonprofits to give homeless individuals and families immediate rental assistance and housing placement, as well as 18 months of supportive services. The vast majority of placements are in private rental units.

22. The agency's guide to the development of Safe Havens is available at **www.hud.gov/offices/cpd/homeless/library/havens/index.cfm.**

23. City of Philadelphia/Project H.O.M.E. Outreach Coordination Center Census, "Street Homelessness in Center City by Year; Average Across All Seasons."

24. Burt et al., "Strategies for Reducing Chronic Street Homelessness," **www.urban.org/uploaded*PDF/1000775.pdf.**

25. Most of the funding for Rapid Exit comes from a HUD Supportive Housing Program grant. Funds for the screeners come from a state program called the Family Homeless Prevention and Assistance Program (FHPAP). Established by the legislature in 1993, the program uses state legislative appropriations to encourage local homeless response systems to focus on homelessness prevention. For the 2006-7 state biennium, FHPAP had $7.43 million to spend on these efforts. Local governments compete for the funds under an RFP process administered by the Minnesota Housing Finance Agency.

26. Susan D. Einbinder and Tanya Tull, "The Housing First Program for Homeless Families: Empirical Evidence of Long-Term Efficacy to End and Prevent Family Homelessness," Institute for Research, Training and Technical Assistance, Beyond Shelter, June 2005.

27. Partners include the state departments of Mental Health and Addiction Services, Social Services, and Economic and Community Development; the state Office of Policy and Management, the Connecticut Housing Finance Authority, and the Corporation for Supportive Housing, a nonprofit intermediary.

28. "Manna for the Mentally Ill," *The Fresno Bee,* June 2, 2006.

29. James Tassos, "Using the Housing Credit for Supportive Housing; An Assessment of 2005 State Policies," Enterprise Community Partners, Inc. and Corporation for Supportive Housing, 2006, **www.practitionerresources.org/cache/documents/637/63766.pdf.**

30. The program is a collaboration among the New Jersey State Parole Board, the state Departments of Corrections, Human Services (through its Division of Mental Health Services), and Community Affairs, and the New Jersey Housing and Mortgage Finance Agency.

Seattle Captures Private Investment
To Sustain Public Housing

On a hill overlooking downtown Seattle is an expanse of 561 low-income apartments housing about 1,200 residents. Like public housing elsewhere in the country, Yesler Terrace has long provided a home to struggling families, seniors on fixed incomes, immigrants, and other very low-income people. One-time residents of this, the nation's first racially integrated public housing project, include musician Jimi Hendrix and former Washington Governor Gary F. Locke.

The Seattle Housing Authority is attempting to save this important resource by allowing other uses on what is a very valuable piece of land. Though Yesler Terrace isn't falling apart, its $1 million annual operating costs consume an ever-greater share of diminishing funds, leaving less for maintenance than at other complexes. The housing authority believes that the most promising scenario involves using the proceeds from the lease or sale of some parcels to private developers to subsidize the construction of new public housing units, perhaps mixed in with high-end condominiums or apartments.

The planning is part of the authority's wider effort to sustain public housing and revitalize neighborhoods by unlocking the value of the agency's underlying assets. The authority is replacing four other isolated public housing complexes spread out over more than 300 acres with new, more densely developed and better designed communities. By selling more than 1,000 lots of public housing to private developers to build market-rate homes, the authority is subsidizing the cost of replacing every public housing unit, either on site or elsewhere in the city. What is more, a unique profit-sharing agreement with the homebuilders granted access to authority landholdings may generate millions more for authority activities.

A BETTER PLACE

Leveraging Public Housing Assets To Improve Communities and Lives

2

About 1.2 million low-income individuals and families live in public housing. More than half are elderly and/or disabled. Of those who are neither elderly nor disabled, half rely on earned wages, according to the Council of Large Public Housing Authorities (CLPHA). Some public housing families are headed by single parents or grandparents. Some are immigrants. Some are on welfare, and some are juggling more than one job.

By providing housing affordable to low-wage workers in high-growth industries such as hospitality and food service, public housing provides tangible economic benefits to local communities. A recent study finds that direct spending on public housing capital improvements and operations generates a roughly equivalent amount of indirect economic activity.[1] Moreover, public housing is an economic and social asset that cannot be created or sustained by the private market. Excluding land costs, it would take approximately $145 billion to replace the existing stock of public housing without generating returns for private investors.

As Seattle and other cities have demonstrated, well-functioning public housing agencies with sound housing stocks and entrepreneurial management can preserve shelter for their communities' lowest-income citizens while tackling their broader regional housing needs. Policy changes in the 1990s, designed in part to reduce the concentration of public housing, gave public housing authorities more flexibility to operate like private real estate managers, albeit with a social mission.[2] Already, many public housing authorities have shed old bureaucratic traditions for a new, entrepreneurial mindset.

Housing authority leaders must continue (or start) to move beyond being a franchise of the federal government to being a responsive local housing provider. They must use their land, properties, and federal income streams to leverage additional public and private resources—all with an eye toward preserving public housing and creating new affordable housing for a range of underserved populations.

Growing needs, diminishing federal resources, escalating building costs, and new rules requiring that all public housing authorities move to project-based management and accounting by 2011 will bring more authorities into alignment with private sector management practices.

The decision to expand beyond basic public housing management into new developments and partnerships can, however, be controversial. Local advocates may criticize the move as a shift in mission that will leave the lowest-income residents out of the picture. Authorities need to be clear that the new activities will help sustain support for low-income people while having a positive impact on the entire city.

Housing authorities are testing new ways to use their assets to secure private financing or loans for upgrades and new housing development. For example, a growing number are looking at bonds backed by federal Capital Fund allocations or, for smaller agencies, joining bond pools. Although HOPE VI funding levels have been declining, program successes have created a new market of private investors and lenders who want to invest in mixed-income, mixed-finance public housing—plus a cadre of architects and designers who specialize in such projects.

In addition, a handful of innovative housing authority leaders are diversifying their holdings with nonpublic housing, and, in some cases, spin-off service companies. This shift unburdens agencies somewhat from the vagaries of federal funding streams while giving authorities increasing freedom to engage in broader revitalization programs. Municipalities should continue to aid public housing redevelopment projects with expedited review processes, infrastructure investments such as tax incentive programs, housing levies, and, importantly, top-level affirmation by the mayor or county leader. By emphasizing school reform as integral to neighborhood revitalization, municipalities can also engage the business community in public housing redevelopment efforts.

RECOMMENDATIONS FOR LOCAL ACTION

1 Access Capital Markets to Accelerate Improvements To Public Housing

The nation's approximately 3,100 public housing authorities own and operate about 1.2 million housing units. Between 47,000 and 82,000 units are considered distressed.[3] While no current figures exist on the unfunded backlog of capital needs, some officials have put the total at upwards of $18 billion, with about $2 billion annually in new needs arising from depreciation.[4] Capital needs include such major projects as replacement of building systems, modernization of kitchens and baths, weatherization, and site work.

Housing authorities get about $6 billion annually through HUD for operating costs and capital needs. The operating subsidy, provided through the Public Housing Operating Fund, helps cover the gap between the rent that housing agencies are legally permitted to collect and operating costs such as insurance, maintenance, salary and benefits, and compliance with HUD regulations. Funding for capital needs comes through the Public Housing Capital Fund.

Federal funding, however, has failed to keep pace with increasing costs and changes in tenant rents. In the past eight years, the operating subsidy has covered 85–99 percent of need, according to the National Association of Housing and

Redevelopment Officials (NAHRO). With the implementation of a new funding formula in fiscal 2007, NAHRO reports that agencies received 76 percent of subsidy needed in the first quarter.[5] Funding for the capital program has also been on the decline, down about four percent annually from 2000 to 2006. The capital fund appropriation proposed by Congress for fiscal 2007 only slightly exceeds the amount needed to keep pace with ongoing depreciation, hardly addressing the backlog.[6]

Housing authorities must obligate capital fund monies within two years and spend them within four. Historically, the inability to save up years of funding has hampered authorities' capacity to complete big projects. Reforms passed in 1998 did, however, allow debt on public housing properties, opening up new financing opportunities. Housing authorities can now use the expected income from their future year federal capital fund allocations as collateral for private financing. To take advantage of this opportunity, authorities must welcome the scrutiny of bond agencies or lenders. Authorities are starting to use these opportunities to clear modernization backlogs and fund large-scale revitalization projects.

▼ CASES IN POINT

Large Authorities Issue Bonds Against Future Federal Receipts

Under HUD's Capital Fund Financing Program, authorities or intermediaries issue bonds using the expected capital fund receipts from the federal government as collateral. Among the handful of large housing authorities issuing sizable bonds are Chicago ($291 million), New York City[7] ($600 million in two increments), and Puerto Rico ($700 million). In the New York and Puerto Rico deals, HUD required another entity to share some risk. Bond-rating agencies usually insist on debt service coverage ratios of at least three to one, implying that agencies can pledge up to about a third of their annual allocation to repay the bond.[8]

The upshot for the authority is a large infusion to fund improvements in the short term, but a third less every year to spend on other public housing over the 20-year life of the bond.[9] Eligible uses of funds are mixed-finance projects that include public housing and improvements to building systems such as HVAC, windows, doors, and deferred maintenance. For example, the Chicago Housing Authority is using its 2001 bond issue—to be repaid with a portion of its $139 million annual capital fund allocation— to help fund a 15-year plan to rehabilitate or rebuild 25,000 public housing units.

Philadelphia Enhances Bond Issue with Tax Credits

The Philadelphia Housing Authority is the first housing authority to use private activity tax-exempt bonds backed by public housing capital funds to leverage Low-Income Housing Tax Credit (LIHTC) equity.[10] Projects involving rental housing can apply for four-percent tax credits from the state under the federal government's private activity bond cap. Under this arrangement, a separate entity—usually a limited partnership— takes ownership of the units. The authority must lend the capital fund proceeds to the limited partnership, which then invests the loan proceeds and tax-credit equity in public housing.

Philadelphia used this innovative financing structure to redevelop Tasker Homes, a distressed public housing site built in the 1940s. The $150 million in bond proceeds included $96 million in governmental purpose bonds and $54 million in private activity tax-exempt bonds, all secured by future allocation of capital funds ($12 million annually for 20 years). The $54 million in private activity tax-exempt bonds leveraged approximately $28 million in Low-Income Housing Tax Credit equity. Funds from other sources brought the total raised to $195 million. With the construction cost savings and leveraging the LIHTCs, the authority used roughly $165 million to demolish Tasker Homes in 2002 and build the new, lower-density Greater Grays Ferry Estates mixed-income community (completed in 2006). The remaining $30 million was used to renovate more than 200 units at two other public housing complexes that housed Tasker residents during construction.

Smaller Authorities Form Bond Pools

By going jointly to the bond market, smaller authorities without sizable capital fund appropriations can spread their expenses. The first such pool was the $131 million bond issue by 37 Alabama agencies in 2003. The agencies set up a nonprofit to serve as the "traffic cop." Similar pools have since been created in Illinois, Maryland, Massachusetts, New Jersey, and Pennsylvania.

Authorities Pledge Capital Funds to Obtain Loans

A growing number of public housing authorities are taking out direct loans from Fannie Mae and banks, pledging a portion of the capital fund as security for those loans. Because they are less expensive, direct loans make much more sense than capital fund bonds for smaller authorities whose annual allocations are $2–5 million, according to Standard & Poor's. Like the bond-rating agencies, lenders usually require debt service coverage ratios of three-to-one or more. Fannie Mae's Modernization Express product provides capital fund-backed loans ranging from seven to 20 years.

Voucher-backed Loans Provide a Promising Strategy

A handful of authorities have secured loans with properties funded by project-based vouchers to replace public housing. For example, the San Francisco Housing Authority's North Beach Place, an award-winning HOPE VI redevelopment project, included mortgage financing from Citibank based on project-based vouchers.

2 Make Strategic Choices to Sell Assets

As they engage in capital improvements, some housing authorities recognize that it makes more sense to sell some properties rather than keep them in portfolio. In such situations, federal Low-Income Housing Tax Credits can be a useful tool for keeping the units affordable. Under one arrangement, the authority sells a site to a developer who assembles a financing package that includes project-based vouchers, bonds, and four-percent tax credits, with the tax-credit units serving households at 50–60 percent of area median income.

Sale of Distressed DC Complexes Ensures Housing for Tenants

The Housing Authority of the District of Columbia has used the strategic disposition of assets several times. For example, sale of the Edgewood Terrace senior housing development to an affiliate of the Community Preservation and Development Corporation (CPDC) will help preserve the complex for low-income senior citizens. The high-rise property needed extensive repairs. With its long track record in rental preservation, CPDC was able to assemble a financing package to both rehabilitate the building and keep it affordable for tenants.[11] Had the housing authority retained ownership, it would not have been able to access that financing mix. In addition, a key component of CPDC's strategy is to offer strong support services to residents, something that housing authorities often lack the staff or expertise to handle.

Meanwhile, the DC housing authority will also sell the land under the highly distressed Arthur Capper and Carrollsburg projects in a neighborhood slated for economic revitalization, including a new ballpark. The land was valued at $37 million in December 2006 and is expected to net even more at the time of closing. The revenue will enable the authority to replace every unit of public housing that is razed. In addition to a significant number of affordable units, developers will build market-rate homes, office buildings, and retail space on the site.

Vancouver, WA Auction Nets Millions for Replacement Housing

The Vancouver Housing Authority auctioned a workforce housing development called Meadowbrook Place to private owners in early 2006. Since the development was financed entirely with tax-exempt bonds, the authority faced no regulatory approvals or barriers to its decision to rebalance its portfolio. Leveraging its equity position, the housing authority raised $4.5 million in unrestricted income to devote to new replacement housing elsewhere, nonfederal capital expenses, and community redevelopment programs.

Atlanta to Replace Public Housing Complexes with Vouchers

Atlanta's more radical approach to asset sales is too new to evaluate but worth watching. In early 2007, the Atlanta Housing Authority announced plans to demolish nearly all of its blighted multifamily public housing complexes and two senior communities, offering residents of the more than 3,000 units vouchers and counseling to move anywhere in the country. The authority, which has already converted 11 of its public housing projects into mixed-income communities, said it would be too costly to renovate the remaining complexes needing significant repairs. The properties will be sold or redeveloped as part of larger community development efforts.[12]

3 Diversify the Portfolio with Workforce Housing And Other For-Profit Ventures

A handful of innovative housing authority leaders have diversified their holdings with nonpublic housing and, in some cases, spin-off service companies. These initiatives unburden agencies somewhat from the vagaries of federal funding streams. In addition, they enable authorities to continue to house very poor families while helping to meet broader housing needs.

▼ CASES IN POINT

Authorities in Pacific Northwest Expand Bond- And Tax Credit-Funded Stock

The Portland, Seattle, and Vancouver housing authorities have used their bonding authority, along with Low-Income Housing Tax Credits, to expand their portfolios of nonpublic housing. The Portland Housing Authority owns more than 70 workforce housing and special needs properties, about half bond-owned and half tax credit-owned. The authority served as developer for 21 of those properties, recycling its developer fees into other endeavors. As of May 2006, the authority owned and operated about 2,400 units of traditional public housing and 3,900 units of work-force and special needs housing—often owned in partnership with other entities.

The Seattle Housing Authority operates approximately 5,400 public housing units and owns and manages, without operating subsidy, about 1,000 units of senior housing and 1,000 units of workforce housing. Using its bonding authority and tax credits to create housing for middle-class renters is part of a broader plan to reduce reliance on federal funding sources and help ensure that it can provide housing for as many extremely low-income people in the future as it does today. In 1998, 96 percent of the authority's revenues came from the federal government. By 2005, that share had decreased to about 75 percent.

The Vancouver Housing Authority (VHA) has used its public housing asset of 515 units as a base to build a portfolio of 2,200 workforce housing units, funded primarily by private activity bonds and federal Low-Income Housing Tax Credits. The authority acts as a developer or co-developer, thus earning fees. Like a private development company, it maintains multiple lines of credit with bank partners, using the funds to acquire sites and carry the cost of predevelopment as it assembles financing.

Workforce projects provide net cash flow to support new developments. For example, the Vancouver Housing Authority uses income from its workforce housing to subsidize the operation of four emergency shelters, owned by VHA and leased to nonprofits. By 2005, less than half of the authority's operating budget came from federal sources. The goal is to reduce this share to a third, in part through new ventures in industrial and commercial revitalization. Such ventures will tap new sources of financing, such as New Markets Tax Credits, industrial revenue bonds, and state-authorized tax increment financing.

Macon Housing Authority Creates Multiple Subsidiaries, Owns Trust Fund

The Housing Authority of the City of Macon, Georgia has created more than two dozen not-for-profit subsidiaries, most being single-asset entities that own tax-credit developments (and, unlike quasi-governmental entities, can compete for certain tax credit set-asides). One nonprofit subsidiary is a housing foundation that accepts tax-deductible gifts of cash or property that can be transferred to other subsidiaries. In the works are a nonprofit property management firm and a multifamily maintenance company, designed to handle the portfolios of the authority, its affiliates, and other affordable housing sponsors.

Macon's housing authority also has a for-profit subsidiary that serves as a managing general partner in a tax credit-funded development, offering investors more advantageous tax treatment of depreciation. These capabilities are enhanced by the authority's ability to issue tax-exempt revenue bonds and acquire land by eminent domain. The authority has issued three single-family mortgage revenue bonds totaling $38 million. A consortium of local banks used the proceeds to offer below-market financing, most with downpayment assistance, to more than 400 first-time homebuyers.

In addition, the authority plays a lead role in Georgia HAP Administrators Incorporated, a consortium of 10 housing authorities and the state housing finance agency that administers 300 project-based Section 8 properties in the state. The company recently won a contract for HAP administration of 500 properties in Illinois. Macon reinvests its share of this business, amounting to several hundred thousand dollars a year, in putting together tax-credit deals.

Finally, the housing authority created and endowed a $1.7 million trust fund that collects nonfederal funds earned through development and contract management activities. The fund provides front-end capital for affordable housing and community development ventures sponsored by the authority's local partners and affiliates. According to executive director John Hiscox, this may be the only such fund created by a public housing authority.

4 Implement Effective Site-Based Management And Operational Reforms

Following passage of the Quality Housing and Workforce Responsibility Act in 1998, Congress tasked researchers with estimating what it costs to operate well-run public housing. Based on the study results, Congress is requiring that all public housing authorities move to project-based management and accounting by 2011. Instead of getting an annual lump sum for operating costs based on the number of units, authorities will have to track revenues and expenses at each public housing complex. This rule forces authorities to align their systems with private-sector rental housing conventions.[13]

▼ CASES IN POINT

Portland Takes the Lead in Project-based Management

The Housing Authority of Portland, Oregon implemented project-based management and accounting to accommodate a portfolio of projects with increasingly different financing structures, resident populations, and housing types. Management of the public housing operations recently underwent a dramatic change. A central supply warehouse was closed, with purchasing authority given to on-site managers. The site managers now do more of the work that directly affects their properties, including being responsible for work orders, preventive maintenance, tenant applications and waiting lists, and lease enforcement and other issues associated with tenant turnover.

Applicants now apply for housing at the apartment communities rather than at a central intake office. An extensive team-based program trains staff to handle its new responsibilities. The authority is using its growing capacity to forecast revenues and costs by property to identify outdated public housing sites for revitalization. As it adapts to these and other strategic initiatives, the agency has removed barriers to cooperation between individual operating units. To reduce demands on staff and improve services, the agency partners with more than 100 public, private, and nonprofit organizations that provide supportive services to families living in authority-managed units.

Authorities Share Costs by Merging Staff Operations

The Laurinburg, North Carolina Housing Authority manages operations for two other very small housing authorities in its region, the Southern Pines and Maxton housing authorities. Laurinburg staff administers all programs under contract to each authority's board. While still fairly uncommon, this type of arrangement may become more widespread as small authorities attempt to take on new responsibilities, such as project-based accounting, with declining resources.

5 Replace Concentrated Public Housing With Mixed-Income Communities

Created by Congress in 1992, HOPE VI grants provide seed money to tear down and replace severely distressed and geographically isolated public housing complexes with more livable, mixed-income communities connected to their cities. HOPE VI essentially taught the public housing community how to attract private capital. To make it work, HUD for the first time stated that entities other than public housing authorities could own units as long as the owners follow public housing regulations. This allowed authorities to set up separate development entities (limited partnerships and limited liability corporations) that could use Low-Income Housing Tax Credits and other funding sources such as the Federal Home Loan Bank program.

With HOPE VI, authorities used their affiliates to develop mixed-income projects. Under one structure for such projects, a third of the units are market-rate, a third are funded with tax credits and thus affordable to families making up to 50–60 percent of the area median income, and a third are public housing. The income from the more expensive units may thus subsidize the less expensive units. Land sales or rents for community centers, health clinics, and other facilities also provide revenues. As of December 2006, 127 housing authorities were awarded HOPE VI revitalization grants, with some winning several grants for different projects.

Research suggests dramatic improvements in the neighborhoods near some HOPE VI developments, including rising resident incomes, falling unemployment, and less concentration of poverty. Two studies of Philadelphia Housing Authority redevelopments found that property values in the surrounding communities increased by 142 percent from 1999 to 2000—more than 2.5 times the citywide rate.[14] One of the studies estimated that the increases generated an additional $4 million annually in property taxes.

A cost-benefit analysis of the revitalization of East Lake Meadows, once one of Atlanta's most distressed housing projects, looked at the return on equity invested during the revitalization. The study found that the redevelopment improved social and economic welfare by $197 million, with every dollar invested generating a $2.90 net benefit.[15]

Despite its successes, HOPE VI funding fell from $575 million in fiscal 2000 to $99 million in fiscal 2006, and the program's future is uncertain. Fortunately, HOPE VI has created a new market of private investors and lenders who want to invest in mixed-income, mixed-finance public housing. HOPE VI experiments with innovative designs have also created a cadre of architects and designers who specialize in such projects.

▼ CASES IN POINT

San Francisco Community Fully Replaces Public Housing

The San Francisco Housing Authority and lead developer BRIDGE Housing Corporation have gained national recognition for the $108 million North Beach Place development. The project replaced a "prison-like" public housing project "beset by rodents and sewage problems" with a mixed-income complex that enhances the surrounding North Beach area.[16] With some HOPE VI-funded projects, the number of new affordable units falls short of the number of public housing units lost. Not so with North Beach Place.[17] The development replaced 229 public housing units with 341 affordable apartments, including 138 public housing units, 119 project-based Section 8 units, and apartments funded by tax credits and affordable to families with up to 50 percent of the area median income.

A $20 million HOPE VI grant to the San Francisco Housing Authority in 1996 seeded the redevelopment. The development partnership, led by BRIDGE Housing Corporation, received $17 million in tax credits from the State of California and about $38 million in federal Low-Income Housing Tax Credits—reportedly the largest allocation to a single project at the time. Other funding sources include a $10 million loan from the city, $1 million from the Federal Home Loan Bank of San Francisco, and $56 million for interim financing from Citibank (of which $24 million was converted to permanent financing). The housing authority retains ownership of the site through a 75-year lease to the development partnership.

Philadelphia Revitalizes Community Without HOPE VI Funds

Philadelphia's Greater Grays Ferry Estates is an example of a HOPE VI-like project that did not rely on HOPE VI grants. The Philadelphia Housing Authority's most ambitious development, Greater Grays Ferry Estates replaced the highly distressed and crime-ridden Tasker Homes project with an open, suburban-style development. Although the new community has about half of Tasker's 1,081 units, many of the original units had been vacant or practically uninhabitable. The new community features 125 for-sale single-family homes affordable to households making from $21,000 to $55,000 a year, 357 units of public housing family rental units, 72 enhanced-services apartments for seniors, a workforce training center and maintenance facility, and a community center/ office building. (The housing authority also plans to convert 125 of the family rental units to homeownership at the end of the 15-year tax credit compliance period.) The $165 million funding package set the standard for innovative mixed financing.

---

6 Engage Key Stakeholders in Redevelopment Plans

Municipalities should support revitalization efforts of housing authorities by inviting in stakeholders. Important stakeholders include key city staff in the planning, housing, and economic development departments, local bankers, residents, public housing tenants, foundations, and the business community, as well as representatives of any major industry that has a large presence in the community.

Municipalities themselves have an important role to play in supporting public housing redevelopment. For example, they can expedite processes, make infrastructure investments and, importantly, provide top-level affirmation by the mayor or county leader. Jurisdictions can also offer their own tax incentive programs, such as the tax increment financings in Chicago and San Bernardino, California. In addition, housing levies can support authority-led mixed-income developments.

For example, an $89 million housing levy passed in Seattle in 2001 provides funds for the developers that partner on Seattle Housing Authority projects.

Many Join Chicago Housing Authority's Plan for Transformation

Chicago's $1.6 billion, 15-year plan to rebuild or rehabilitate 25,000 public housing units is a city- and statewide effort involving more than 160 partners. Launched by the Chicago Housing Authority (CHA) in 2000, it is the largest public housing reconstruction in US history and will transform some of the nation's most notorious projects into mixed-use, mixed-income neighborhoods.

The plan replaces or rehabilitates 14 family public housing complexes with 20,000 units (just under 9,000 of which were habitable and occupied) into new communities totaling more than 22,000 units. The communities include roughly 8,000 public housing units and more than 14,000 affordable and market-rate apartments and homes. The plan seeks to provide housing for every resident who was lease-compliant as of October 1999, along with better access to services such as job training, daycare, and drug treatment.

Both the city Department of Housing and the Illinois Housing Development Authority are contributing substantial allocations of Low-Income Housing Tax Credits, as well as other loan funds, to the affordable units in the new communities. The city has invested more than $500 million of its own funds for infrastructure, including new streets and sewers, lighting, schools, parks, and police and fire stations. Other public agencies have mobilized to support the plan. For example, the city Department of Planning and Development has created a significant number of Tax Increment Financing (TIF) districts in areas of public housing and assessed ways to foster retail, commercial, and housing development at the sites.[18] The Parks Department is helping to create additional park space, while the school system is creating charter and magnet schools for the communities. This coordination is supported by monthly meetings among the mayor and key department heads.

Leveraged funds are also coming from the philanthropic sector. The John D. and Catherine T. MacArthur Foundation worked with the city and the public housing authority to arrange a tax increment financing facility to provide funds for redeveloping public housing sites. Under the arrangement, Fannie Mae and the Methodist Pension Fund lent $15 million, backed by the expected increase in tax revenues in the revitalized neighborhoods. The MacArthur Foundation guaranteed the loan.

The MacArthur Foundation and other leading civic institutions created The Partnership for New Communities to support the "Plan for Transformation." The partnership intends to raise $15 million to invest in strategic, high-impact initiatives in key communities, including employer-assisted housing and job training for public housing residents. The partners are also engaged in other ways. For example, the Illinois Institute of Technology is offering forgivable downpayment grants to employees who buy homes in the new mixed-income development near campus. The University of Chicago is also matching downpayment funds of teachers, police officers, and firefighters who choose to move into the developments.

7 Improve Relocation Services for Displaced Residents

While redevelopment of public housing has enormous benefits, it does displace tenants. Residents of properties slated for revitalization are moved into other public housing or given Housing Choice Vouchers to find rental units in the private market. Although HOPE VI was designed to enable residents to move back into their former communities, some tenants have financial and credit issues, health or substance abuse problems, disabilities, or other conditions that make their return difficult.[19] These "hard-to-house" tenants are also likely to face barriers to finding decent housing elsewhere.

Housing authorities must assess the quality of their relocation services to help former tenants succeed in their new homes or return to redeveloped sites. In their 2005 report, "Public Housing Transformation and the Hard-to-House," Urban Institute researchers outline the services that housing authorities should provide hard-to-house tenants, including search assistance and post-move support, transitional and permanent supportive housing, service-enriched SRO units, and counseling and support for households with one-strike problems.

The housing authorities in Tucson and Seattle are among those providing extensive and successful relocation services, according to a 2004 report from the Urban Institute and The Brookings Institution, "A Decade of HOPE VI: Research Findings and Policy Challenges." In Tucson, relocation counselors escorted tenants seeking to move off-site to potential apartments and held one-on-one sessions to discuss the merits of various neighborhoods. The authority also offers job training and educational services. The Chicago Housing Authority has improved its tenant relocation efforts with services similar to Tucson's, along with relocation clinics, budget and housekeeping training, and mobility counseling to encourage residents to move to lower-poverty neighborhoods.

8 Balance Tougher Screening Policies with New Tenant Support

In keeping with the view that the public housing stock is an asset, authorities have tightened their screening policies and implemented requirements more like the private sector. Policies may include conducting background checks, credit checks, home visits, and reference checks from previous landlords. To go beyond "housing of last resort," authorities must implement these tougher rules carefully—balancing them with family self-sufficiency programs, homeownership programs, job training, and other supportive services.

Mixed-Income Community Offers Youth Facilities, Resident Services

Like other authorities, the Housing Authority of Portland has incorporated various tenant supports in its HOPE VI redevelopment projects. For example, the 82-acre New Columbia redevelopment includes not only a mix of public housing, workforce rentals, and for-sale homes but also a new public elementary school, a Boys & Girls Club, and a lifelong learning center. Created through a partnership with Portland's community college, the state department of employment, and the regional workforce investment organization, the center helps people seeking higher-paying jobs with counseling, computer training, and a range of classes.

Authorities Connect Residents with Work, Job Training

The Atlanta Housing Authority (AHA) requires that non-disabled, non-elderly recipients of rental subsidies have a job, go to school, or be in a job training program. AHA contracts with service providers to connect residents with practical employment, job training and educational experiences that can lead to permanent jobs, and supports to sustain that employment. For example, the Atlanta Workforce Development Agency gives priority job placement to AHA residents who have been relocated because of public housing redevelopment. If residents need childcare, the Department of Labor covers the costs. In the first year after AHA imposed the work requirement, compliance was nearly 70 percent.

As part of its plan to transform public housing into new mixed-income communities, the Chicago Housing Authority (CHA) requires adult occupants of public housing in the new communities to work or attend school at least 30 hours per week. To assist CHA residents and voucher recipients seeking work, the authority partners with the Department of Human Services, job training agencies, and more than 150 employers. Between 1999 and the end of 2006, these efforts helped more than 3,000 CHA tenants find work, lifting the employment rate (for both full and part-time workers) from 25 percent to 39 percent. The CHA, the city, the state, and philanthropic partners have pledged $22.5 million to place another 3,000 public housing residents by 2009.

To help the 14,000 households it serves succeed in their residency, the Housing Authority of Portland has used its Moving to Work authority to devote significant resources to its Family Self-Sufficiency (FSS) program. FSS is a HUD-assisted program that assigns case management staff to work with selected public housing residents and voucher recipients to create five-year plans for achieving self-sufficiency goals, such as enhanced employment or homeownership. As of the end of 2005, 485 participants had graduated from the FSS program and left public assistance, and 40 percent had become homeowners.

Chicago, Cambridge Aid Youth Educational Attainment

As part of its plan to transform high-rise public housing into new mixed-income communities, the Chicago Housing Authority has funded case managers to help teenagers apply for college or jobs and to help place younger children in Head Start, daycare, and after-school activities. It has also brought in new foundation partners to expand a program that has provided 665 college scholarships since 1997.

In Cambridge, Massachusetts, the housing authority operates an education and employment program for youth who live in public housing or in voucher-subsidized units. The program, called The Work Force, enrolls children in the eighth grade and follows them through high school. It provides after-school life-skills classes, a literacy program, preparation for the state graduation test, staff for homework help centers, college prep activities, and a modest scholarship to attend two- or four-year colleges. The program also offers "try-out" jobs with 45 area employers who serve as worksite mentors. Participants work in medical offices, engineering firms, law offices, nonprofits, and non-fast food retail establishments. In operation since 1984, the program is funded primarily by HUD and a variety of local governmental and private sources, including Cambridge Public Schools. As of 2006, 135 youth were enrolled. All of the seniors graduated and 88 percent matriculated at two- or four-year colleges.

9 Develop Partnerships to Provide Assisted Living

A growing share of public housing residents—about 52 percent—are low-income elderly and/or disabled households.[20] Most public housing for seniors, which usually accommodates disabled persons as well, is about 20–35 years old and without the amenities and design considerations for people with special needs. Especially lacking is funding for the services necessary to support seniors and people with disabilities in an independent, healthy lifestyle.

Some authorities are using innovative financing strategies and partnerships to retrofit public housing so that people can age in place rather than go to more expensive nursing homes. One emerging trend is to combine public housing subsidies and capital funds with Medicaid waivers to create affordable assisted-living units.

▼ CASES IN POINT

Milwaukee Complex Allows Seniors to Age in Place

Milwaukee's Lapham Park complex is the nation's first assisted-living facility within a public housing development. Concerned about the need for health services for the mostly elderly and frail residents, the Housing Authority of the City of Milwaukee, the Milwaukee County Department on Aging, and several service agencies formed Lapham Park Venture.[21] The initiative brought together practitioners in planning, housing, gerontology, and social services to provide on-site medical care to residents. Services include pharmacy, home healthcare, physical therapy, podiatry, and dental care.

The housing authority raised more than $1.3 million in a capital campaign to transform the building's basement into a 1930s streetscape with a "storefront" exam room, physicians' offices, pharmacy, whirlpool baths, and a gym. According to one estimate,

Lapham Park Venture is saving taxpayers over $1 million annually in Medicaid nursing home costs by providing a continuum of care that allows fully 96 percent of elderly residents to age in place.[22]

Philadelphia Uses Medicaid Waivers to Help Fund Senior Complex

As part of the 554-unit Greater Grays Ferry Estates mixed-income development, the Philadelphia Housing Authority built an enhanced senior services complex with 72 apartments for seniors. The building is designed to nursing home standards with wider hallways and beds, plus other amenities such as a first-floor barbershop. Through a partnership with Program of All-Inclusive Care for the Elderly (PACE), a senior medical services agency, the project accessed Medicaid waivers to help fund construction and ongoing maintenance of the complex.

State Trust Fund Monies Aid Vancouver, WA Assisted Facilities

To better serve very low-income seniors, the Vancouver Housing Authority (VHA) in 1996 converted six stories of a public housing high-rise to offer assisted-living services in concert with a private provider. This effort was expanded in 2000 with construction of Arbor Ridge Assisted Living and Arbor Ridge Senior Apartments, two adjoining properties co-developed by the VHA and Columbia Non-Profit Housing. CNPH developed 40 high-quality senior apartments using the HUD 202 Program, as well as an allocation of state housing trust fund monies. The adjacent assisted-living property consists of 60 dwelling units financed with private activity bonds and tax credits, as well as state housing trust fund revenue.

---

10 Leverage Housing Authority Resources To Improve Public Schools

City leaders and housing officials increasingly recognize the key role that schools play in neighborhood revitalization plans. In a 2003 lecture, Richard D. Baron, Chairman and CEO of McCormack Baron Salazar, Inc., said that improving schools must be the centerpiece of creating vital communities in once-distressed urban areas.[23] Schools affect housing markets and home values, influencing whether individuals and companies will invest in neighborhoods and whether neighborhoods can retain their residents.

▼ CASES IN POINT

Rebuilt School Becomes One of Atlanta's Top Performers

In the mid-1990s, the Atlanta Housing Authority and partners replaced the former Techwood/Clark Howell Homes with a new mixed-income community called Centennial Place. As part of the project, a poorly performing school was razed and rebuilt just beyond the housing community, so that it became part of the broader neighborhood. Working with the Georgia Institute of Technology across the street, the school district created an entirely new curriculum. Now Centennial Place Elementary is one of the highest performers in the school system even though more than half of the students are from low-income households. Each of the revitalization plans for AHA sites includes a strategy for producing an excellent neighborhood school.

Public-Private Partnership Launches Milwaukee Cyber School

The Housing Authority of the City of Milwaukee partnered with HUD, Johnson Controls, and the Central City Cyberschool (C3) to build a $7 million state-of-the-art technology school within Parklawn, a HOPE VI community. C3, a charter school serving 350 students in grades one through eight, opened in 2000. Every student has a laptop computer and can log onto the Internet from anywhere in the building. Johnson Controls provided access to financing to help build the school with integrated HVAC, security, fire alarm, and lighting controls under a 15-year lease-to-own contract.

OPPORTUNITIES FOR STATE ACTION

1 Help Local Authorities Access Capital Markets

In a few cases, a state housing finance agency has served as the lead agency for bond pools, issuing the bonds under HUD's Capital Fund Financing Program and loaning the proceeds to pool participants. Expanding this kind of partnership may require establishing closer relations between local housing authorities and state housing finance agencies.

In November 2005, the Pennsylvania Housing Finance Agency (PHFA) issued a $22 million bond for seven housing authorities across the state. Most of the authorities are using the funds to cover deferred maintenance, but at least one will undertake some new construction. PHFA plans to issue another bond pool in early 2007. State housing finance agencies in Illinois, Maryland, Massachusetts, and New Jersey have also led such bond pools.

2 Support Mixed-Income Communities

State housing finance agencies can support mixed-income developments by giving preference to such communities—or public housing agencies in general—in their Low-Income Housing Tax Credit allocation plans. This can be done formally or informally. For example, the Chicago, Philadelphia, and San Francisco housing authorities are among those that have built strong relationships with their state housing finance agencies, which helps them compete for tax credits. As of 2005, the Philadelphia Housing Authority received more tax credits than any other entity in the state.

In a collaborative effort, the Association of Washington Housing Authorities has worked with the Washington State Housing Finance Commission on policies to ensure HOPE VI replacement housing projects are financed in a timely manner without "crowding out" other low-income housing developments. Under this partnership, the legislature provides local housing authorities a set-aside of not less than 10 percent of the state's allocation of private activity bonds, providing predictability for local housing authorities that want to diversify their portfolios.

Other state policies can encourage a mix of incomes and uses in development projects. For example, the State of Washington requires that only 51 percent of units in projects financed with housing authority bonds must be low-income (affordable to people who make up to 80 percent of the area median income). That is not true in all states. In Oregon, the policy with respect to bond-financed properties is more restrictive, requiring all units to be affordable to people below 80 percent of area median income. In states that do not allow market-rate housing to be mixed with affordable units, authorities must find private partners to develop these units, potentially adding to the cost.

3 Ease the Way for Local Housing Authorities To Diversify Their Portfolios

State leaders should reexamine the myriad rules and regulations that prevent housing authorities from branching out into other income streams. Some states, for example, have procurement rules that hamstring authority efforts. Under Pennsylvania law, housing authorities must bid out anything costing more than $20,000, compared with a limit of $100,000 under federal law.

At the same time, states can explore new ways to help authorities' development programs. For example, some housing finance agencies have favored HOPE VI or other public housing redevelopment efforts in their allocation of nine-percent Low-Income Housing Tax Credits. More of this should be done. These agencies could also sub-allocate some of the private activity bond cap to local housing authorities, if that is necessary in their state.

In addition, states can offer direct grants for affordable units that housing authorities can use. A number of California housing authorities have successfully leveraged funds made available from the state's $2.1 billion bond issue (known as Proposition 46), along with other funds, to increase affordable housing projects.

States could foster innovation among smaller public housing agencies that do not have the staff, expertise, or funds to launch new ventures. States should consider establishing a grant or loan program providing seed money to smaller agencies to undertake different kinds of projects.

Increasingly, states have empowered housing authorities to act as community development or redevelopment agencies, creating a synergy among housing development and commercial revitalization, workforce development, and resident self-sufficiency programs. For example, Minnesota and Virginia both merged their housing and redevelopment agencies for administrative efficiency. California and Washington have also embraced and facilitated an expanded role for well-managed local housing authorities. California mandates a set-aside of tax increment financing for affordable housing development. For its part, Washington gives cities and counties the option of designating housing authorities or port authorities as community renewal agencies.

AFFORDABLE HOUSING FINANCE
www.housingfinance.com/ahf/

Magazine regularly covering innovative public/private partnerships to redevelop public housing and other public housing issues. The May 2006 issue focuses on the future of public housing and includes the article, "PHAs Test Ways to Deliver Aid."

THE BROOKINGS INSTITUTION
www.brookings.edu

Private nonprofit organization devoted to independent research and innovative policy solutions. The Brookings Metropolitan Policy Program has published reports and briefs on the transformation of public housing, including "Public Housing Reform and Voucher Success: Progress and Challenges," January 2005.

COMMUNITIES & BANKING
www.bos.frb.org/commdev/c&b/index.htm

Quarterly publication of the Federal Reserve Bank of Boston reporting on regional and national trends in community development, affordable housing, and financial services. Among the articles involving public housing are "A New Approach to Public Housing," Winter 2007, and "Elderly Public Housing & Assisted Living," Summer 2004.

COUNCIL OF LARGE PUBLIC HOUSING AUTHORITIES (CLPHA)
www.clpha.org

Represents 60 of the nation's largest public housing authorities, providing a forum for developing and promoting innovative and effective approaches to housing development and management. CLPHA has published a 2007 report on the economic benefits of public housing, an article examining the ability of redeveloped public housing complexes to effect economic improvement in surrounding communities, a Moving to Work backgrounder, and success stories about how public housing is being revitalized in cities across the nation.

HOUSING POLICY DEBATE
www.fanniemaefoundation.org/programs/hpd.shtml

Quarterly journal published by the Fannie Mae Foundation covering housing and community development issues. Articles of note include "Public Housing Transformation and the Hard-to-House" and "The HOPE VI Program: What About the Residents?"

RESOURCES

LOCAL INITIATIVES SUPPORT CORPORATION
Housing Authority Resource Center
www.lisc.org/whatwedo/programs/harc/

Brokers relationships between local housing authorities and other community developers in neighborhoods across the country. In part through alliances with its partners, HARC provides a range of services for business-minded housing authorities, including strategic planning. The website features a July 2005 report from the HARC symposium, "Breaking New Ground: Entrepreneurial Approaches for Housing Authorities."

NATIONAL ASSOCIATION OF HOUSING AND REDEVELOPMENT OFFICIALS
www.nahro.org

Association of administrators of HUD programs such as Public Housing, Section 8, CDBG and HOME. Its public housing resource web page links to fact sheets on public housing, including spending levels. An overview of public housing innovations, "Innovative Public Housing Initiatives: An Annotated Bibliography," is also available on the website.

PUBLIC HOUSING AUTHORITIES DIRECTORS ASSOCIATION
www.phada.org

Represents the professional administrators of approximately 1,900 housing authorities throughout the US. PHADA works closely with members of Congress to develop sensible and effective public housing statutes and obtain adequate funding for low-income housing programs. The association also serves as an advocate before HUD on a variety of regulations governing public housing nationwide. The PHADA website offers an extensive set of guidebooks and manuals on various management issues.

TRANSPIRE INC.
www.transpire.org/alliance.html

Nonprofit subsidiary of the National Association of Housing and Redevelopment Officials (NAHRO). Transpire provides agencies expanding beyond traditional public and assisted housing activities access to working capital lines, bond financing, and other financial and technical assistance products.

US DEPARTMENT OF HOUSING AND URBAN DEVELOPMENT
Office of Public and Indian Housing
www.hud.gov/offices/pih/

Sponsors conferences with training on capital fund financing, capital improvement planning, and accessing financing for modernization and/or mixed-finance development. The Office of Public and Indian Housing is also developing training for public housing authorities about basic procedures for good project-level management, including project-based accounting and budgeting.

THE URBAN INSTITUTE
www.urbaninstitute.org

Gathers and analyzes data, conducts policy research, evaluates programs, and educates Americans on issues and trends to promote public debate on national priorities. The institute has published numerous reports and studies on elements of public housing transformation, including "Distressed Public Housing—What it Costs to Do Nothing" and "A Decade of HOPE VI: Research Findings and Policy Challenges."

ENDNOTES CHAPTER 2

1. Econsult Corp, "Assessing the Economic Benefits of Public Housing: Final Report," report prepared for the Council of Large Public Housing Authorities, January 2007.

2. The Moving to Work demonstration program authorized by Congress in 1996 allowed a certain number of housing authorities to negotiate waivers from certain HUD rules, such as those governing housing vouchers. It also allows them to combine their operating, capital, and voucher funds into one funding pool. As of August 2006, 31 agencies had participated at some time and 24 agencies were currently participating. Congress took some of the lessons learned from Moving to Work when it passed the Quality Housing and Workforce Responsibility Act (QHWRA) in 1998. The act further changed the rules by allowing public housing authorities to secure debt by mortgaging their properties.

3. Senator Barbara Mikulski (D-MD) cites this estimate in her 2005 HOPE VI reauthorization bill (**thomas.loc.gov/cgi-bin/query/z?c109:S.1513:**). The estimate derives from Margery Austin Turner et al., "Distressed Public Housing—What It Costs to Do Nothing," The Urban Institute, April 2005. Based on his read of the research, in his paper for The Brookings Institution, "Public Housing Reform and Voucher Success: Progress and Challenges," Rod Solomon offers the more conservative estimate of almost 47,000 distressed public housing units.

4. HUD Secretary Alphonso Jackson has used the $18 billion figure in congressional hearings, as did Barbara Mikulski's 2005 HOPE VI reauthorization bill. The $18 billion is believed to be an estimate as of about 2003, subtracting presumed reductions in the backlog from an estimate of the unfunded backlog in 1998. A 2000 study by Abt Associates Inc. found a 1998 unfunded backlog of $24.6 billion (or $21.6 billion in 1990 dollars when adjusted to compare with an earlier capital needs study).

5. As of February 2007, the pending bill in Congress, HJ Res 20, may include an additional $300 million for operating subsidy, which would bring funding up to about 84 percent of need for the year, according to NAHRO. The president's budget proposal for FY2008 would supply about 84 percent of the projected operating subsidy need for the public housing program.

6. Rod Solomon, *Journal of Housing and Community Development*, September/October 2006. The president's budget proposal reduces funding to just over $2 billion, a cut of more than $400 million. The budget document states that $1.96 billion is provided for annually accruing capital needs, but there is no funding marked to address the backlog.

7. In some cases, another entity will issue the bond for the housing authority. For example, the New York City Housing Development Corp. issued the bond for the New York City Housing Authority and then made a loan to the housing authority, using the loan payment to repay bondholders.

8. Although these transactions rely on substantial debt service coverage and stable federal allocations, HUD and bond rating agencies will also look at authorities' financial and legal strength, performance on construction and modernization projects, planning and wherewithal to spend money within HUD guidelines, checks and balances, experience with special types of projects outside of traditional public housing modernization, and board and senior staff relationships, according to Standard & Poor's.

9. Bond or loan proceeds may be about four times the amount of the annual capital grant, and must be spent within four years.

10. LIHTCs are allocated by the federal government, but allocated by the states through a competitive process. Developers usually sell the credits to investors and use the proceeds, or equity, to fund the project. There are two types of tax credits: nine-percent credits and four-percent credits, allocated in conjunction with a "bond cap" that allows the issuance

of tax-exempt bonds. The recipient of an allocation of private activity bond cap has the option to claim the four-percent LIHTCs associated with the bonds. This credit may be syndicated to investors to raise additional funding for the development. For more information on the tax credit program, see **www.ncsha.org/uploads/20040311_HC_factsheet.pdf**.

11. The package includes a HUD Section 202 capital grant plus public housing and project-based Section 8 units, both subsidized in part with Low-Income Housing Tax Credits.

12. S. A. Reid, "Atlanta to raze most of its public housing complexes," The Atlanta Journal-Constitution, February 15, 2007.

13. Organizations such as NAHRO have an expanded course offering, including workshops on newer topics such as asset management. Other sources of training include universities. Consulting firms that provide training on project-based accounting include Casterline Associates, PC and Nan McKay and Associates. At the Philadelphia Housing Authority, which has implemented asset-based management, all property managers are accredited by the Institute for Real Estate Management.

14. The studies, by Applied Real Estate Analysis, Inc. (AREA) and Econsult Corp., were commissioned by the Philadelphia Housing Authority and released in 2005. For more information, see **www.pha.phila.gov/press/index.asp?id=22**.

15. McKinsey & Company, "East Lake—A Model for Successful Community Revitalization," presentation materials, August 4, 2006. The analysis compared net differences in current and previous rates of crime, employment earnings, public housing assistance use, and residential property values.

16. "Community Impact/San Francisco, Winner: North Beach Place, San Francisco," *San Francisco Business Times,* March 28, 2005.

17. Donna Kimura, "Readers' Choice: Family Projects: Grand Ideas Realized at North Beach Place," *Affordable Housing Finance,* August 2005.

18. Tax increment financing districts help cities fund redevelopment projects in economically distressed areas by diverting new tax revenues generated by rising property values back to the district. To raise money quickly, cities usually sell tax increment bonds to investors, pledging future tax increment flows to repay the bondholders.

19. Other hard-to-house residents include grandparents caring for grandchildren, very large households, and families with multiple barriers such as low education, criminal records, little work history, or mental health issues, according to Susan J. Popkin et al., "Public Housing Transformation and the Hard-to-House," *Housing Policy Debate,* 16:1.

20. HUD's Resident Characteristics Report for the period August 1, 2005–November 30, 2006.

21. Lapham Park Venture is one of 11 innovative models in elderly public housing that HUD identified at **www.hud.gov/offices/pih/pihcc/innovationmodels.cfm**, accessed December 8, 2006.

22. Michael Davidson, "2004 National Social Advocacy Award, Lapham Park Venture, Milwaukee," *Planning,* April 2004, **www.planning.org/affordablereader/planning/milwaukee0404.htm**.

23. James W. Rouse Lecture on the American City, October 16, 2003. Baron's for-profit company has served as the lead developer for many public housing redevelopment efforts, including the Atlanta Housing Authority's flagship HOPE VI project, Centennial Place.

Voucher and Mobility Counseling Provides Disabled Man a Ticket to a New Life

John Price's new apartment in West Haven, Connecticut may be modest, but it's bright and clean and safe. And the view from here is worlds away from where he's been.

John once made a decent living as a maintenance worker at Yale University. After developing a degenerative spine disease, he lost his job and his pension, ending up in a New Haven apartment next door to a drug dealer. After a drive-by shooting outside his window, he'd had enough. John already had a federal Housing Choice Voucher, a ticket out of his dangerous environment. Mobility counseling enabled him to use that ticket.

Working with the nonprofit HOME Inc., John found a new apartment in a bustling neighborhood in suburban West Haven. Outside the window, instead of gunshots are the sounds of traffic on a busy thoroughfare lined with coffee shops, family restaurants, and other commercial establishments. When he leaves in the morning to catch the bus outside his door to Gateway Community College, he doesn't have to step around empty drug needles on the sidewalk. He's going back to school to get his associate's degree in engineering. At 51, John Price feels he is getting a new start.

A NEW START

Using Housing Vouchers
To Expand Life Opportunities

3

The Housing Choice Voucher program is the main vehicle specifically intended to provide permanent shelter for the poorest US families. Approximately two million very low-income families and individuals have an affordable home through the program. Families with vouchers live in privately owned rental apartments, generally paying 30 percent of their household income for rent and utilities. The voucher, provided by the US Department of Housing and Urban Development through a public housing agency, covers the rest (up to a maximum set by the agency).[1]

Housing Choice Vouchers are an important tool in an overall housing strategy that seeks to boost the supply of affordable housing while improving the economic well-being of low-income citizens. The program—commonly referred to as Section 8[2]—has traditionally enjoyed bipartisan support, with policymakers across the political spectrum viewing it as an effective way to help low-income families find safe and affordable homes of their choice.

But the full potential of vouchers remains unrealized unless they are distributed and administered in ways that create new opportunities for households and serve as a springboard for personal and economic advancement. Voucher programs should help people move to quality housing near good schools and job centers. Research backs up the commonsense notion that where you live shapes your life chances. Many studies have shown that living in distressed, high-poverty neighborhoods affects health and limits opportunities.[3] In contrast, more stable and economically advantaged communities generally offer greater access to jobs, better public schools, safer parks and public spaces, and less crime and violence.

In the past, public housing authorities received a set allocation of vouchers and were reimbursed for the actual cost of administering those vouchers, even when tenants moved from lower-cost to higher-cost neighborhoods. Starting in 2004, however, the program switched to a budget-based or fixed-funding formula, producing shortfalls for housing authorities nationwide.[4] In 2005 and 2006, authorities received a set amount based on what they spent in the middle of 2004, plus inflation. Under a budget-based system, authorities that want to help a small number of people move to more expensive communities must reduce the number of people they serve overall.

Continuing appropriations legislation covering fiscal 2007 recalculated the formulas yet again, distributing voucher funding on the basis of authority costs during the most recent 12 months for which voucher cost information was available. Although still budget-based, this "recent-cost formula" may distribute funding more efficiently to meet local housing authority renewal funding needs and to improve incentives to lease up a maximum number of vouchers. The law also sets aside $100 million to reimburse authorities for added costs due to portability (and other factors). Later in 2007, Congress is expected to consider other improvements to authorizing legislation.

Given funding constraints, however, many public housing authorities will find it hard to fund mobility and tenant support programs out of their voucher administration fees. Moreover, given the lack of incentives in the federal system, they are likely to focus on their core operations. State and local governments should support these important efforts by providing their own assistance and incentives. In addition, they can make sure housing officials are taking full advantage of other enrichment programs—such as Family Self Sufficiency (FSS) and Section 8 Homeownership— that can enhance economic if not geographic mobility. Finally, local and state governments can bring public housing agencies into joint purchasing arrangements or offer other in-kind aid that does not add new costs but can help authorities save operating dollars for mobility and other services.

In turn, voucher program administrators can look outside their standard income streams for funds to support mobility and tenant services. Although programs such as Moving to Opportunity and Regional Opportunity Counseling[5] no longer receive federal allocations, some localities have found ways to keep pieces of their programs using funds freed up by their Moving to Work designation, by forming strategic partnerships, or by using other public or philanthropic support.

Improving opportunities for housing voucher holders is tough but important. Many of the approaches outlined here align with bipartisan goals of helping poor families build assets and leave welfare. Mobility and self-sufficiency services demonstrate how housing assistance can be a hand up, rather than simply a handout.

RECOMMENDATIONS FOR LOCAL ACTION

1 ### Create Programs to Help Families Move Closer To Jobs and Schools

Mobility counseling programs provide the most direct way to help voucher holders move closer to jobs, better schools, and other opportunities. Vouchers are portable, allowing recipients to move from one housing authority's jurisdiction into another after one year.

Research on relocation programs has shown that families moving to greater opportunity neighborhoods experienced significant improvements in their environments and notable improvements in the well-being of both adults and children. For example, studies tracking outcomes for the Gautreaux families (Chicago public housing families who received vouchers to move throughout the region) found that those who relocated to middle-income suburbs had higher employment rates than those who moved to low-income city neighborhoods. Studies also show that the children of families who move to the suburbs are more likely to go to college than children of families who move within the city, while families that relocate to neighborhoods with more educated residents are less likely to remain on welfare.[7]

Where possible, voucher programs should specifically seek to send holders into neighborhoods and situations where they can succeed. This is a different strategy than focusing simply on getting voucher holders out of certain neighborhoods. People who move to unfamiliar communities need support handling the challenges of their new environment.[8]

▼ CASES IN POINT

Outreach, Post-Move Support Key to Voucher Mobility in Chicago

In 1999, the Chicago Housing Authority converted some of its regular allotment of vouchers to funds for a much broader mobility program. The Housing Opportunity Program, administered by CHAC, Inc., is one of the largest voluntary mobility programs in the nation. Between 1999 and the end of 2005, nearly 9,000 families received counseling and leased apartments. Of those, more than 3,000 moved from high- to low-poverty communities. The program has also helped another 1,800 or so families living in low-poverty neighborhoods stay in those areas when they made a move.

While any family that has a voucher can enroll, the program targets so-called "second movers" because they are not under as much pressure to find an apartment as first-time recipients. CHAC also indirectly targets people most likely to move by marketing to participants of the Family Self-Sufficiency program and to other families that are employed but living in high-poverty areas. Outreach methods include notices in a magazine and neighborhood van tours. Counselors help applicants overcome barriers to relocating, such as poor credit. CHAC administers a $225,000 revolving interest-free loan fund offering security deposits to families moving from high- to low-poverty areas.[9]

In recent years, CHAC has stepped up post-move support, helping families become part of their new communities through such activities as introductions to churches or block groups. Families with young children are encouraged to get involved with the school system or mentoring program. Staff reconnect with families about a year after a move to check how they are doing. As of 2005, about 85 percent of families that had relocated from high- to low-poverty neighborhoods were still living there two years later.

Security Deposit Assistance Is Crucial in High-Cost Boston, San Diego

The Community Choice Voucher Program (CCVP) of the Metropolitan Boston Housing Partnership is a federally funded housing voucher initiative for minority families wanting to move to more diverse communities. The program is a result of a 1978 lawsuit by the NAACP, charging HUD with segregating minorities in public housing developments. The partnership took a significant portion of the budget to create a fund for security deposits, application fees, and moving costs to support voucher holders. With this assistance and landlord outreach, the organization was able to get mobility program participants quickly into communities that traditionally had few subsidized renters.

Through its Relocation Fund, the Fair Housing Council of San Diego offers $300 for security deposits to voucher holders moving from high- to low-poverty areas. The city allocated $15,000 to create the fund,[10] which has helped more than 100 people move to better neighborhoods.

Baltimore Movers Receive Deposit Aid, Vehicles

Families moving to job-rich but less urban areas need reliable automobile transportation to sustain their new housing. Since 2002, the Abell Foundation of Baltimore has supported two housing mobility programs. As of November 2006, the foundation had provided more than $300,000 in grants to pay for security deposits for families moving from public and assisted housing in Baltimore City to subsidized housing in low-poverty, low-minority suburban areas. Averaging $463 apiece, these grants assisted 647 families. Through the Vehicles for Change program, the foundation has also awarded grants totaling $122,150 to subsidize the purchase of cars for voucher holders.[11]

2 Avoid Restricting Subsidized Housing To High-Poverty Neighborhoods

A series of class-action lawsuits starting in the late 1960s launched a national conversation about the failures of a public housing system that isolated poor, predominantly African-American families in communities wracked by intergenerational poverty and lawlessness. The lawsuits were fought and won on the argument that economic and racial segregation is bad for families and, when government-sponsored, violates their civil rights.

The desire to reduce the concentration of poverty and new federal policies have led authorities nationwide to create new, mixed-income communities and scatter subsidized housing regionwide. Vouchers have helped to accomplish this goal, allowing residents of demolished public housing complexes to move to new neighborhoods if they wish. Housing agencies do, however, have the obligation to monitor the impacts of their policies and ensure they are encouraging integrated neighborhoods of choice.

▼ CASES IN POINT

Atlanta's Voucher Program Incorporates Site and Neighborhood Standards

The Atlanta Housing Authority, a national leader in creating new mixed-income communities, does not approve voucher use in locations that have a high concentration of subsidized units. The authority also considers the conditions of the neighborhood before approving a location, and will reject areas with boarded-up units, vacant buildings, trash and debris, excess graffiti, and abandoned cars.

Dallas Limits Voucher Use in Single Buildings, High-Crime Areas

The Dallas Housing Authority prohibits property owners from leasing more than 30 percent of units in any one complex to voucher holders. From 2005 through mid-2006, the authority was also required to limit the use of rental vouchers in high-crime areas as part of the final judgment in a desegregation lawsuit. Under this policy, voucher recipients were not sent to neighborhoods where the crime rate exceeded the citywide average for more than six months. Those already living in high-crime areas had the opportunity to move. According to authority officials, property owners were notified in advance if their area crime rate had risen above the city average. Although the requirement has since ended, the authority continues to monitor voucher use in high-crime areas, with informal assistance from the police department.

Chicago Program Reverses Voucher Growth Rates in Concentrated Areas

In 1995, CHAC, Inc., a Chicago subsidiary of Quadel Consulting[6] of Washington, DC, was hired to administer Chicago's housing voucher program under an innovative performance-based contract. In 2003, the housing authority asked CHAC to create a special program to help slow the nearly 10-percent annual growth in voucher use in six neighborhoods that had both high poverty rates and high concentrations of assisted housing. By expanding its already extensive mobility counseling program and specifically targeting residents in those areas, CHAC has been able to reduce the number of vouchers in use in the neighborhoods by about 2.2 percent annually since 2004.

---

3 Make the Voucher Program More Attractive to Landlords, Including Those in Low-Poverty Areas

To bring new landlords into the program, voucher administrators must pay sufficient rents.[12] Though agencies are limited in the rent they can pay and in the federal funds available for administration, they can pursue other local funding sources for landlord incentives. For example, the Cuyahoga Metropolitan Housing Authority offers security deposit assistance through a $25,000 grant from the Cuyahoga County Department of Development's block grant allocation. Authorities can also offer signing bonuses for landlords, perhaps through local trust fund monies. These bonuses would be similar to the payments some authorities offer to deal with underutilization of vouchers.

▼ CASES IN POINT

Landlord Education Expands Portland Program

The Housing Authority of Portland (HAP) serves all of Oregon's Multnomah County, managing about 2,400 public housing units and administering about 8,000 Housing Choice Vouchers. In the mid-1990s, the authority embarked on an aggressive program to extend voucher participation to landlords in every part of the county. HAP established a landlord advisory committee, expedited processing and paperwork, allowed landlords to choose the tenants they wanted to rent to, and instituted other reforms. The authority also launched an extensive landlord education program that includes regular newsletters, periodic training on such topics as landlord-tenant law and fair housing, and a plain-language guide to how the voucher program works. Housing staff attend trade shows, landlord association meetings, and chamber of commerce events to describe the program and hand out the guides. Within a decade, the program expanded to 3,500 landlords.

Fast-Track System Improves Processing in Chicago

CHAC, Inc., the private firm administering Chicago's voucher program, has a "fast track" alert built into its computer system. When a staff member enters a new request for tenancy approval, the screen blinks with a message that the request is coming from a participant in the agency's mobility program. Requests flagged in this way become a top priority for processing through inspection, rent determination, and lease-up. Counselors hand-deliver contracts for signature and bring them back to the office for immediate entry so that the property owner gets the first check quickly. To smooth operations further, CHAC's landlord outreach workers and several housing mobility counselors have been certified as housing inspectors who can fill in if the regular inspectors are busy.

Illinois County Program Creates New Suburban Homes for Voucher Holders

Through the Project Opportunity program, the Housing Authority of Cook County, Illinois and its partners offer low-cost loans for investors to buy and rehabilitate single-family homes in suburban neighborhoods. The homes, which are rented only to housing voucher holders, must be in areas with a minority population of less than 13 percent and a poverty concentration of less than 10 percent. Units must remain affordable for a minimum of 15 years. An authority affiliate, Turnstone Development, administers the program.

The investor puts up 15 percent of the purchase price, and a private lender provides a first mortgage covering up to 35 percent of the balance. The Illinois Housing Development Authority and the Cook County HOME Program provide loans at one-percent interest for the remaining amount. A $6,000 grant from the Chicago Federal Home Loan Bank helps to cover closing costs. The Metropolitan Planning Council ensures that the homes meet certain criteria, such as being close to jobs and transportation. Lutheran Child and Family Services of Illinois offers mobility counseling and trains the tenants in home maintenance and financial management. Launched in 2002, the program had created 40 units by 2006.[13]

Tenant Mediation, Landlord Appreciation Enhance Mobility in Boston

The Metropolitan Boston Housing Partnership (MBHP) is one of eight regional nonprofits that administer the Housing Choice Voucher program for the Commonwealth of Massachusetts. MBHP handles the Boston metro area. Faced with an increasingly tight housing market, the organization shifted the focus of its program to treat property owners as customers on par with voucher holders. A new director of property services was hired to conduct landlord-tenant mediation and organize workshops on topics ranging from discrimination law to maintenance. MBHP also started an annual appreciation evening to recognize landlords for their support. According to program officials, providing added value to landlords has been crucial to improving mobility for voucher holders.

Online Locater Services Aid Rental Searches in Portland, Spokane

With help from a US Department of Commerce Technical Opportunities Program grant, the City of Portland's Bureau of Housing and Community Development and the Bureau of Technology Services launched Housing Connections (**www.housingconnections.org**) in 2002. The service links voucher recipients and other families with affordable and special needs housing throughout the Portland metropolitan area. The site is designed to help property managers and landlords in four counties easily list their properties and to allow renters to customize their search. As of December 2006, the service listed more than 52,000 units.

In 2006, the Spokane Low Income Housing Consortium launched a similar service, OneStopHousing.org, with funding from Spokane's housing authority, Northeast Washington Housing Solutions, and others. The listings serve households with up to 60 percent of area median income. The 2,200 units in the service are dispersed throughout Spokane and Spokane Valley.

4 Use Project-based Vouchers to Create More Housing In Opportunity Areas

A lack of affordable housing in higher-opportunity areas limits mobility for voucher holders. Housing authorities can use project-based vouchers to support housing opportunities in areas with good access to jobs, good schools, and other amenities. With vouchers, tax-credit and other types of housing developments can serve people at a broader range of income levels.

HUD allows public housing authorities to use up to 20 percent of their voucher funds for project-based assistance. Under the program, the vouchers are attached to a unit rather than a renter. Participating property owners agree to set aside a specific number of units for voucher families for up to 10 years (renewable indefinitely). When families move, they receive priority for the next tenant-based voucher available through the housing authority's ordinary turnover, and the project-based voucher unit becomes available to another family. When combined with services from other sources, project-based vouchers can be an integral part of a strategy to create supportive housing for the elderly or persons with disabilities.

▼ CASES IN POINT

San Bernardino, Cambridge Authorities Ensure Opportunities In Higher-Income Communities

The Housing Authority of the County of San Bernardino, California creates housing opportunities for subsidized renters in higher-income communities by acquiring or building new properties in those locations. Acting as the developer, the authority adds project-based Section 8 vouchers to its housing complexes after the property is built (rather than using them as part of the initial financing package to leverage other monies). This gives the authority full control to pursue poverty deconcentration goals. The authority has completed 16 such projects. Profits from serving as the Section 8 landlord are recycled into more affordable housing efforts.

To ensure the long-term affordability of units in affluent neighborhoods, the Cambridge, Massachusetts Housing Authority has used its Moving to Work authority to convert 423 vouchers to project-based vouchers. As of fall 2005, authority affiliates had created almost 320 units with the vouchers, leveraging over $69 million in public and private financing. In addition, the housing authority's board recently authorized sponsor-based vouchers, providing nonprofit groups and others with service-rich or transitional housing programs easier access to voucher subsidies for their work. In this way, the authority acts like a finance agency, supporting city and nonprofit efforts to maintain housing affordability in the region.

Illinois Agencies Pool Vouchers to Develop Homes In High-Opportunity Neighborhoods

Four housing authorities in the Chicago region, the Illinois Housing Development Authority, and the Metropolitan Planning Council have worked together to create voucher-supported homes in suburban and city neighborhoods with access to jobs and transportation. In 2002, the Chicago, Cook County, and Lake County housing authorities created a pool of over 300 unused tenant-based vouchers and transformed them into project-based vouchers. The McHenry County Housing Authority later joined this effort, contributing additional vouchers.

Under the Regional Housing Initiative (RHI), developers and owners of mixed-income rental housing near jobs and transit can use the pool to fund up to 25 percent of their units with subsidies. Proposals that include housing for people with special needs and/ or disabilities can qualify for a higher percentage of funded units. As an added incentive, developers get four extra points on their applications for Low-Income Housing Tax Credits. To further guarantee quality, the properties must meet other criteria established by the Metropolitan Mayors Caucus. As of November 2006, almost 30 units had been created and more than 100 were in the pipeline.[14]

Minneapolis Helps Families With At-Risk Children Achieve Stability

The Minneapolis Public Housing Authority makes about 18 percent of its voucher allocation project-based to provide transitional housing for at-risk youth and nearly homeless families in more stable neighborhoods. For example, the authority allocated eight project-based vouchers to the developer of a 24-unit complex in southwest Lenhurst, an affluent neighborhood with few rental units. The complex is located on a transit line and near a new school, library, and grocery store.

The authority also operates a separate but complementary program called "All About the Kids." Under the program, the authority works with Lutheran Social Services and schools to identify children who are struggling with their studies because their families are constantly moving. The program sets aside 150 vouchers for these homeless or near-homeless families so that they can live in stable environments. According to program officials, test scores for children in the families served have improved.

5 Adopt Local Laws Protecting Voucher Holders From Housing Discrimination

Jurisdictions should consider enacting "source of income" laws as a means of enhancing voucher holders' choice. In some localities, property owners cannot refuse to rent to anyone based on their source of income. Indeed, some laws explicitly prohibit discrimination based upon the use of Housing Choice Vouchers as a source of income. A 2001 study on success rates found that voucher families in jurisdictions with laws that bar discrimination based on source of income were more than 12 percent more likely to succeed in leasing a unit than enrollees in other jurisdictions.[15]

In addition, federal provisions require that certain types of landlords—such as owners of complexes developed with Low-Income Housing Tax Credits—accept voucher holders. Local housing leaders should work with fair housing groups to advocate for such laws, educate landlords about their responsibilities, and ensure that the regulations are followed.

6 Develop Regional Partnerships For Voucher Administration

Housing authorities in the same region should coordinate their voucher programs to streamline operations and overcome the administrative barriers to mobility. Through regional partnerships, authorities can alleviate the mismatch between job growth and availability of affordable housing in the suburbs and the concentration of voucher holders in the cities.

Although vouchers are technically portable, HUD regulations and the "administrative geography" of the program can discourage mobility. More than 2,400 agencies nationwide administer vouchers, and their jurisdictional boundaries do not reflect the way people live and move. If a voucher holder relocates from one jurisdiction to another, the authority in the new jurisdiction can either "absorb" the voucher into its program or bill the original authority for the cost of the voucher plus a portion of the administrative fee. This creates time- and resource-consuming paperwork for the authorities as well as delays for the renter.

Furthermore, with the move to fixed-budget funding in 2004, the system essentially stopped compensating public housing authorities for the cost of subsidizing a higher rent in a lower-poverty area. In recognition of this mobility barrier, Congress made some adjustments for fiscal 2006 and appears likely to make even more changes in fiscal 2007. It is unclear, however, if additional changes will restore the level of flexibility to movers that existed before 2004.

Regional structures for voucher administration would create more options for families, including the opportunity to move to suburban areas where there are more jobs, better schools, and newer housing. For small housing authorities, forming a consortium to administer the voucher program creates economies of scale. By sharing expenses and resources, agencies can expand mobility and support activities that are crucial to running an effective program.

Massachusetts System Emphasizes Regional Mobility and Self-Sufficiency

Massachusetts has a fully developed regional system for rental assistance that emphasizes mobility and self-sufficiency. The state Department of Housing and Community Development contracts with eight regional nonprofits to administer roughly 19,000 federal Housing Choice Vouchers and more than 4,000 state-funded vouchers. The regional groups share a centralized waiting list.

One outcome of the Massachusetts approach has been to build considerable capacity in the nonprofit network. Organizations that started out small and focused primarily on administering the voucher program have now expanded into development, homeownership counseling, homelessness prevention, and other activities. For example, the Metropolitan Boston Housing Partnership (MBHP), the largest regional administrator, operates numerous programs such as mobility counseling and a state-funded housing consumer education center. MBHP administers about 6,000 vouchers for the 30 communities in the greater Boston metropolitan area. Voucher holders can move freely from one community to another without incurring any additional paperwork. MBHP housing inspectors and staff maintain relationships with property owners throughout the region.

Centralized Waiting List Simplifies Section 8 Applications in Massachusetts

Following the lead of the voucher program, approximately 60 of the public housing authorities in Massachusetts that administer their own Section 8 programs instituted a centralized waiting list in 2003. The Massachusetts chapter of NAHRO administers the list. Instead of visiting numerous authorities to put their names on individual lists, prospective voucher recipients need only apply to one of the participating housing authorities. Each authority does, however, rank applicants according to its own residency preferences.

Nevada Jurisdictions Share Voucher Administration

Under a memorandum of agreement, the housing authorities of the Cities of Las Vegas and North Las Vegas and the Clark County Housing Authority share administration of the housing voucher program. The three authorities use the same information system to determine rent reasonableness, reducing paperwork for the administrators and allowing tenants to move more freely among jurisdictions. If a voucher-holder from the Housing Authority of the City of Las Vegas rents an apartment in Clark County's service area, for example, the Las Vegas housing authority handles inspections and payments following the county's payment and utility allowance.

7 Partner with Service Providers to Help Voucher Recipients Move to Self-Sufficiency

By helping their tenants move to self-sufficiency, public housing authorities position themselves as a community asset rather than a provider of housing of last resort. That can enhance their public standing and increase political support for their development projects and other activities. It also makes good business sense. Tenants who earn more can pay more in rent. Those who earn enough—and perhaps even buy homes—then free up valuable vouchers for new applicants.

Housing authorities can also increase the availability of work-promoting services to tenants by tapping grant programs that are uniquely available to them. Programs include Resident Opportunities and Self-Sufficiency, HOPE VI Community and Supportive Services, and Neighborhood Networks.[16]

The Family Self-Sufficiency (FSS) program is another HUD program that helps tenants increase earnings and work toward economic independence.[17] Of the roughly 68,000 FSS program participants in October 2006, 87 percent had tenant-based Section 8 subsidies. According to a recent HUD program evaluation, participants experience much greater income gains and much larger welfare declines than nonparticipants. FSS graduates also accumulate about $3,300 in savings through the program.[18]

▼ CASE IN POINT

Portland GOALS Participants Triple Earnings

In keeping with its strategic goal of helping households succeed in their residency, the Housing Authority of Portland (HAP) operates an active and effective family self-sufficiency program called GOALS. Case managers and participants create a five-year plan covering not just employment and financial goals but also social relationships, mental health, and housing.[19] Case managers encourage participants to take charge and find their own solutions to problems. As of the end of 2005, about 600 households—10 percent of the HAP's Section 8 and public housing tenants—were participating in the program. Another 485 participants had graduated and no longer required Temporary Assistance to Needy Families (TANF) aid. Of the graduates, 195 had bought homes. Graduates had increased their average earnings by 196 percent, working in a variety of positions ranging from entrepreneurs and college professors to social workers and construction workers.

The program is funded in several ways. As a Moving to Work site, the authority can combine public housing, voucher FSS funds, and public housing Resident Opportunities and Self-Sufficiency (ROSS) grants. The use of ROSS grants has been a critical element. Underemployed people who are not normally eligible for Workforce Investment Act (WIA) services can access those services through a ROSS employment-training grant to the housing authority. For its part, the WIA program gets help meeting its service targets, with the benefit that referrals from the housing authority simultaneously receive job assistance and supportive case management. GOALS coordinators also provide fee-for-service counseling for some residents of tax credit-funded properties, which helps subsidize their earnings. The housing authority plans to significantly increase the number of GOALS participants over the next several years, in part by using the FSS program to leverage case management services funded by TANF.[20]

---

8 Expand Use of Vouchers to Help More Families On the Path to Homeownership

Renters who graduate from subsidized housing into homeownership demonstrate how vouchers can offer economic as well as geographic mobility. The Housing Choice Voucher homeownership program is a natural extension of mobility and opportunity services—and perhaps the only means by which very poor people can attain the American Dream.

As of June 2006, more than 500 public housing authorities operated voucher homeownership programs.[21] Under such programs, the voucher essentially goes to a bank to pay off a mortgage rather than to a landlord. In most cases, nonprofit agencies provide counseling and support. Only four percent of programs surveyed by HUD reported any foreclosures.

To launch a homeownership program, housing authorities can enlist the support of community development corporations, organizations that serve people with disabilities, homeownership counseling organizations, and other partners seeking to increase homeowning among their constituents. Community developers tend to favor voucher homeownership programs because they help people remain in gentrifying communities and benefit from rising property values and improved services.

▼ CASES IN POINT

Portland FSS Program Provides Access to Homeownership

The Portland Housing Authority is one of many local authorities using its Family Self-Sufficiency program as a pipeline to homeownership. At the end of 2005, some 195 of its GOALS program participants had become homeowners.

Chicago Produces Most Voucher Homeowners

The Chicago Housing Authority (CHA) has produced more Housing Choice Voucher homeowners than any other public housing authority in the country. Between 1999 and November 2006, the program helped 183 people earning an average of $22,196 annually to become homeowners. Twenty-four homeowners used their FSS escrow accounts to help fund closing costs, and about one-fourth moved from high- to low-poverty neighborhoods.

CHAC, Inc., manager of the voucher program, works with four counseling agencies and bank partners that offer very favorable loan products. One of its most critical partners is the Economic Development Law Project of the Chicago Lawyers Committee for Civil Rights. The pro bono attorneys help ensure that homebuyers clearly understand what the closing documents mean.

Sacramento Makes Partnering Key to Homeownership in High-Cost Market

The success of the Sacramento Housing and Redevelopment Agency (SHRA) with Section 8 homeownership proves that partnering can be critical in high-cost housing markets. In October 2005, the minimum household income needed to purchase a median-priced home in California was $128,480.[22] Still, between the program's inception in 2002 and November 2005, the agency was able to help 59 voucher recipients and public housing residents buy homes costing $85,000 to $260,000, even though most of the families had incomes only a fraction of the typical new homeowner. Five of the homeowners have since refinanced into mortgages that they can afford on their own.

The key is layering financial assistance from many partners. The agency sets aside what the client would otherwise pay in rent in a special account. Through Citibank, the agency offers Individual Development Accounts that clients can use to save for the downpayment. After 10 months, the bank matches what the client puts into the account. The Federal Home Loan Bank of San Francisco offers a three-to-one match for the amount that clients save. SHRA's redevelopment arm also offers forgivable, soft second mortgages of $30,000–40,000 through the American Dream Downpayment Initiative.[23] In addition, Sacramento Neighborhood Housing Services, a local nonprofit, provides forgivable grants of $10,000 to program participants who remain in their homes for five years.

Colorado Voucher Program Helps People with Disabilities Buy Homes

Colorado's Supportive Housing and Homeless Programs, a division of the state Department of Human Services, administers housing choice vouchers statewide, primarily for persons with disabilities. As of November 2005, the programs had helped 68 disabled families and one non-disabled family purchase homes with housing choice vouchers. The state housing finance agency offers below-market-rate loans to persons with disabilities, along with downpayment assistance. A nonprofit partner also provides downpayment assistance. Service agencies work with persons with disabilities before, during, and after closing to support their homeownership.

OPPORTUNITIES FOR STATE ACTION

1 Support Landlord Incentives to Rent To Voucher Holders

States should consider providing funds for landlord incentives, either through grants or tax programs. The State of Illinois offers property tax abatements of up to 19 percent of the equalized assessed value to property owners who rent to people with Housing Choice Vouchers. The savings depend on the size of the property and the number of qualified units. The property must be located within a census tract with less than 10 percent poverty. No more than two units or 20 percent of the total in any one multifamily building are eligible. The Housing Choice Voucher Tax Savings

Program is administered by 19 public housing authorities in the nine eligible counties in conjunction with the county clerk.

---

2 Enact Policies Supporting Voucher Portability

State governments should implement policies that make vouchers more portable by encouraging regional agreements to make fewer distinctions between central waiting lists and those administered by housing authorities. States could work with local authorities to create a central reserve fund from which vouchers "porting" from jurisdiction to jurisdiction could draw.

Under Ohio law, county housing authorities administer the voucher program for the entire county. For example, the Cuyahoga Metropolitan Housing Authority administers about 14,000 vouchers for every municipality in the county. There are no administrative barriers to moving from one jurisdiction to another. The authority has achieved a good geographic balance of voucher use, with about 60 percent of recipients living in Cleveland and 40 percent in the outlying suburbs.

States such as Michigan that run their own federal voucher programs are more able to promote mobility goals. Since the 1970s, the Michigan State Housing Development Authority (MSHDA) has administered vouchers for areas not served by public housing authorities. As of 2005, it administered more than 22,000 vouchers through performance-based contracts with nonprofits or limited liability companies operating throughout the state. In the last few years, several smaller public housing authorities that had run their own voucher programs asked MSHDA to take over. The state authority can offer services that small authorities cannot. For example, MSHDA runs the largest FSS program in the country, with close to 2,500 participants. It also has an award-winning Section 8 homeownership program.

The Connecticut Department of Social Services also administers vouchers for the state. The department funds a Regional Mobility Counseling Program with three different contractors serving three different areas of the state. Housing Choice Voucher administrative fees fund the program. HOME, Inc., a New Haven nonprofit, administers the program in its service area.

---

3 Fund Work and Self-Sufficiency Services For Voucher Recipients

States can appropriate money for work and self-sufficiency services, or allocate funds such as CDBG for work services. State job development funds can also support these activities, with childcare or transportation agencies contributing funds. State and local agencies can seek out housing authorities to compete for programs such as the Job Access and Reverse Commute grants administered by the US Department of Transportation. State agencies can also allocate TANF funds to help Section 8 voucher recipients locate stable housing. In addition, state housing finance agencies can enrich tax-credit developments with service coordination or FSS-type activities. The Illinois Housing Development Authority, for example, contributed $5 million in 2006 toward the Chicago Housing Authority's workforce development program for current and former CHA residents.

RESOURCES

THE BROOKINGS INSTITUTION
www.brookings.edu

Private nonprofit organization dedicated to independent research and innovative policy solutions. The Brookings Metropolitan Policy Program has published several reports and briefs on housing vouchers, including "Public Housing Reform and Voucher Success: Progress and Challenges," 2005.

CENTER ON BUDGET AND POLICY PRIORITIES
www.cbpp.org

Conducts research and analysis to inform public debates over proposed budget and tax policies that affect low-income households. The organization also develops policy options to alleviate poverty, particularly among working families. The website provides a good primer on the housing voucher program.

FSS PARTNERSHIPS
www.fsspartnerships.org

Initiative dedicated to promoting asset-building opportunities for families in public housing and HUD's Section 8 voucher program. Background information on HUD's Family Self-Sufficiency Program and descriptions of local programs, along with many other reports and resources, can be found on the website.

HOUSING POLICY DEBATE
www.fanniemaefoundation.org/programs/hpd.shtml

Quarterly journal published by the Fannie Mae Foundation. The publication has covered many voucher debates, including "Who Should Run the Housing Voucher Program? A Reform Proposal."

MASSACHUSETTS NONPROFIT HOUSING ASSOCIATION
www.masshousinginfo.org/mnpha

Umbrella group for the eight regional nonprofits that administer the statewide housing voucher program.

METROPOLITAN PLANNING COUNCIL
www.metroplanning.org

Nonprofit, nonpartisan group of business and civic leaders that promotes and implements sensible planning and development policies necessary for an economically competitive Chicago region. Web resources provide more details on the Regional Housing Initiative and Project Opportunity.

NATIONAL ASSOCIATION OF HOUSING
AND REDEVELOPMENT OFFICIALS (NAHRO)
www.nahro.org

Association of administrators of such HUD programs as public housing, Section 8, CDBG and HOME. NAHRO offers resources on voucher management programs. For example, the January/February 2005 issue of NAHRO's *Journal of Housing & Community Development* addresses ways that public housing authorities are achieving cost-efficiencies by forming consortia to administer their voucher programs.

NATIONAL COUNCIL OF STATE HOUSING AGENCIES
www.ncsha.org

Resource for innovative programs run by state housing finance agencies.

NATIONAL LOW INCOME HOUSING COALITION
www.nlihc.org/about/index.htm

Seeks to pass legislation that provides new funding for production of rental housing for extremely low-income people. It also conducts public education, organizing, and research, including many informative publications on voucher use and strategies.

NEW AMERICA FOUNDATION
www.newamerica.net

Nonprofit, post-partisan public policy institute that sponsors a wide range of research, writing, conferences, and public outreach on major global and domestic issues. The foundation published an issue brief, "Shoring Up HUD's Family Self-Sufficiency Program: Recommendations for Congressional Action," describing the FSS program and recommending congressional action to stabilize funding for the program.

POVERTY & RACE RESEARCH ACTION COUNCIL
www.prrac.org

Sponsor of a Housing Mobility Initiative that brings together mobility counseling agencies, public housing agencies, and housing integration advocates to develop research and advocacy strategies to influence the debate over voucher policy. The initiative recently published "Keeping the Promise: Preserving and Enhancing Housing Mobility in the Section 8 Housing Choice Voucher Program."

RESOURCES

URBAN INSTITUTE
www.urbaninstitute.org

Gathers and analyzes data, conducts policy research, evaluates programs, and educates Americans on issues and trends to promote public debate on national priorities. The institute has produced an extensive series on public housing vouchers, mobility programs, and HOPE VI.

US DEPARTMENT OF HOUSING AND URBAN DEVELOPMENT
www.huduser.org

Offers numerous grant programs and best practice studies to support voucher mobility and resident self-sufficiency programs. Among other resources, the website provides information on the Homeownership Voucher program and a list of public housing authorities that administer Section 8 homeownership programs.

1. Under HUD requirements, 75 percent of households newly admitted to the program must have incomes at or below 30 percent of the area median income (AMI). The rest may have incomes of up to 50 percent AMI (or 80 percent, if negotiated with HUD). Voucher values vary per household to ensure that the recipient pays at least 30 percent of adjusted income on rent and utilities. To calculate the value of the voucher, the agency subtracts 30 percent of the family's adjusted income from a set rent and utilities rate for the area, called the payment standard. If the rent and utility costs for the unit are less than the payment standard, the family still pays 30 percent of its adjusted gross income, with the voucher covering the rest. If the rent and utilities exceed the payment standard, tenants end up paying more than 30 percent of their income because they must make up the difference between the value of the voucher and the higher rent. For a complete description of voucher rents, see the Center on Budget and Policy Priorities, "Introduction to the Housing Voucher Program," **www.cbpp.org/5-15-03hous.pdf**.

2. Section 8 refers to the section of the US Housing Act authorizing the program. There are different kinds of Section 8 assistance. For example, under another Section 8 program, HUD contracted directly with multifamily property owners (or with state housing finance agencies contracting with owners) to provide subsidy funding in exchange for renting units to eligible tenants for a set period of time. Public housing agencies have no direct role in this privatized, decentralized approach. When housing advocates talk about expiring Section 8 developments, they are referring to this private-owner Section 8 program.

3. See, for example, Margery Austin Turner and Dolores Acevedo-Garcia, "The Benefits of Housing Mobility: A Review of the Research Evidence," in Philip Tegeler, Mary Cunningham, and Margery Austin Turner, eds. "Keeping the Promise: Preserving and Enhancing Housing Mobility in the Section 8 Housing Choice Voucher Program," Conference Report of the Third National Conference on Housing Mobility, November 2005, **www.prrac.org/pdf/KeepingPromise.pdf**.

4. In the appropriations bills, Congress fixed funding for voucher programs based on costs in May through July of 2003. A study of fiscal 2004 changes in federal funding for the renewal of the Section 8 Housing Choice Voucher program, conducted by the National Association of Housing and Redevelopment Officials (**www.nahro.org/pressroom/2004/200410renewalstud y.pdf**) concluded that nearly 500 housing agencies would be left with a shortfall of as much as $93 million for the year. The shortfall was forcing about a quarter of the agencies to increase households' rents by an average of 9 percent. It was also preventing 4,517 households served by about half of the agencies from moving to new neighborhoods with greater educational and employment opportunities.

5. Congress established the Moving to Work (MTW) demonstration program in 1996 to allow a certain number of public housing authorities greater flexibility to experiment—for a fixed but extendable period—with their voucher and public housing programs by waiving certain regulatory and reporting requirements and allowing the merger of operating, capital, and voucher funding streams. While 31 agencies have participated in the program over time, 24 were participating as of August 2006. Congress has been considering authorizing MTW status for additional agencies. Congress also enacted the Regional Opportunity Counseling (ROC) program in the 1990s, a five-year program providing 16 metro regions with grants for mobility counseling for Section 8 voucher holders.

6. Jack Kemp serves on the Board of Directors for Quadel Consulting.

7. James Rosenbaum, "Black Pioneers: Do Their Moves to Suburbs Increase Economic Opportunity for Mothers and Children?" *Housing Policy Debate* 2:4, 1991, 1179–1213; "Changing the Geography of Opportunity by Expanding Residential Choice: Lessons from the Gautreaux Program," *Housing Policy Debate* 6:1, 1995, 231–70; "Residential Mobility: Effects on Education,

Employment and Racial Interaction" in J. C. Bolger and J Wegner, eds., *Legal and Social Changes in Racial Integration in the US, 1995;* Len Rubinowitz, and J. E. Rosenbaum, *Crossing the Class and Color Lines,* University of Chicago Press, 2000; and James Rosenbaum and Stefanie DeLuca, "Is Housing Mobility the Key to Welfare Reform? Lessons from Chicago's Gautreaux Program," The Brookings Institution Center on Urban and Metropolitan Policy Survey Series, 2000.

8. To be effective, mobility programs must address such barriers as lack of funds for a security deposit, notes Gene Rizor of Quadel Consulting in "Essential Elements of Successful Mobility Counseling Programs." Through work with a company that manages mobility programs for Baltimore, Chicago, and Memphis, Rizor assembled a list of other elements for success: well-run and efficient processing of leases and rent payments; specific and communicated definitions of who is eligible and to what neighborhoods they can move; outreach to eligible households; signing bonuses and awards programs and other landlord recruitment and retention tools; relationships with service providers in the new neighborhood to help residents adjust; pre- and post-move counseling; search assistance that includes transportation to prospective complexes; credit repair services; loans for security deposits; and specific performance goals for the program administrator.

9. Over 70 percent of the more than 3,000 families moving from high- to low-poverty areas from 1999 to 2005 received and repaid loans averaging $578 apiece.

10. The Relocation Fund was created in 2001 to complement a mobility counseling program that the Fair Housing Council operated under a federal Regional Opportunity Counseling grant. Though that grant program has ended, the council maintains the fund with city support.

11. The foundation also made a $30,000 grant to Homes for America to pay the predevelopment costs of building 57 units of subsidized housing in unaffected areas. The homes will be set aside for families relocated from one of the HOPE VI developments in Baltimore City under the Thompson consent decree. Finally, Abell awarded $40,000 to a faith-based affordable housing coalition, BRIDGE, to advocate for the adoption of inclusionary zoning policies in Baltimore suburbs.

12. To calculate the value of the voucher, the agency subtracts 30 percent of the family's adjusted income from a set rent and utilities rate for the area, called the payment standard. The payment standard is based upon what HUD considers a fair market rent. HUD policies that encourage mobility include an increase in fair market rent standards in certain high-cost areas and an authority's discretion to set payment standards up to 110 percent of fair market value. In more expensive housing markets, a higher payment standard increases the number of housing opportunities available to voucher holders. Housing authorities may also appeal to HUD to offer benefits above the metropolitan-area standard.

13. For more information on the program, go to **www.metroplanning.org/articleDetail.asp?objectID=3508&keyword=Project+Opportunity** or **www.turnstonedev.org**.

14. More details on the RHI initiative can be found at **www.regionalhousinginitiative.org**.

15. Meryl Finkel and Larry Buron, "Study on Section 8 Voucher Success Rates," report prepared by Abt Associates Inc. for HUD's Office of Policy Development and Research, Vol. 1, November 2001, 3–17, **www.huduser.org/Publications/pdf/sec8success_1.pdf**.

16. For more information on the ROSS program, go to **www.hud.gov/offices/pih/programs/ph/ross/about.cfm;** for HOPE VI, go to **www.hud.gov/offices/pih/programs/ph/hope6/css;** and for Neighborhood Networks, go to **www.hud.gov/offices/hsg/mfh/nnw/nnwaboutnn.cfm**.

17. Public housing agencies provide case management services to help voucher holders or public housing tenants connect with welfare agencies, schools, businesses, and other local partners to get the skills and support they need to obtain living-wage jobs. Families whose earnings rise

as a result of increased work do pay more in rent, but the higher rent they pay due to higher earnings is deposited into an escrow account. The funds can be used to buy a home, buy or repair a car, pursue post-secondary education, start a business, pay down high-interest debt, save for retirement or children's education, or for other purposes. Although there have been a few wrinkles in funding in recent years, HUD generally covers the costs of the escrow accounts and the costs of one or two (and occasionally more) case managers per agency, but does not provide funds for services or for additional case management.

18. Robert C. Ficke and Andrea Piesse. "Evaluation of the Family Self-Sufficiency Program, Retrospective Analysis, 1996 to 2000," report prepared for HUD Office of Policy Development and Research, April 2004, **www.huduser.org/publications/econdev/selfsufficiency.html**.

19. Coordinators help participants access services through HAP partnerships with multiple providers. For example, the Portland Housing Center and the Portland Community Land Trust provide homeownership counseling and loan products. The Portland Housing Center also offers money management training. People who need employment referrals and job training access the one-stop training centers funded by the federal Workforce Investment Act. Other agencies provide health-related, domestic abuse, GED, and substance abuse services.

20. Under a pilot program, two community colleges that have contracts to offer TANF training will accept people on the GOALS waiting list who are also TANF clients. By essentially offloading case management to TANF staff, the GOALS program can serve more people without having to add its own staff.

21. Voucher Homeownership Study, **www.huduser.org/publications/homeown/voucherhomeown.html**. According to the findings, purchasers generally moved to neighborhoods with more homeowners and single-family homes and slightly lower poverty rates. The majority of purchasers, however, were living in low-poverty neighborhoods both before and after purchasing their homes. The three most common approaches to applying the housing assistance payment toward the mortgage are to use it as a direct offset to the mortgage payment, to use it as payment for a second mortgage, and to count it as income in determining the amount that can be borrowed.

22. California Association of Realtors®, **www.car.org/index.php?id=MzU2OTY**.

23. The American Dream Downpayment Initiative is a Congress-authorized pool of funds for homeownership administered under the federal HOME program. It offers downpayment and closing costs, targeting primarily lower-income and minority households. For more information, see **www.hud.gov/offices/cpd/affordablehousing/programs/home/addi/index.cfm**.

Bipartisanship Brings New Life
To Twin Cities Property

Every Wednesday afternoon, the St. Paul Public Library Bookmobile stops by a comfortable, well-managed, safe, and attractive apartment building called Skyline Tower. Library staff dispense everything from the latest Harry Potter novel to books on American history to the Hmong, East African, and African-American children living in and near the 504-unit complex.

Since being "reborn" after a close shave with demolition, Skyline Tower has become a neighborhood gathering spot. During the day, a steady flow of residents can be seen entering the first-floor Advantage Center community rooms to attend career training sessions, citizenship classes, parenting and school readiness programs, and youth recreation activities. For its largely immigrant tenants, Skyline Tower is a steppingstone to success.

And it exists today in part because visionary local leaders on both sides of the political aisle recognized that affordable rental housing is a key asset worth protecting. Built in the early 1970s with HUD assistance, the privately owned complex had become well-known for all the wrong reasons—drug trafficking, gang violence, shot-out windows, and worse. The owner considered selling to a buyer who would rehabilitate the property and charge market rents.

Reasoning that it would cost less to save the building for its low-income tenants than serve them in shelters or build new homes, the city's Republican Mayor Norm Coleman (now a US Senator) and Democratic County Commissioner Susan Haigh crafted a rescue plan. In 1999, the city and county used $15 million in tax-exempt bond funds to leverage tax credits and bank investments to transfer the site to the state's largest nonprofit affordable housing provider. The provider, CommonBond, renovated the property, keeping it affordable and transforming a virtual disaster into a civic asset.

Preserving and Expanding The Affordable Rental Supply

4

Decent, affordable rental homes and apartments allow individuals and working families to live in stable environments and within their means. Families that spend a reasonable amount on rent and utilities can reserve funds for weathering the unexpected—job losses, health problems, car repairs, and other hardships. Decent, affordable rentals can also forestall the kind of bill-juggling that often leads to poor credit and enables tenants to save for homeownership. Well-maintained and attractive rental housing in turn contributes to neighborhood stability and helps alleviate crime and other social ills.

But the supply of such housing is disappearing. A recent study reports that some two million low-cost rental units were razed or withdrawn from the inventory between 1993 and 2003.[1] Among the low-cost units being lost are complexes like St. Paul's Skyline Towers—properties with private or nonprofit owners and built with assistance from HUD. Other properties received Low-Income Housing Tax Credits.[2] As the contracts governing the subsidies expire, owners in gentrifying neighborhoods or facing expensive maintenance costs may opt out of the program, either raising rents to levels beyond the means of current tenants or selling to private developers of market-rate housing. Privately owned rental units built without public subsidies are also disappearing due to demolition, rent hikes, and condo conversions.

True to the laws of supply and demand, rental costs are rising rapidly. From 2000 to 2007, rents were up 28 percent—almost twice the 15 percent increase in low-income workers' incomes.[3] With housing costs outpacing wages, renters must spend more of their income for shelter. Indeed, nearly half of all renter households now pay more than 30 percent of their incomes on housing, compared with about a third of renter households in 1980.[4]

In 2006, the hourly wage required to afford the rent and utilities on a modest, market-rate two-bedroom rental unit was $16.31 nationally, or $33,925 a year. Entry-level professional staff at schools, hospitals and police departments in many communities across the country make less than this amount.

The high cost of rental housing is not just a challenge for individual households, but also for communities and local economies. In communities across the nation, thousands of people are on long-closed waiting lists for federally subsidized housing. Families that have to move because of a financial or personal crisis have to take children out of school, and some become homeless. Employers now worry about losing workers while civic leaders are concerned about how far away their police workers and first responders must live to afford housing.

Fortunately, some local leaders have focused on the preservation and production of affordable rental homes. They are enlisting developers well-schooled in avoiding warehouse-type building design and other mistakes of the past. The partnerships are rehabilitating or creating attractive, affordable apartment complexes that blend into the community while allowing the kind of diversity that gives neighborhoods their distinctive character.

Communities at the forefront of this change view housing preservation as a complement rather than a competitor to production programs. Preservation has become particularly important in high-cost markets where land values make new development too expensive as a stand-alone strategy. Experts estimate that it costs 50–75 percent less to preserve affordable housing units than to build new ones.[5]

Successful programs apply lessons learned in the treatment of homelessness—namely, the importance of services as a component of housing programs. Improvements, such as the Advantage Center added to Skyline Towers in St. Paul, can make properties work better for their communities.

The range of tools that communities have at their disposal allows a flexible, multi-faceted strategy for preserving and producing needed rental housing. As communities assess their options and debate their choices, they should keep in mind that often the most valuable thing that local leaders can provide is "moral suasion." Some of the programs that have worked well are not necessarily unique, but they have had a powerful champion in a mayor, governor, or other local leader.

RECOMMENDATIONS FOR LOCAL ACTION

1 Provide Tax Breaks, Rehabilitation Assistance, and Other Supports To Affordable Multifamily Property Owners

A major impediment to sustained affordability, particularly in gentrifying neighborhoods, is the property tax rate. A sudden hike in assessments often triggers the sale of subsidized rental housing to market-rate developers. Tax increases can drain funds from needed maintenance and put the squeeze on nonprofit owners committed to low rents. In addition, high taxes may dissuade owners from joining subsidy programs that limit their ability to raise rents to cover costs.

Municipalities should consider directing some of their resources to help owners of rental housing, fund needed renovations or get the properties into the hands of responsible rehabbers. Often, the lack of money to bring projects up to code precipitates the decision to court a market-rate buyer. Incentives for rental property owners to upgrade and preserve buildings as affordable can come in the form of tax breaks, grants, density bonuses, and low-interest or forgivable loans, perhaps through HOME funds. Pairing the loans with housing vouchers may provide a further incentive to owners.

Local governments should work with local financial institutions and other partners to provide owners of smaller rental properties with the skills and resources to manage their units profitably. Although often overlooked, these owners are a critical resource given that about two-thirds of all lower-income families live in small, privately owned rental properties. Unfortunately, there is a marked lack of suitable financing options for owners of such properties.

Cook County Tax Program Supports Mixed-Income Projects

The Class S program in Cook County, Illinois encourages owners of project-based Section 8 multifamily housing in high-cost markets to keep their units affordable by reducing the tax assessment by up to 33 percent. The Class 9 program offers a similar reduction to developers who complete new construction or major rehabilitation of multifamily buildings and reserves 35 percent of the units as affordable. In 2001, Cook County extended the program from just low-income census tracts to all areas of the county, an important strategy for encouraging mixed-income development. To prevent conversions of rentals to condos, the county is lowering the property tax assessment for apartment buildings from 26 percent to 20 percent by 2008. According to the assessor's office, the reduction will have a minimal impact on the tax base and result in only a 1.9 percent countywide shift to other classes of property taxes.

New York City Offers Tax Breaks on Renovation

In any given year, between 70,000 and 100,000 housing units are renovated under New York City's J51 Program. The program provides real estate tax exemptions and abatements to multifamily buildings that are renovated or rehabilitated according to certain requirements. Buildings converted from lofts or other nonresidential uses to residential use are also eligible. Affordable housing projects generally qualify for a 34-year exemption from the higher real estate taxes resulting from the improvement. The tax break allows owners to recoup the costs of repairs. From fiscal 1980 to the end of 2006, these incentives spurred essential upgrades and system replacements for more than 2.4 million units.

Development Rights Transfer Program Provides Millions for Rehab in Seattle

Under Seattle's Transferable Development Rights (TDR) program, commercial developers who want more density than allowed under zoning can purchase unused density from owners of downtown properties with affordable housing, landmark buildings, or major open space. To enhance efficiency, nonprofits that need funds to repair and preserve their properties can sell the development rights to the city, which deposits them in a "TDR Bank" for later sale to office and hotel developers on an as-needed basis. The program is a critical tool for preserving low-income housing in the downtown area. Between 1986 and 2005, developers paid owners of over 900 units of low-income rental housing about $7.8 million.

Los Angeles Helps Mom & Pop Rental Owners with Repairs

Los Angeles has used data from its award-winning rental inspection program to create a rehabilitation assistance program for the "mom and pop" owner-occupants of duplexes and four-plexes who lack funds for repairs. Many of these low-income landlords are seniors living on retirement benefits. By providing three-percent deferred loans as well as grants for lead paint removal and exterior improvements, the Mom & Pop Program also helps preserve homeownership by serving owners who are vulnerable to high-cost refinancings. A related program provides three-percent, fully amortized rehabilitation loans to properties of up to 28 units occupied by low-income tenants.

Triage Services Help Maryland's Montgomery County Owners

The National Housing Trust's February 2006 issue of *Preservation Outlook* describes Montgomery County's use of "triage, moral suasion, and just plain common sense" to preserve affordable rental housing. County officials enlisted the trust to help identify which properties were most likely to opt out of the federal Section 8 program. The county executive met with owners' representatives from seven properties and found that risk of loss was the biggest concern. In response, the county agreed to help cover costs and rent losses caused by excessive tenant damage, and to front money in the event that HUD is late with its payments. The $60,000 or less spent annually on the program has been well worth the $3.4 million annual federal subsidy to the residents, the county says. Only once in five years has the county had to cover tenant damages.

2 Encourage Responsible Ownership Through Code Enforcement

By maintaining the quality and safety of existing units, code enforcement is a critical tool for preserving affordable rental housing. Local leaders should ensure that their code enforcement programs are rigorous and support wider preservation goals.

▼ CASES IN POINT

LA's Systematic Inspections Lead to Over a Billion in Reinvestment

Through its Systematic Code Enforcement Program (SCEP), the Los Angeles Housing Department inspects all rental properties with two or more units—about 760,000 to 780,000 buildings—on a four-year cycle. In effect, the program forces owners to keep up their properties, preventing the deferred maintenance that can seriously undermine the condition of the housing stock. By the end of the first inspection cycle (December 2005), SCEP had identified 1.9 million violations that spurred an estimated $1.7 billion in plumbing, heating, carpentry, and other repairs.

Code Enforcement Becomes a Rescue Tool in Chicago

Vigorous code enforcement was an integral factor in Chicago's takeover and resale of 1,100 units of distressed subsidized housing—reportedly the nation's largest-ever rescue of a troubled Section 8 complex.[6] City inspections discovered 1,800 code violations at

104 apartment buildings owned by two separate private landlords in North Lawndale, helping to instigate HUD foreclosure proceedings. HUD sold the developments to the city for a total of $20. To save the housing, the city distributed the parcels among 25 for-profit, nonprofit, and faith-based developers who agreed to rehabilitate their portion within two years and keep the units affordable for 20 years. HUD provided $33.5 million for the renovations.

3 Enact Notification and Right-to-Buy Laws

More than 1.4 million HUD-assisted multifamily rental units face expiring rent and mortgage subsidies in the future—and at least 860,000 within the next decade. Perhaps as many as 640,000 units are considered most at risk because their contract rents are comparable to or below market rate. Already, 300,000 such units have been lost.[7] Most at-risk units were developed under HUD's private owner Section 8 program, while others were developed through other rental assistance programs or with a HUD-subsidized mortgage.

Jurisdictions should enact laws requiring property owners operating under HUD-assisted programs to notify officials of the intent to convert to market rate. Although HUD must be notified when any of its subsidized properties are to be sold or converted, cities are often left out of the loop. With notification, municipalities can solicit nonprofit housing developers or other buyers committed to long-term affordability. Denver, Portland, Sacramento, San Francisco, and Washington, DC are among the cities that already require up to a year's notification before any private owners opt out of HUD's Section 8 program.

Cities should also consider pairing notification laws with measures that grant the first opportunity to purchase to tenant organizations, nonprofits, public agencies, or other entities that commit to specific preservation terms. Under a "Right of First Refusal" ordinance, when a prospective buyer makes an offer, a designated purchaser can step in and acquire the property by matching the offer. According to the National Housing Law Project, such measures can apply to all federally assisted properties or be limited to, for example, prepayments of HUD-subsidized mortgages. In many cases, designated buyers waive their rights to the property by persuading the market buyer to keep some or all of the units affordable for a certain number of years.

Funding programs for nonprofits and tenant groups seeking to purchase and rehabilitate at-risk housing can enhance the effectiveness of notification and purchase rights laws. Lining up partner nonprofits can facilitate use of such laws. For example, organized tenant groups in the District of Columbia and Montgomery County have turned their rights over to Community Preservation Development Corporation, a large regional developer, and NHT/Enterprise Preservation Corporation.[8] These organizations raise money through tax credits and other sources to rehabilitate the properties and maintain a long-term management interest.

DC's Right of First Refusal Law Helps Preserve Affordability

The District of Columbia's Tenant Opportunity to Purchase Act helped to preserve thousands of affordable homes (many in gentrifying neighborhoods) while making it possible for low-income renters to purchase homes.[9] The city's unusually broad "Right of First Refusal" law requires all residential rental property sellers to first offer their properties to any tenants in the building at a fair market price. This law enables tenants to find "friendly buyers" who will purchase the property and preserve its affordability.

Some large Washington area affordable housing developers have partnered with tenant groups to arrange complex purchase and rehab deals, often involving LIHTC financing. For example, Somerset Development and NHT/Enterprise Preservation Corporation worked with the tenants to acquire and rehabilitate Galen Terrace, a federally subsidized 84-unit community in serious disrepair and threatened with sale. The DC Housing Finance Agency provided $5.6 million in tax-exempt bonds and $4.65 million in tax-credit equity toward the acquisition and renovation, while the Department of Housing and Community Development provided $3.25 million in CDBG funds. HUD renewed the complex's Section 8 contract for another 20 years.

Montgomery County Agencies Exercise Right to Match Offers

Under Montgomery County, Maryland laws, the county and its public housing/housing finance agency—the Housing Opportunity Commission (HOC)—have the right to match contracts on rental facilities built before 1981 or on rental buildings being sold for conversion to condominiums. Certified tenant associations also have the right to match the contract on rentals built prior to 1981. The right can be waived if the purchaser commits to preserving the building as a rental property for five years at rents acceptable to the county. The county, either through HOC or a designated nonprofit housing developer, has exercised the right of first refusal at least six times. For example, to preserve some naturally occurring affordable units and hard-to-find three-bedroom units, the HOC bought an unsubsidized 1950s apartment building and is renovating it for moderate-income tenants.

Rights of First Refusal Provisions Save Locally Subsidized Housing

To preserve the affordability of housing built under local programs, some municipalities attach rights of first refusal provisions to such homes. For example, Carlsbad, California has an inclusionary housing program that requires developers to set aside units in their projects for affordable housing, earning density bonuses in return. The city retains the right to purchase any projects built under the program that go on the market.

4 Support Community-based Preservation Partners

Spearheading some successful preservation programs are local nonprofit developers who specialize in affordable housing production, preservation, and other community development activities. Local governments should support the work of effective local partners through general revenue funds, federal pass-through of HOME and CDBG funds, and assistance in securing federal Low-Income Housing Tax Credits.

Local governments that partner with such groups can leverage additional resources offered by regional and national intermediaries such as NeighborWorks® America, Enterprise Community Partners, Inc., Local Initiatives Support Corporation (LISC), the Housing Assistance Council, and the Rural Community Assistance Corporation. Intermediaries and their affiliates syndicate Low-Income Housing Tax Credits, provide up-front equity financing to low-income rental developments sponsored by community developers, and pull together development partnerships among local nonprofit builders, banks, foundations, local governments, and other entities.

The NeighborWorks® Multifamily Initiative is a portfolio management program for the more than 90 NeighborWorks organizations that develop, own, and manage affordable multifamily housing. The initiative supports its members by providing asset management training, consultation, and quarterly comparative portfolio performance data; offering development grants and access to predevelopment and interim acquisition loans; creating opportunities for risk management education and lower-cost insurance pools; and sharing best practices and developing certification in resident services. The initiative can serve as a resource by introducing seasoned multifamily owners to new communities.

5 Generate More Local Resources for Rental Preservation and Development

Preservation efforts are most effective when developers who specialize in affordable housing are equipped to step in and purchase properties that are distressed or being put on the market. Local governments should foster this capacity by generating new local funding streams to cover gaps in financing. The large regional and national developers that can serve as partners to local governments have become adept at accessing various sources of funding for rental rehabilitation and new production.[10] But they tend to flourish most in states and localities that invest their own resources in affordable housing, whether through housing trust funds, generous bond allocations, or local appropriations.

These groups produce many hundreds of units each year and manage portfolios with thousands or even tens of thousands of units.[11] Many have offices in multiple states, units that specialize in preservation, and their own loan funds.[12] Major national funders such as the John D. and Catherine T. MacArthur Foundation also support their preservation efforts. The foundation's $75-million, 10-year initiative to purchase and maintain 100,000 units of affordable rental housing nationwide provides grants and low-cost loans to nonprofit preservation owners and helps lenders provide specialized financing for preservation transactions. As of October 2006, the initiative had helped long-term affordable housing owners secure over $2.6 billion for preservation projects totaling more than 35,000 rental units.

▼ CASES IN POINT

Virginia Suburbs Dedicate Tax Revenues to Preservation

In 2005, both Fairfax County and the City of Alexandria adopted "One Penny for Housing" programs, dedicating a cent of the real estate tax to affordable multifamily housing preservation. In Fairfax County, the fund receives $18–22 million annually, which is leveraging private financing, CDBG, and other resources such as developer contributions to preserve more than 1,000 units of affordable housing by the end of 2007. Alexandria's penny fund has generated approximately $3 million annually. The city has used the expected income stream from the new tax to back $22.1 million in bond issues to preserve an estimated 134 rental units. Penny fund monies, combined with other local and federal funds, are expected to develop or preserve 150–200 rental units annually. Other jurisdictions with housing trust funds used for preservation include Boulder, the District of Columbia, and more than a dozen states.

$100 Million Fund Expands Rental Pipeline in Los Angeles

The Los Angeles Housing Trust Fund has an annual level of $100 million, including $8 million in city general funds, entitlement funds, tax increment financing funds, project-based Section 8 vouchers, state grant dollars, and other resources.[13] The fund is the main vehicle for leveraging outside dollars and developer partnerships to create a production pipeline for multifamily rental housing.[14] Sixty percent of trust fund monies are earmarked for multifamily rental projects serving households with incomes up to 60 percent of the area median. Since its first funding round in 2003, the fund has awarded about $200 million and leveraged an additional $800 million, for a total investment of $1 billion that was used to create about 4,800 rental units.

Linkage Fees in Boston and San Francisco Support Housing for New Workers

Boston and San Francisco are among the municipalities using linkage fees to fund affordable housing development. These programs assess fees on new commercial developments under the rationale that such projects increase property values and bring in more workers who need housing. Since its inception in 1983, Boston's linkage fee program has committed more than $81 million to projects creating or preserving 6,159 affordable housing units in 115 developments.[15] In San Francisco, revenues are deposited into an affordable housing fund. The program raised about $45 million between 1989 and the end of 2005, producing more than 1,000 (primarily rental) units.

New York Targets Billions to Housing Construction and Preservation

New York City's 10-year New Housing Marketplace Plan aims to create or preserve 165,000 units of affordable housing between 2004 and 2013. The city allocated

$4.4 billion from the capital budget to create a leveraged pool of $7.5 billion for the initiative. As part of the effort, the city plans to preserve 73,000 units of affordable housing, particularly units with expiring subsidies. The preservation component includes a $230 million site acquisition fund and partnerships with HUD to obtain troubled FHA-insured housing at discounted rates by circumventing standard foreclosure auction sales, offering refinancing products to owners of properties subsidized under the city's Mitchell-Lama program, and helping owners of tax-credit properties that are reaching the end of their 15-year compliance periods with financial restructuring.

6 Allocate New Property Tax Revenues For Affordable Multifamily Housing

In strong markets where condominium values are much higher than rental values, municipalities should consider using tax increment financing (TIF) to capture some of the windfall revenues from the condos to support affordable rental housing. Under TIF, a city government designates the boundaries of a redevelopment district. New tax revenues generated by rising property values flow to the TIF district. Often, to jump-start redevelopment, the district issues bonds backed by the future revenue stream to finance projects and infrastructure improvements.

▼ CASES IN POINT

Chicago TIF Funds Generate $200 Million for Housing

Between 1994 and the end of 2006, Chicago spent more than $200 million in TIF revenues on projects to create or improve nearly 8,000 affordable housing units. TIF funds in the form of grants, loans, upfront financing, or mortgage interest subsidies support new housing construction and rehabilitation, including units built under the city's Affordable Requirements Ordinance.[16] In addition, TIF funds allocated under the TIF-Neighborhood Improvement Program have helped owners of small rental properties complete exterior renovations. Finally, TIF funds have also helped the city make greater use of its tax-exempt bonding authority by filling financing gaps in projects accessing four-percent tax credits.

San Francisco, Portland TIF Set-Asides Target Affordable Housing

The San Francisco Redevelopment Authority has used tax increment financing to acquire distressed rental properties and lease them to nonprofits for renovation. In 2006, the city made a major affordable housing commitment—to dedicate 50 percent of the tax increment revenue in the 1,300-acre Bay View Hunters Point redevelopment area to housing for very low- to moderate-income residents. The pledge may generate more than $90 million for housing over 45 years.[17]

Portland, Oregon sets aside 30 percent of tax increment financing in urban renewal areas for preserving and developing affordable housing. Enacted in October 2006, the requirement is expected to generate $121 million for affordable housing over a five-year period. Chicago and Portland are among the list of cities that have used TIF financing for mixed-income housing developments.

7 Reuse Abandoned Properties and Surplus Public Land

Vacant and abandoned or surplus public land is a hidden asset that can be used to generate affordable housing. Returning abandoned parcels to productive use is both a challenge and an opportunity. Some cities have created programs to get vacant and abandoned property into the hands of affordable housing developers for both multifamily and single-family housing.

Architects are becoming adept at turning old factories, schools, hospitals, nursing centers and other structures into affordable rental housing, particularly for senior citizens. Developers often tap historic preservation tax credits and Low-Income Housing Tax Credits for such projects. Local governments can foster these developments by designating surplus government-owned sites to be used for affordable housing, either by notifying developers when sites become available or pursuing developers more aggressively.

In some cases, school districts can sell or lease unneeded property to affordable housing developers, subject to state restrictions. Public agencies can also support efforts to transfer nonpublic sites to affordable developers.

▼ CASES IN POINT

Chicago Saves Troubled Buildings from Blight

Launched in 2003, the City of Chicago's Troubled Buildings Initiative prevents large apartment buildings from becoming so distressed that they need to be razed. The initiative is funded by $4 million in city funds and a $2 million federal community development financial institution (CDFI) grant. Community Investment Corporation (CIC), a pooled-risk mortgage lender specializing in multifamily rehabilitation projects, administers the program.

Program officials urge owners or purchasers of large, distressed apartment buildings to make necessary repairs and offer small subsidies (up to $5,000 per unit) for renovation. If the owner won't make the repairs, CIC and the city gain temporary control of the structure and pass it to new owners who will. In its first three years, the program covered 272 buildings with 5,100 units. Of these, 132 buildings with 2,439 units were either repaired or are being rehabilitated. Only nine buildings with 278 units were demolished—a significant achievement given recent loss rates.

New York Multi-Agency Partnerships Deliver Land for Housing

Now that it has almost eliminated vacant and abandoned properties, the New York City Department of Housing Preservation and Development (HPD) is building its affordable housing pipeline through targeted land use collaborations with city and state partners. For example, HPD and the New York City Housing Authority (NYCHA) have begun work on nearly 6,000 units of low-income affordable housing on underutilized NYCHA-owned land. HPD is also forming new relationships with agencies not typically associated with housing development, including the Department of Transportation, the Health and Hospitals Corporation, the Human Resources Administration, and several New York state agencies. In some cases, agencies have surplus property they are willing to transfer to HPD for affordable housing development. Together, these city and state agency partnerships are expected to generate over 20,000 units of new housing by 2013.

Enterprise-NYC Partnership Builds Local Capacity

One noteworthy property referral initiative is the Neighborhood Entrepreneurs Program (NEP), a partnership between the New York City Department of Housing Preservation and Development (HPD) and Enterprise Community Partners, a national community development intermediary. The program focuses on small, locally based entrepreneurs to help build real estate capacity. Clusters of city-owned apartment buildings—vacant or occupied—are targeted for renovation and matched with neighborhood-based private property managers, selected through an RFP process. The buildings are sold to the Neighborhood Partnership Housing Development Fund Corporation (NPHDFC), a subsidiary of Enterprise, for $1 each and then leased to the entrepreneurs. The entrepreneurs oversee the rehabilitation, using city and bank loans and Low-Income Housing Tax Credits secured with the help of the NPHDFC. City financing and proceeds from the sale of LIHTCs fund ongoing operations, enabling the owner to keep rents affordable. The entrepreneur is also matched up with a local nonprofit that assists with building stabilization and provides tenant support and training. As of December 2006, more than 8,000 units had been created through the program.

Michigan Land Banks Support Rental Development

Land banks—public authorities that acquire, manage, and convey vacant, tax-foreclosed properties—can support affordable rental development. State legislation provides these entities with title-clearing mechanisms and other legal and financial tools to recycle abandoned properties. Among the most successful is the Genesee County Land Bank, created in 2002 by Genesee County, Michigan, the City of Flint, and Flint Township. The land bank has acquired about 5,400 parcels and prepared sites for reuse by cleaning up empty lots and demolishing abandoned homes. As of late 2006, more than 150 foreclosed tenant-occupied properties had been sold to nonprofits to develop as affordable rental or for-sale homes or for other neighborhood stabilization projects. Genesee County's land bank has pioneered a way to self-finance redevelopment by using the financial returns on the sale of one property to support the costs of holding other properties—an approach that ultimately reduces municipal costs.[18]

8 Offer Predevelopment and Land Acquisition Funding

Affordable multifamily housing developers need longer-term capital to acquire and develop sites. And they need the money fast, particularly in hot markets. But often banks are unwilling or unable to assume the risk. Local leaders can use trust fund revenues or other sources to provide badly needed land acquisition and predevelopment funding—or use government and foundation funds as a guarantee to secure bank funding. Guarantees from housing finance agencies would significantly aid efforts to secure financing.

▼ CASES IN POINT

NYC Acquisition Fund Helps Affordable Developers Compete for Land

The $230 million New York City Acquisition Fund, launched in August 2006, is an integral component of Mayor Bloomberg's plan to preserve 73,000 affordable housing units by 2013. The fund provides early-stage acquisition loans to developers through for-profit and nonprofit lenders, including Enterprise New York, LISC, the Corporation for Supportive Housing, and the Low Income Investment Fund. The fund is a product of an innovative partnership that combined $8 million in city funds[19] with $32.6 million in grants and investments from nine foundations, creating a $40 million "guarantee pool." The pool has leveraged an additional $192.5 million in loans from 15 lending institutions. By securing the loans in the event of default, the guarantee pool reduces risks to participating lenders while enabling the city and foundation funding to attract significant private capital for affordable housing.

Washington, DC Trust Fund Leverages Predevelopment Funds

Washington, DC's Department of Housing and Community Development administers a Site Acquisition Funding Initiative for Affordable Housing under the city's Housing Production Trust Fund Program. The initiative provides low- or no-interest loans to a select group of lenders, who then underwrite projects that need bridge financing for quick purchase. The $20 million in program funding for fiscal 2005 and 2006 is leveraging private funds to provide site acquisition and predevelopment loans, purchase options, and technical assistance to nonprofit developers. As of the end of 2006, 13 loans had closed under the program for projects to preserve or produce an estimated 800 housing units.

Nationwide CDFI Offers Predevelopment/Bridge Financing

The National Housing Trust Community Development Fund is a nationwide community development financial institution (CDFI) dedicated to providing predevelopment and bridge financing to preserve and improve affordable multifamily properties. Since its inception in 1999, the fund has made over $5.1 million in loans, supporting the private investment of over $280 million and helping to preserve more than 3,600 units of affordable housing across the country.

9 Encourage Formation of Bank Consortia

In many cities (Chicago, Portland, New York) and states (Massachusetts, Washington), bank consortia are making sure that money and loans are available for rehabilitation of multifamily housing. Local leaders should encourage the creation of such consortia. They should also encourage lenders to design products suitable for the smaller, private rental property owners who manage so many of the units occupied by lower-income families.

▼ CASE IN POINT

Chicago Pooled-Risk Lender Helps Hands-on Rehabbers

The Community Investment Corporation (CIC) in Chicago is a pooled-risk mortgage lender specializing in multifamily rehabilitation in lower-income neighborhoods. The company was capitalized by 47 banks, Fannie Mae, Peoples Energy, and the United Methodist Pension Fund to create a revolving loan fund totaling $550 million.

CIC has been able to deliver creative financing tools to rehabber-owners in older low-rent neighborhoods, a very important but often overlooked segment of the rental industry. Often, owners of smaller rental complexes handle property management with relatively low operating costs and excellent maintenance, without much overhead or government engagement. The company offers a range of products, including low-rate construction and permanent financing for up to 90 percent of a property's appraised value.

Among other initiatives, the CIC works with the city departments of housing, buildings, and law to restore blighted apartment complexes through Chicago's Troubled Buildings Initiative. It also partners with Neighborhood Housing Services of Chicago, Inc. Between April 1984 and the end of 2006, CIC made 1,360 loans totaling $777 million for the rehabilitation of 39,000 units of affordable rental housing for roughly 113,500 Chicago area residents.

10 Foster Mixed-Income Developments to Preserve Affordability in High-Cost Markets

Mixed-income developments use a blend of locally generated public funds, Low-Income Housing Tax Credits, private financing, and, occasionally, public housing vouchers to create communities that include market-rate along with lower-cost housing. Sponsors are making the numbers work by mixing market-rate, for-sale units with lower-cost rentals. With such developments, the income from the more expensive units can help subsidize the less expensive units. Land sales or rents for community centers, health clinics, and other facilities also provide revenues.

DC's New Communities Initiative Pledges One-for-One Replacement Of Affordable Units

Washington, DC has combined bond proceeds with trust fund monies to support the New Communities Initiative, a program to redevelop three to five large-scale neighborhoods over five to twelve years. In 2002, the city council dedicated 15 percent of the district's real estate transfer tax to the Housing Production Trust Fund. The city council has authorized using $12 million of trust fund monies annually to secure an estimated $150 million in bond issues for the initiative. The funds will leverage other public and private funds. The redevelopments will replace a significant amount of publicly subsidized and unsubsidized substandard rental housing (as well as for-sale homes) with new mixed-income communities. Under the program, city officials pledged to replace every affordable unit demolished with a new unit. As of December 2006, the city launched three of the new communities representing over $2 billion of redevelopment, including 6,000 units of affordable and market-rate housing.

Project Preserves Affordability in Affluent Virginia Suburb

Fairfax County's Madison Ridge development mixes for-sale condos with low-cost rentals, providing affordable homes in the high-priced Washington, DC market. An existing affordable complex was slated to become 100-percent market-rate condominiums until the county stepped in to provide the critical investment to keep the building affordable. Fairfax County contributed $8.6 million to the financial package that allowed the nonprofit Wesley Housing Development Corporation of Northern Virginia to purchase the 216-unit complex. Funding included $5.1 million from the county's Housing Trust Fund, $2.5 million from the One Penny for Affordable Housing Fund, and $1 million from the county Preservation Loan Fund.[20] Ninety-eight of the units will remain affordable rentals and 118 units will be converted into condominiums sold at affordable prices in the $210,000–290,000 range. The Fairfax County Redevelopment and Housing Authority will purchase ten of the condos to lease as permanently affordable rental units.

For-Sale Homes Cross-Subsidize Rentals, Prevent Displacement In Washington Area

The nonprofit Community Preservation and Development Corporation (CPDC) and partners are using a variation on the mixed-income strategy to help tenant groups in greater Washington, DC acquire rental housing put up for sale. Built in 1963, Hampshire Towers is a 448-unit apartment community in Takoma Park, Maryland. The property was purchased in 2006 by a joint venture between CPDC and Tenacity Group. CPDC will retain 216 units as affordable rental housing and Tenacity will convert 232 units into affordable homeownership, with units first offered to tenants at special "insider" rates (affordable for households making up to 80 percent of the area median income). Tenants also have the option of remaining renters or taking a buyout. The condos will be priced at different levels, depending on their upgrades.

About $2.5 million in revenues will help subsidize the rehabilitation of the rental units, half of which will be affordable to households with incomes up to 50 percent of the area median and half to households with incomes up to 60 percent of the area median. The financing package for the rental tower includes four-percent tax credits and tax-exempt bonds, $7 million from the Montgomery County Housing Initiatives Fund, and likely "soft" funds through a state program supplementing four-percent tax-credit deals.

Atlanta Housing Authority Uses Vouchers for Rental Preservation

As of early 2006, the Atlanta Housing Authority (AHA) had committed close to 2,000 project-based vouchers to private, tax-credit-financed housing developments as a means of creating mixed-income communities. For example, a 342-unit apartment complex for seniors in the affluent Buckhead area was deteriorating due to lack of capital funding. The only way to modernize the property was to convert it to market rents. The AHA partnered with the owner to provide a capital investment of $2 million as secondary financing at below-market rates, along with a project-based operating subsidy on 205 of the units.

New York City Tax-Exempt Bonds Fund Mixed-Income Complexes

The New Housing Opportunities Program at the New York City Housing Development Corporation (HDC) finances mixed-income rental complexes. HDC uses the proceeds from the sale of tax-exempt private activity bonds (credit-enhanced by Fannie Mae), together with its corporate reserves, to make one-percent second-mortgage loans. The first mortgage makes cash available to build the project, while the second helps increase the number of affordable units. As of December 2006, the program had created 1,630 units.

11 Help Colleges and Universities Build Student Housing

In tight rental markets, widespread student use of private apartments can be a serious problem. In some neighborhoods, competition between students and non-students for housing can damage town-gown relations. Community leaders should work with local institutions to ensure that the demand for student housing does not exacerbate the shortage of neighborhood-based affordable housing.

▼ CASE IN POINT

Boston Takes the Lead in Freeing Up Rentals in Tight Market

When it launched a campaign to increase affordable housing opportunities, the City of Boston recognized the need to do all it could to alleviate pressure in the extremely tight rental market. The Boston Redevelopment Authority is working with local colleges and universities to provide more on-campus housing for students. By the end of 2008, officials expect the partnerships to add close to 7,300 dorm beds, freeing up more than 1,800 apartments for non-student households.

12 Offer Density Bonuses to Multifamily Developers

Density bonuses allow developers to build more units on a given site than local zoning laws would normally allow. Higher densities reduce per-unit development costs, thereby boosting per-unit profits. Developers may find it more profitable to build some low-cost apartments along with market-rate units if they can build more units overall.

Density bonuses have worked well within single-family detached and town-home developments. They have also been offered to builders as part of a city's inclusionary zoning program that requires or encourages developers to set aside a certain percentage of units in new projects for low- and moderate-income households. Density bonuses work less well for high-rise and, to some extent, mid-rise properties, although they can still be effective.

Density bonuses need not be limited to residential construction. For example, municipalities could offer hotel developers density bonuses in exchange for building some affordable housing (or contributing to a fund).

▼ CASES IN POINT

New York City Rezoning Generates Thousands of Rentals

A voluntary inclusionary zoning program allowing higher densities in projects that include affordable housing is a key element of New York City's ambitious preservation plan. City rezonings allow higher housing densities in formerly industrial areas targeted for redevelopment. In exchange, builders working in those areas must set aside a portion of the units with varying levels of affordability. To further encourage affordable units, the city also assists developers working in such districts with financing for land acquisition and construction subsidies. For example, the Greenpoint-Williamsburg rezoning opened two miles of waterfront to create 54 acres of open space, including a continuous public esplanade and a 29-acre park, while also preventing inappropriate heavy industrial uses. The plan will spur development of 10,800 new units of much-needed housing. Through a powerful combination of zoning incentives, housing programs, and city-owned land, more than 3,500 of those units will be affordable. One year after the rezoning was enacted in 2005, there were already 1,000 affordable units in the pipeline for near-term construction on the waterfront alone.

Density Bonus Creates Affordable Rentals in Virginia Suburbs

To encourage affordable units in high-rise multifamily developments, Arlington, Virginia offers a density bonus of up to 25 percent to developers who provide one affordable unit for every two to four market-rate units. In addition, any developer seeking rezoning to build projects larger than currently allowed must either build some affordable units on site, build a slightly higher number of affordable units elsewhere in the county, or make a cash contribution to the county's Affordable Housing Investment Fund.[21] Projects with a density above a 3.24 floor area ratio are expected to replace existing affordable housing on a one-for-one basis. Units created with density bonuses must remain affordable for at least 30 years.

---

13   Employ Tools to Assure Long-term Affordability

To sustain their investment, local leaders can use a variety of instruments to assure long-term affordability of the units they help to create. In some cases, as with Boulder, Colorado's preservation grants and Boston's rental projects funded with linkage fees, covenants attached to the assisted units require affordability in perpetuity. New York City attaches "restrictive declarations" (akin to deed restrictions) to its inclusionary housing units that run lifelong with the property. In addition, many of New York City's tax programs and enriched benefit offerings require either written or regulatory agreements governing projects built using the benefit. Chicago uses developer agreements to ensure multifamily properties aided by the city are affordable, usually for at least 30 years. Community land trusts are another increasingly popular tool for preserving long-term affordability.

OPPORTUNITIES FOR STATE ACTION

---

1   Prioritize Tax Credits for Preservation and Coordinate with Other Resources

Local preservation and development activities are often fueled by state housing finance agencies using their power to allocate federal Low-Income Housing Tax Credits and private activity bonds. Every year, the federal government gives a designated agency in each state (usually the housing finance agency) millions of dollars in tax credits, depending on population. Some cities get their own allocations. The agencies award the tax credits to developers on a competitive basis or using a lottery system under rules outlined in the agency's Qualified Allocation Plan.

More and more states are giving extra "points" to preservation applicants. As of July 2006, the National Housing Trust (NHT) reported that more than 45 state agencies prioritize preservation in their allocation plans for Low-Income Housing Tax Credits, either by awarding additional points to developers seeking to fund preservation projects or by setting aside a certain percentage of credits for such projects.[22] Wisconsin, for example, has set aside 40 percent of its tax-credit allocations for preservation. Other states giving priority to preservation include Illinois, Michigan, and North Carolina. NHT notes that the number of affordable apartments preserved using LIHTCs increased from around 5,000 in 2000 to more than 56,000 in 2005.

Preservation advocates say more affordable units could be preserved if agencies coordinated funding cycles, application forms, and selection criteria so that developers could apply for tax credits and other resources all at once. Models include Indiana, where developers apply for tax credits and state housing trust fund loans at the same time; Washington State, where projects receiving awards from the state's housing trust fund get extra points in their LIHTC applications; and Florida, where a single application covers tax credits and the State Apartment Incentive Loan program.[23]

Taking a highly targeted approach, Virginia carved out 15 percent of its annual housing credit limit in 2006 for a special noncompetitive credit pool for the suburbs of Washington, DC. The region is experiencing a severe shortage of affordable rental housing because of condominium conversions and other redevelopment activities. The pool helps preservation developers move quickly to acquire sites in the hot market, rather than having to wait for the standard credit-scoring process to play out.[24]

2 Maximize Use of Tax-Exempt Bond Financing with "Automatic" Four-Percent Tax Credits to Preserve Rental Housing

Federal Low-Income Housing Tax Credits are of two types—nine-percent credits, which are allocated to the states based on population, and "automatic" four-percent credits, which are available to projects that meet certain criteria and are financed with the proceeds of tax-exempt bonds. Larger developers and housing agencies have turned increasingly to the four-percent credits as a resource for affordable housing preservation. Financings using both tax-exempt bonds and four-percent credits are generally not subject to the same funding cycles or competitions required for nine-percent credits and can better meet a developer's timetable for closing.

The bond cap for tax-exempt financings has also increased in recent years, making this source of financing more plentiful than in the past. Coupled with the automatic four-percent tax credits, bond financing provides a significant resource for preservation efforts.

3 Enhance Tax-Credit Preservation and Asset Management Efforts

In addition to using LIHTCs to preserve affordable rental housing, states should seek to preserve the affordability of existing tax-credit properties. For example, the Washington State Housing Finance Commission has developed a system to market and sell expiring LIHTC properties to qualified buyers committed to keeping them affordable. It also hosts training sessions to help nonprofits understand how they can participate. Finally, the commission alleviates some of the reporting burdens for property owners remaining in the program beyond 15 years.[25]

Strong asset management is key to any preservation strategy. The Washington State Housing Trust Fund, which currently receives approximately $100 million every two years from the state's capital budget, gives priority to preserving federally subsidized rental properties. In addition to funding preservation, it spearheaded asset management efforts. It helped to develop a Monitoring Task Force group made up of the Washington Housing Finance Commission (administrator of tax credits) and other state funders, HUD, a private lending consortium, the City of Seattle, King County, and other local jurisdictions. The forum allows people working on the asset management side to share strategies about reserves, tax-credit year-15 transitions, and problem projects.

4 Direct Housing Authority Reserves and Other State Supports to Preservation and Rental Development

States are supporting preservation with resources beyond tax credits, including lending money to restructure existing loans, allocating state housing trust fund money to preservation, providing predevelopment and bridge loans, allowing owners equity take-outs, and offering tax incentives to owners who agree to maintain the housing as affordable.[26] For example, Maryland appropriates $15.5 million of general funds to support affordable rental housing. These funds are generally awarded competitively in conjunction with nine-percent tax credits, but a portion of these funds was recently used to reopen the Maryland Housing Rehabilitation Program for Multifamily Housing. This program provides gap financing for the acquisition and rehabilitation of existing affordable rental buildings. Funds can only be used in conjunction with four-percent tax credits and private activity bond financings. The purpose of the program is to preserve the supply of housing with existing federal, state, or local affordability requirements, particularly project-based Section 8 and Rural Development Rental Assistance.

Like many other real estate lenders, the Massachusetts housing finance agency, MassHousing, realized respectable gains during the 1990s and early 2000s as a result of increased loan volumes, investments, interest payments, fee income, anticipated future mortgage payments, and intelligent management of resources. To reinvest those gains into the housing market, MassHousing developed the Priority Development Fund (PDF) to aggregate funds from a variety of sources inside the agency to provide gap financing for smart growth and transit-oriented housing developments. As of early 2007, a total of $65 million in PDF loans had been closed, committed, or were in the pipeline. The funds support 29 rental housing developments with over 3,000 units—more than 1,600 of which will be affordable to low-income residents. The success of the PDF lies in its ability to leverage other funds, providing developers access to more than $283 million in non-MassHousing monies.

The Wisconsin Housing and Economic Development Authority (WHEDA) Saving Our Stock program has set aside $30 million since 2004 for low-cost loans to facilitate transfers of ownership to preserve affordable housing, fund operating deficits that arise from frozen rents and increasing expenses, address capital needs, and restructure and refinance current mortgages. As of early 2007, the Saving Our Stock program had preserved more than 2,000 units.

Massachusetts, Virginia, and Washington have developed nonprofit financial institutions that fund predevelopment and acquisitions or provide bridge financing for preservation transactions. In Massachusetts, the publicly chartered Community Economic Development Assistance Corporation (CEDAC) manages over $39 million in revolving loan funds serving nonprofit developers. Among its many roles, CEDAC helps community organizations and municipalities negotiate the extension of current affordability restrictions or the sale of such subsidized rental complexes to nonprofit owners, as well as secure new capital to meet deferred maintenance or system replacement needs. CEDAC has also developed an Acquisition Loan Program, which makes loans to developers to buy sites if they must make the purchase before they can secure all of the necessary financing.

States are also taking other creative approaches to spur rental housing development. For example, the California Housing Finance Agency launched a new program to foster more affordable rental development by addressing a barrier to investor interest. Under the new 30/15 program, developers finance projects for 30 years but may repay the loan after year 15. Although the developer is no longer locked into the loan for the full term, the units financed must remain affordable for the entire 30 years.

5 Enact Notification and Right-to-Buy Laws

States as well as local jurisdictions should require owners of federally assisted multifamily housing to notify officials of the intent to convert their properties to market rate and/or grant some form of "right of first refusal." With notification, states can help ensure that local jurisdictions have an opportunity to arrange for properties to be sold to buyers committed to long-term affordability. State laws that grant tenant organizations and other groups the first opportunity to purchase properties at risk of conversion can be accompanied by a variety of procedural requirements and enforcement mechanisms that give tenants, nonprofits, and other interested parties important tools to advance the preservation policy.[27] States with rights of first refusal and notification laws include California, Illinois, Maine, Maryland, Rhode Island, and Texas.

California has what many preservation advocates consider the nation's strongest notification program. All owners of HUD-subsidized housing and expiring Section 8 projects who intend to terminate the subsidy for any reason or prepay their mortgages must give a year's notice to tenants, the state housing authority, the local housing authority, and local governments. The notification program is paired with a right of first refusal that allows state-registered preservation buyers to match offers from other parties under certain circumstances.[28]

In 2006, Rhode Island strengthened its Two Year Notice Law that requires owners of HUD-subsidized housing who intend to exit the program to inform tenants and the state two years in advance. The amendment also requires that owners offer to sell their properties to the tenant association, the state and local housing authority, and the municipality.

6 Reduce Property Taxes and Adopt an Income Approach To Tax Assessments

State laws should provide some property tax relief for affordable rental projects. California, Florida, and Wisconsin allow property tax exemptions for nonprofit affordable housing providers. In Minnesota, the tax rate for apartments that receive federal Section 8 housing subsidies or meet other qualifications is 60 percent of that for market-rate rentals. The Minnesota Housing Partnership estimated that this tax break saved developers and other eligible entities approximately $9.4 million in 2006.

States should direct tax assessors to value rental units based on their income, factoring in rent restrictions rather than the "highest and best use." This would provide relief for complexes in high-cost areas that, due to rent restrictions, cannot increase revenues. Alaska, Colorado, Connecticut, Florida, Illinois, and Iowa all have statutes addressing the valuation of rent-restricted properties.

7 Create a State Affordable Housing Tax Credit To Leverage Other Resources

Missouri, North Carolina, and Illinois have state tax-credit programs that help to stretch funds. Such credits are equally useful in both hot and distressed markets. In hot markets where an affordable developer cannot afford to pay a high price for a property, the donation tax credit can help make up the difference between the seller's asking price and what the new owner can afford. In distressed markets, appraisers can still find some value, providing owners who donate property to an affordable housing developer a way to handle exit taxes.

The Illinois Affordable Housing Tax Credit program provides a $0.50 state income-tax credit for every $1.00 invested in a qualified housing activity. The $13 million in credits available each year generate up to $26 million statewide. In Missouri, the credit equals $0.55 for every donated dollar. The credits are transferable, making them useful to donors with low tax liabilities. North Carolina's tax-linked bonus is a little different. Under that program, projects awarded LIHTCs that meet certain criteria receive a bonus in the form of check.

8 Streamline Laws Governing Vacant And Abandoned Properties

Since state law governs the way municipalities handle properties with tax liens, state legislatures are critical partners in local efforts to recycle vacant and abandoned properties for affordable housing. New Jersey's Abandoned Properties Rehabilitation Act, passed in 2004 and fine-tuned in 2005, makes it easier for local governments to develop abandoned properties by expediting tax foreclosures. First, it clearly defines what constitutes an abandoned property for legal purposes. Second, it provides a route for spot blight eminent domain. Local governments generally seize private real estate for public use only if the property is within an area designated as blighted. Spot blight laws allow governments to seize individual nuisance properties without having to go through the whole redevelopment process. Third, the vacant property receivership provision enables municipalities (or community developers acting as the municipality's agent) to order owners to return abandoned properties to productive use or hand them over to nonprofit developers for redevelopment as affordable housing.

9 Give Priority to Affordable Housing When Selling Surplus State Properties

State agencies selling land should give priority to affordable housing developments or mixed-income developments with at least some affordable housing. States could also authorize sale of state-owned land at below-market prices to nonprofits for the development of affordable housing. California law, for example, requires that surplus lands held by state, county, and local jurisdictions first be made available to uses for the public good, including affordable housing. When land is scheduled for disposition, public agencies and some nonprofits receive notification (although the land is usually sold at market price). Agencies such as CalTrans, the state transportation agency, have used the law to work with developers.

10 Provide for Use of Local TIF Revenues For Preservation

Under California's Community Redevelopment Law, at least 20 percent of all tax increment financing (TIF) revenues must be used for low- and moderate-income housing. According to a 2006 report by the Center for Housing Policy, the revenues made redevelopment agencies one of the biggest sources of funding for affordable homes in California, generating more than $1.2 billion in fiscal 2004–2005 alone.[29] Maine also has authorized TIF districts to fund affordable housing.

RESOURCES

CAMPAIGN FOR AFFORDABLE HOUSING
www.tcah.org

National nonprofit organization dedicated to dispelling the negative stereotypes that surround affordable housing. The website features several resources, including a catalog of successful campaigns and a review of public opinion research on affordable housing.

CONSORTIUM FOR HOUSING AND ASSET MANAGEMENT
www.cham.org

Collaboration of Enterprise Community Partners, the Local Initiatives Support Corporation, and NeighborWorks®America. CHAM offers resources and training on property and asset management, including a certification program for asset managers.

ENTERPRISE COMMUNITY PARTNERS
www.enterprisecommunity.org

Provides financing and expertise to community and housing developers. A for-profit subsidiary, Enterprise Community Investment, offers tax-credit financing and asset management services. Enterprise has also formed a joint venture with the National Housing Trust to preserve affordable rental housing.

HOMES FOR WORKING FAMILIES
www.homesforworkingfamilies.org

Focuses on policy changes that increase access to affordable, good-quality homes for America's working families.

HOUSING PARTNERSHIP NETWORK
www.housingpartnership.net

Peer network and business cooperative of 86 large affordable housing nonprofits operating city- or region-wide. Members forge entrepreneurial partnerships among the business, community, and government sectors to create and sustain affordable housing.

JOHN D. AND CATHERINE T. MACARTHUR FOUNDATION
www.macfound.org

Philanthropic foundation that is investing $75 million in rental preservation efforts through its "Window of Opportunity" initiative.

RESOURCES

KNOWLEDGEPLEX® WEEK IN REVIEW
www.knowledgeplex.org

Newsletter summarizing housing and related development articles from newspapers nationwide, including regular coverage of local and state rental production programs.

LOCAL INITIATIVES SUPPORT CORPORATION (LISC)
www.lisc.org

National intermediary providing capital, technical expertise, training, and information to help community-based developers create affordable housing and commercial, industrial and community facilities. LISC's affiliate, National Equity Fund, Inc., syndicates tax credits, providing equity capital for multifamily housing projects. LISC's Affordable Housing Preservation initiative helps nonprofit community development corporations acquire and preserve housing developments.

NATIONAL ASSOCIATION OF AFFORDABLE HOUSING LENDERS
www.naahl.org

Represents private sector lenders and investors in affordable housing and community economic development, including but not limited to banks, loan consortia, financial intermediaries, and pension funds.

NATIONAL COUNCIL OF STATE HOUSING AGENCIES
www.ncsha.org

Association of state housing finance agencies as well as more than 350 for-profit and nonprofit firms in the affordable housing field. NCSHA's members administer the Low-Income Housing Tax Credit program. A fact sheet providing background information on the tax-credit program is available on the website.

NATIONAL HOUSING CONFERENCE
www.nhc.org

Represents all segments of the housing industry and engages in advocacy for national policies that promote suitable housing in a safe, decent environment. NHC's nonprofit research affiliate, the Center for Housing Policy, examines the impact of policies and programs developed to address America's affordable housing challenges.

NATIONAL HOUSING LAW PROJECT
www.nhlp.org

National housing law and advocacy center that promotes housing justice for the poor. The organization provides legal assistance, advocacy advice, and housing expertise to attorneys, low-income housing advocacy groups, and others who serve the poor.

NATIONAL HOUSING TRUST
www.nhtinc.org

Nonprofit organization that seeks to preserve and improve affordable multifamily homes for low- and moderate-income people. NHT provides training, technical assistance, and loans to local nonprofits, government agencies, and tenant groups acquiring and preserving properties. It also operates a clearinghouse on HUD-assisted properties and develops public policy. Among the many resources available through the website are "Change in Project-Based Multifamily Units in HUD's Inventory Between 1995 and 2003," and the regularly updated working paper, "State and Local Housing Preservation Initiatives." NHT's monthly newsletter, *Preservation News,* is also available on the website.

NATIONAL LOW INCOME HOUSING COALITION
www.nlihc.org

Seeks to pass legislation that provides new funding for the production of rental housing for extremely low-income people. NLIHC also conducts public education, organizing, and research. NLIHC produces an annual interactive study comparing the full-time hourly wage a person would need to earn to pay the Fair Market Rent in a given area while spending no more than 30 percent of income on housing.

NATIONAL MULTI HOUSING COUNCIL
www.nmhc.org

Represents the interests of larger US apartment firms, including owners, developers, managers and financiers. An NMHC paper, "From NIMBY to Good Neighbor," summarizes reports that indicate that apartments are not a threat to local property values and can even help raise values in certain neighborhoods. An NMHC-commissioned report, "Higher-Density Development: Myth and Fact," compares the advantages and drawbacks of higher-density development.

NATIONAL RESIDENT SERVICES COLLABORATIVE
www.residentservices.org

Provides certification training, conferences, and publications on resident services best practices.

RESOURCES

NATIONAL VACANT PROPERTIES CAMPAIGN
www.vacantproperties.org

Launched by Smart Growth America, LISC, and the International City/County Management Association in 2003 to advocate for property reclamation and offer technical assistance to communities.

NEIGHBORWORKS® AMERICA
www.nw.org

National nonprofit organization created by Congress that provides financial support, technical assistance, and training for community-based revitalization efforts. More than 240 organizations in 50 states are members. The NeighborWorks® Multifamily Initiative is a collaborative of nonprofit housing developers that produce, preserve, own, and/or manage affordable multifamily housing. The initiative provides grants, loans, and training and technical assistance in the areas of asset management, resident services, and real estate development.

STEWARDS OF AFFORDABLE HOUSING FOR THE FUTURE
www.sahfnet.org

Association of national nonprofit organizations that acquire and preserve multifamily housing as affordable to low-income families, seniors, and disabled individuals. Members include Mercy Housing Inc., National Affordable Housing Trust, National Church Residences, Inc., NHT/Enterprise Preservation Corporation, Preservation of Affordable Housing, Inc., Retirement Housing Foundation, and Volunteers of America.

1. Joint Center for Housing Studies of Harvard University, "America's Rental Housing—Homes for a Diverse Nation," 2006, Table A-10,
   www.jchs.harvard.edu/publications/rental/rh06_americas_rental_housing.pdf/.

2. Low-Income Housing Tax Credits are allocated by the federal government and then allocated by the states through a competitive process. Developers usually sell the credits to investors and use the proceeds, or equity, to fund the project.

3. National Low Income Housing Coalition, "Out of Reach 2006," Seven Slide Summary of the Data, **www.nlihc.org/oor/oor2006/sevenmaps.pdf**.

4. Keith Wardrip and Danilo Pelletiere, "Recent Data Shows Continuation, Acceleration of Housing Affordability Crisis," National Low Income Housing Coalition, Research Note #06-05, December 11, 2006. The share of renter households paying more than 30 percent of their income on housing increased from 34 percent to 49 percent between 1980 and 2005.

5. NAHRO 2005 Legislative and Regulatory Agenda,
   www.nahro.org/legislative/2005/05NAHROLegAgenda.pdf.

6. Antonio Olivo, "City Turns Over Beleaguered Housing Units," *Chicago Tribune,* January 19, 2006.

7. The National Housing Trust, "Changes to Project-Based Multifamily Units in HUD's Inventory Between 1995 and 2003," April 2004, **www.nhtinc.org/documents/PB_Inventory.pdf**. Data on units lost and remaining units are as of 2003. Data on units at risk of loss over the next decade are as of December 2006.

8. NHT/Enterprise Preservation Corporation. is a joint venture between the National Housing Trust and Enterprise to buy and hold affordable housing units in areas without local nonprofits engaged in rental preservation. As of September 2006, the organization had preserved 3,000 units in the Mid-Atlantic, Midwest, South, and Southeast regions.

9. Georgetown University Law Center, Harrison Institute for Public Law, "An Analysis of the Strengths and Deficiencies of Washington, DC's Tenant Opportunity to Purchase Act," 2006, **content.knowledgeplex.org/kp2/cache/documents/1834/183436.pdf**.

10. Tax credits alone are never sufficient to finance an entire project. Affordable rental developers must combine tax credits with local or state trust fund monies or bond funds, bank loans, and below-market government loans or subsidies, often through such federal sources as CDBG or the HOME program. Developers also use commitments of project-based Section 8 rental assistance vouchers as part of the financing package. Such vouchers are the primary federal tool for serving extremely low-income families.

11. Regional developers include such entities as BRIDGE Housing in San Francisco, CommonBond in Minnesota, Community Preservation Development Corporation in Washington, DC, and Greater Miami Neighborhoods. Many belong to the Housing Partnership Network, an association of large regional developers that operates its own lending and investment arm, the Housing Partnership Fund. National nonprofits engaged in preservation include Mercy Housing, Inc., National Church Residences, NHT/Enterprise Preservation Corporation, Preservation of Affordable Housing, Inc., Retirement Housing Foundation, and Volunteers of America.

12. Mercy, for example, developed 19,100 units of housing (as of December 2006) for families, seniors, homeless and formerly homeless populations, and people with HIV/AIDS. An arm of the organization specializes in acquiring "expired use" properties in danger of being converted to market-rate housing.

13. Created in 2002 with a pledge of $100 million annually in public funds, the Los Angeles Housing Trust Fund was funded at lower levels until 2006 and 2007, when it received an annual allocation of $100 million comprised of HUD entitlement funds, special appropriations from several city departments, and city general funds. As of early 2007, the fund was on track for another $100 million in 2008.

14. The Los Angeles Housing Department has tightened up underwriting criteria, increased the number of developer partners from dozens to hundreds, and shifted from working almost exclusively with nonprofits to a more even nonprofit/for-profit balance. By expanding beyond a small set of the usual players that serve certain geographic areas, the city is reaching more neighborhoods within its 468 sq.-mile service area. Larger nonprofit and for-profit developers are better able to acquire land, a critical need in a region of excessive land costs.

15. In Boston, all nonresidential construction or rehabilitation projects exceeding 100,000 square feet and requiring zoning relief pay a fee that goes either to the city's Neighborhood Housing Trust or the Neighborhood Jobs Trust. Developers may build housing or create a job training program in lieu of the fee.

16. Under this ordinance, developers of projects with 10 or more units receiving reduced-priced city land or city financial assistance must set aside 10 percent and 20 percent of the units, respectively, for affordable housing. In early 2007, the city was considering extending the 10 percent requirement to developers seeking zoning changes to increase density and to planned developments.

17. Paul Shigley, "SF Project Emphasizes Housing in Poor Neighborhood," *California Planning & Development Report*, Redevelopment Watch, September 2006.

18 Lavea Brachman, "Vacant and Abandoned Property: Remedies for Acquisition and Redevelopment," *Land Lines* 17:4, October 2005.

19. The funds come from the New York City Housing Trust Fund, which in turn is funded by $130 million in revenues from the Battery Park City Authority, which collects revenues from leasing land at the southern tip of Manhattan to private developers and collecting payments in lieu of taxes.

20. The Housing Trust Fund receives developer contributions and occasional budget allocations, leveraging private, corporate, and other public funds. The Preservation Loan Fund is capitalized with trust fund monies. Under a deal with the county, the Housing Partnership Network (a membership organization of the nation's top-producing nonprofit housing developers) matches or exceeds the amount that the Preservation Loan Fund puts into a deal for short-term acquisition financing. Madison Ridge was the first deal under the partnership arrangement. When it is repaid in December 2007, the funds can be used for another project.

21. The formula, spelled out in the 2005 Affordable Housing Ordinance, gives site plan developers the option of providing affordable units on-site at 5 percent of gross floor area, providing the units off-site at 7.5–10 percent of gross floor area, or making specified cash contributions.

22. National Housing Trust Working Paper, "State and Local Preservation Initiatives," updated July 2006, **www.nhtinc.org/data_reports/DC_Preservation_2006.pdf**.

23. SAIL provides low-interest loans on a competitive basis to developers that build or renovate affordable rental properties. Developers often use the money to bridge the gap between the development's primary financing and the total cost of the development.

24. Donna Kimura, "Housing Agency Executives Discuss Challenges, Solutions," *Affordable Housing Finance,* June 2006.

25 National Housing Trust, *Preservation Outlook*, February 2006, **www.nhtinc.org/Newsletter_Feb.asp**.

26. Michael Bodaken, "Preservation of Affordable Multi-Family Stock, The National Landscape," National Housing Trust presentation, 2004.

27. National Housing Law Project, **www.nhlp.org/html/pres/state/index.htm**, accessed August 9, 2006.

28. For a description of the statutes, see the California Housing Partnership Corporation website, **www.chpc.net**.

29. Jeffrey Lubell, "Increasing the Availability of Affordable Homes: A Handbook of High-Impact State and Local Solutions," Center for Housing Policy, 2006, **www.homesforworkingfamilies.org/resources.dyn/Final_Handbook_12.21.06.pdf**.

Public-Private Partnership Boosts Homeownership in Milwaukee

A unique public-private partnership has helped to transform Lindsay Heights from one of Milwaukee's most blighted neighborhoods into a thriving community. At the same time, the program is providing many low-income and minority families with their first opportunity to build assets through homeownership.

While the financial details have evolved since the program's inception in 1997, the basic tenets remain the same. The city offers borrowers under-used lots for $1 and then up to $10,000 for construction costs, funded through tax increment financing (TIF). Builder partners erect manufactured and panelized homes designed to blend with classic Milwaukee home styles. The Wisconsin Housing and Economic Development Authority (WHEDA) provides a low-cost, 30-year fixed-rate mortgages on the homes. Local realtors® and lenders work with WHEDA to get the word out about the program.

As of December 2006, Lindsay Heights had 160 new residences. About 125 of the homes are owned by African-Americans—no small feat in a city where the homeownership gap between blacks and whites is 20 percent. TIF funds, issued in the form of rehabilitation grants, have helped another 82 homeowners make improvements. Altogether, the new developments in the 44-block district generate about $228,000 more in tax revenues than in 2001. When the city retires the debt in 2011, it will collect $714,000 more in taxes than if the area had not been redeveloped.

A CHANCE TO OWN

Ensuring Access to Homeownership And Wealth-Building

Homeownership stabilizes and enriches families, strengthening communities and sustaining the middle-class prosperity that underpins American society.[1] Families who own homes are much more likely to build wealth and pass it along to the next generation. Indeed, for most owners, more than half of their wealth comes from equity in their homes.[2]

A larger share of US households—69 percent—own their homes than at any time in the past. The widespread availability of affordable mortgage products has helped to increase homeownership rates among all Americans, including historically underserved groups such as low- and moderate-income families, minorities, and female-headed households.

But high home prices and rising interest rates are making it harder and harder for average families to get into the homebuying market. In January 2007, the Center for Housing Policy reported that the annual income required to afford the nation's median-priced home was $84,957—some $38,000 to $48,000 more than the earnings of essential workers such as elementary school teachers, police officers, and licensed practical nurses. It is also over $60,000 more than the annual earnings of most retail salespersons and janitors.[3]

In addition, homeownership rates among minorities are still far lower than those among whites. Boosting minority and low-income homeownership is a critical part of creating stable families and communities and enabling hard-working families the chance to build wealth.

Most municipalities outsource much of their homebuyer assistance and affordable home development activities to local or regional nonprofit organizations that build homes, make low-cost mortgage loans, or provide homeownership counseling and other services. The most effective of these nonprofits operate by building entrepreneurial partnerships among the business, community, philanthropic, and government sectors.

Jurisdictions can make the most of their limited public funds by identifying and working with effective local partners. These organizations can often do the work better than government, but need government capital to expand their programs and fill critical financing gaps. These partners often bring resources to the table from larger national networks.

The recent proliferation of riskier home loans requires vigilant public and private attention to sustaining homeownership. Jurisdictions are responding to rising foreclosure rates with smart and preventive loan servicing, post-purchase counseling, default management, and, in some cases, intervention through foreclosure prevention programs. Because sustaining homeownership is increasingly critical, the entire next chapter is devoted to this topic.

RECOMMENDATIONS FOR LOCAL ACTION

---

1 Offer Comprehensive Homebuyer Assistance Programs That Leverage Private and Public Funds

Homebuyer assistance programs help low-income or first-time buyers overcome the barriers to homeownership posed by a lack of savings for downpayment and closing costs, blemished credit, and inadequate understanding of the purchase process. In higher-cost markets where home prices have far outpaced wage increases, homebuyer programs can help moderate-income buyers who would otherwise be priced out of their communities. In lower-cost areas, homebuyer programs can stimulate investment in the community.

Local governments can use CDBG, HOME, and general revenue funds to offer grants or low- and no-interest second mortgages to cover downpayment and/or closing costs. By taking a subordinate position (agreeing that the bank loan will be paid back first), second-mortgage programs leverage private funds for homebuyer assistance. Bank partners come in with the first mortgage, often at below-market rates and sometimes without requiring private mortgage insurance. The publicly funded second mortgage is often "silent" in the sense that no monthly payment is required. Under silent second mortgages, the loan is paid back when the home is resold or when the first mortgage is refinanced. This approach substantially reduces borrowers' monthly housing costs, and enables the community to recycle the funds to assist other homebuyers.

Homebuyer education must be a prerequisite for assistance.[4] Education can reach people who don't realize that they can buy homes or who think they have to take on high-cost loans to do so. Counseling can also help keep people in their homes by preparing them for the challenges of homeownership and forewarning them about the dangers of costly refinance loans. According to a study by Freddie Mac, high-quality education and counseling reduces delinquencies by up to 34 percent.[5]

Municipal homebuyer programs can stretch resources by aligning with mortgage programs offered by local nonprofits, redevelopment districts, and the state housing finance agency. Coordination is critical. In expensive markets, it may take a mix of supports to get low- and moderate-income residents into homes. In weak markets or ailing neighborhoods, it may take a combination of incentives to get leery homebuyers to invest.

Charlotte, NC Program Strengthens Neighborhoods with Leveraging

Between 1996 and 2006, the House Charlotte second-mortgage program assisted 1,466 Charlotte, North Carolina homebuyers with downpayment and closing costs. Using federal HOME and city funds, the program provides 10-year deferred and forgivable second loans to families with incomes up to 110 percent of the area median who buy homes in one of 87 designated urban neighborhoods. Buyers in threatened or fragile neighborhoods receive up to $10,000, and police officers are eligible for up to $15,000. Participants must complete a pre-purchase homebuyer education program and live in the home.

The program is highly effective. In its first ten years, $9.5 million in city financing generated $139 million in bank financing and another $2 million in borrower equity— leveraging close to 15 private dollars for every city dollar spent on second mortgages. One factor in this success is its coordination with other programs such as those offered by the Charlotte-Mecklenburg Housing Partnership.[6]

Hartford Outreach Partners Support Low-Income Buyers

Since 1995, the Hartford, Connecticut House Hartford program has helped more than 900 first-time buyers purchase homes. The city dedicates about a quarter of its HOME allocation to the program. The program provides an interest-free downpayment loan of five to seven percent of the purchase price to borrowers making up to 80 percent of area median income, or those buying two- to four-family homes with at least one unit for rent to tenants with incomes at or below 80 percent of AMI. The city also offers interest-free loans of up to $3,000 for closing costs. Loans are forgiven after five years (or ten years for loans exceeding $15,000) if buyers remain in their homes. Under the program, the Urban League and Hartford Areas Rally Together provide outreach and credit and mortgage counseling. Clients who complete counseling are referred to lenders approved by Fannie Mae and Freddie Mac for the first mortgage.

One-Stop Shop Eases Coordination in Baltimore

The City of Baltimore helped to sponsor a new organization, Live Baltimore, to attract residents to the city. The program operates the Live Baltimore Home Center, which supports an extensive website (**www.livebaltimore.com/home**) that serves as a clearinghouse for affordable workforce housing in the city. The website lists all available downpayment assistance programs and other housing resources, as well as information on different neighborhoods. Other cities around the country have such clearinghouses, including Boston and Fresno, San Francisco, and Salinas, California. Some agencies have also set up 311 hotlines to serve as information gateways.

2 Ensure Homeownership Resources Reach Minority Markets

Research underscoring the community-wide benefits of homeownership, combined with reports about their vast, untapped buying power, has focused new attention on minority markets. Some of the urgency comes from the desire to reach minority groups with prime products before they obtain high-rate, potentially predatory loans. Another driver is the desire to tackle the persistent wealth gap between white and minority households.

▼ CASES IN POINT

Portland Pledges to Close Minority Homeownership Gap

In 2005, the Portland, Oregon City Council pledged to close the city's minority homeownership gap within a decade. Although the city and its partners were offering a range of affordable mortgage products, they were still not reaching segments of the minority community. City staff, working with a steering committee chaired by the mayor and the housing commissioner, designed a two-pronged strategy—tweaking existing programs to better suit minority needs, and introducing new programs to reach minorities. For example, the city-funded homebuyer education center has changed its marketing strategies and offers bilingual classes. Developers that seek city-disposed properties must demonstrate efforts to reach out to minority communities. The city is also funding homebuyer fairs targeting different segments of the minority community.

City Report on Lending Patterns Spawns Lender Coalition

After the Milwaukee Office of the Comptroller reported wide disparities in lender activity targeting underserved (and predominantly minority) neighborhoods, 50 lenders joined together to improve center-city mortgage programs. Before disbanding in 2003, the group originated $263 million in mortgage loans, with up to 80 percent going to minority homebuyers each year.

3 Increase Lending to Underserved Populations through Loan Pools and Other Risk-Sharing Strategies

Local governments, perhaps working in partnership with nonprofits, should consider leveraging private investment in underserved homeownership markets by providing a modest amount of capital to absorb some of the higher perceived risks of lending to these borrowers and neighborhoods. Second-mortgage programs, such as the House Charlotte program described earlier, are a form of risk assumption. Government funds can also be added to the mix using a number or combination of tools, such as loan guarantees, loan pools, revolving loan funds, and loan loss reserve funds.

Government HOME or CDBG monies, and perhaps general revenue or housing trust dollars, can provide subordinate debt and grants to leverage mortgages or development loans from loan pools. Loan pools allow financial institutions to share the costs of underwriting and the risks of investing in certain types of loans by purchasing shares in a portfolio. The pool may provide capital for a revolving loan fund or a lending program that terminates when lenders recoup their investment. By blending public funds with conventional financing, the programs can offer rates and terms affordable to households with lower credit scores and incomes. Programs can be structured so that, even if the conventional lender monies don't revolve, the public dollars are recaptured for other low- to moderate-income borrowers.

Alternatively, a number of cities contribute public monies to the revolving loan funds operated by local NeighborWorks® America affiliates and others. These funds make second mortgages, leveraging first mortgages from conventional lenders. The staff managing these funds understand what risk mitigation and credit enhancements lenders need to issue loans to borrowers perceived as higher risk. According to NeighborWorks, the network's revolving loan funds annually invest approximately $125 million and generate about $2.5 billion in private investment.

Loan loss reserve funds are enhancements attached to loan programs that guarantee lenders some protection against losses due to bad debts or declining equity. Loss reserves are tapped first in the event of foreclosure. Public funds can help seed the loss reserves and a certain portion of interest on the loans can grow the fund to the desired level. When used properly, loss reserves can generate significant leverage.

▼ CASES IN POINT

Chicago Loan Pool Assists Minority Homebuyers

The City of Chicago contributes $3 million in CDBG funds annually to Neighborhood Housing Services (NHS) of Chicago's Neighborhood Lending Program. Over a three-year period, the program had $100 million in capital commitments from 23 lenders. NHS originates prime-rate home purchase, purchase/rehabilitation, home improvement, and refinance loans for low- and moderate-income buyers whose higher debt ratios or credit problems would normally send them to the subprime market.

City funds are used for subordinate loans to cover closing costs and downpayments (or in some cases, to help borrowers at risk of foreclosure reinstate their mortgages). The city's participation in the program leverages approximately $35 million of the $100 million private investment. In the first round of the program (2003–2006), NHS sold certificates at a premium, funneling a certain percentage into the loss reserve.[7] Delinquency rates for the program (30 days or more) averaged less than one percent through 2006, with charge-offs of less than $75,000 on $88 million originated after four years. With that performance record, NHS did not consider a mandatory loss reserve for round two. The new round is expected to assist about 900 borrowers, 90 percent of whom will be minorities. Seventy percent of borrowers will be households making up to 80 percent of area median income (AMI), and 20 percent will be households making between 81 and 100 percent of AMI.

Syracuse Reduces Price Risk for Homebuyers, Owners

Home Headquarters, Inc., a Syracuse-based affiliate of the national NeighborWorks® America network, offers a home equity protection product to current and new homebuyers. The Syracuse Neighborhood Initiative provided a $5 million federal grant to launch the Home Value Protection (HVP) program, which was designed with assistance from Freddie Mac, the Yale School of Management, NeighborWorks® America, and Potomac Ventures, Inc. Under the program, homeowners pay a one-time fee of 1.5 percent of the value of their homes for the protection. When they sell their homes, HVP will pay down the mortgages (or pay the seller directly) if prices within the zip code have dropped. As of late 2006, 134 customers had purchased Home Value Protection.

4 Support Savings Incentives to Help Very Low-Income People On the Path to Homeownership

While many affordable mortgage products and homeownership programs target low- and moderate-income families, far fewer resources exist for very low-income families. Local communities should consider using their CDBG and HOME funds to support lease-purchase and other savings incentive programs that help these families accumulate assets—an essential step toward homeownership. Local CDBG programs and state housing finance agencies should also partner with housing authorities to help qualified families use their federal housing vouchers to purchase homes.

▼ CASES IN POINT

Nine Out of Ten Clevelanders in Lease-Purchase Program Buy Homes

The Cleveland Housing Network's Lease-Purchase program enables families that are not quite ready to become homeowners rent homes with the option to buy. Using Low-Income Housing Tax Credits, city HOME funds, and state monies, the program acquires vacant homes and lots, and builds or rehabilitates properties for lease to low-income families. Reduced first-mortgage interest rates and "soft-second" funds contributed by the city and state help keep costs down for tenants. After 15 years, Lease-Purchase residents who have made timely payments and repaired their credit can buy homes for far less than the appraised value with no downpayment.[8] As of June 2006, 2,300 new or rehabilitated homes had been created through the program. Over 90 percent of the 152 residents who became eligible to buy their homes did so.

Low-Income San Franciscans Save, Invest Under IDA Program

In San Francisco, the nonprofit EARN offers Individual Development Accounts (IDAs) that are matched by federal funds as well as city allocations of Temporary Assistance to Needy Family (TANF) dollars, CDBG, and city general funds.[9] At the end of 2006, 1,300 people earning less than $20,000 a year on average had opened IDAs. Some 216 used their accumulated funds to buy homes, open businesses, or pursue educational opportunities. The $885,000 total investment (matched funds as well as participants' savings) has leveraged over $15 million in the form of mortgages, educational grants and loans, and small business capital. EARN, founded by local chamber of commerce and government leaders, is working to embed asset-building activities throughout city programs.

Programs Expand Use of Earned Income Tax Credits

Many communities have outreach campaigns that help eligible working families obtain Earned Income Tax Credits (EITCs).[10] Four local jurisdictions and 19 states (including the District of Columbia) go further by offering matches to the federal EITC. The San Francisco Working Families Credit, created by elected officials partnering with nonprofit and private organizations, benefited nearly 10,000 families in its first year.[11]

On a national level, a data service known as the Benefit Bank helps counselors assist low- and moderate-income people in applying for EITCs and other public benefits such as child tax credits and energy assistance programs. According to program officials, nonprofit and government agencies can use the service to bring people closer to financial self-sufficiency.[12]

---

5 Redesign Homeownership Programs to Ensure Revenue Streams And Shrink Growing Affordability Gaps

The most basic form of funds recycling involves converting grant and forgivable loan programs into "silent" second mortgages with deferred payment schedules. The silent second mortgage fills the gap between the approved first mortgage and the purchase price. Total monthly mortgage payments are kept down because payments on the silent second are deferred until the first loan is paid or the home is sold or refinanced. At minimum, this ensures the jurisdiction gets back its principal.

Another increasingly popular tool, particularly in gentrifying areas, is the "shared appreciation" or "equity finance" mortgage. In these cases, homebuyers who receive mortgage assistance share some of the increase in equity from rising home values with the lender. Public entities using this model are able to feed additional assistance dollars back into their programs. Many California jurisdictions have switched, or are considering a switch, to the shared-appreciation model.

In addition, programs must be updated to meet current needs. For example, it may be necessary to raise price caps or income eligibility to keep pace with market changes.

▼ CASES IN POINT

Visalia, California Recaptures HOME Investment

By charging two-percent interest on low-interest, 30-year second mortgages and recapturing the full loan amount when program participants sell or refinance, the City of Visalia roughly quintupled the number of low-income homebuyers it serves with its HOME-funded program. The program offers deferred-payment second mortgages of up to $75,000 toward the purchase of a home costing up to 95 percent of the FHA maximum.[13] If borrowers sell or refinance their homes within 20 years, they must repay the city's loan in full.

A noteworthy provision of the program is to recertify participants' income every five years so that borrowers able to make repayments start to do so. Such provisions help to replenish the loan pool. Without subsidy recapture, the roughly $300,000 in HOME funds dedicated to the program each year would serve four or five families. With the recapture and interest-rate provisions, the Visalia program was able to use revenues of $1.7 million to help 23 families buy homes in 2006.

Santa Cruz Earns Equity Share on Aid to Low-Income Families

Under its First Time Homebuyer Program, Santa Cruz, California borrowers pay no principal or interest on their loans until they either sell or no longer live in the home. The city recaptures the principal amount of the loan plus a share of the borrower's equity upon sale or refinance. Over the past nine years, the city has invested about $1 million in helping 25 low-income families buy homes in a market consistently ranked as among the least affordable in the nation.

Los Angeles Increases Assistance to Retain Middle Class

The median price of a home in the Los Angeles/Long Beach metropolitan area is $525,000. Just over 17 percent of area families are middle income, making LA's middle class the second smallest (after New York City's) among the nation's 100 largest metropolitan areas.[14] To help moderate- and middle-income Los Angelenos buy homes, the Los Angeles Housing Department recently amended or replaced home purchase and rehabilitation programs that were unused because the affordability gap was too great. To close the gap, the department has a new program offering no-interest, deferred-payment second loans of $75,000 to families with 81–120 percent of area median income and no-interest second loans of $50,000 to households with 120–150 percent of area median income.

Portland Offers Transferable Shared Appreciation Product

The Portland, Oregon Development Commission (PDC) offers silent second shared-appreciation mortgages of up to $30,000 to homebuyers earning up to 80 percent of the area median income. Instead of interest accruing on the loan, the PDC takes a share of the appreciation that accrues between loan closing and repayment. The appreciation that goes to buyers increases after seven years and the loan is forgiven after 25 years. By allowing new eligible buyers to assume the mortgage, PDC expands the market for the property to a lower income level while also retaining the unit in the affordable homeownership stock.

Columbia, SC Program Removes Blight, Stabilizes Neighborhoods

By offering home rehabilitation loans rather than the standard grants, the City of Columbia Housing and Loan Administration circulates funds and serves more borrowers. Under the City Purchase Rehabilitation Loan Program, purchasers of homes needing repair in targeted neighborhoods get acquisition loans at zero interest and approvals for permanent loans. When the renovations are complete, the borrower closes on the permanent loan and repays the initial loan. Since 2001, about $4.8 million in loans has enabled the purchase and rehabilitation of 49 properties.

---

6 Offer Tax Breaks to Low-Income Homeowners

For low-income families, property taxes can be a major barrier to buying and keeping a home. In gentrifying neighborhoods, low-income homeowners—particularly elderly households on fixed incomes—may feel pressure to sell their homes because they cannot afford the taxes. In other cases, the cost of property taxes helps boost the purchase price just beyond reach. Municipalities can help preserve and expand homeownership affordability by offering tax abatements to these households. Income tax credits are another means of providing relief to lower-income households.

---

7 Support Developer Partners with Land And Strategic Subsidies

Rather than subsidize deals directly, local governments can use their money more strategically by partnering with nonprofits and for-profits that understand how to leverage private sector participation. By identifying and supporting the more effective of these organizations, jurisdictions can help establish high-volume developers aligned with public policy goals.

Nonprofit developers of affordable for-sale homes face many obstacles, chief among them a scarcity of land and high site acquisition costs, land use restrictions, and a lack of patient capital for site acquisition and development. It takes a long time for nonprofits to acquire sites, assemble financing, and begin construction, and conventional lenders often don't want to invest without some sort of incentive.

LISC reports that its programs with the highest homeownership production—Cleveland, Detroit, New York City, Rhode Island, and Rural LISC—enjoy strong support from local and state governments, which help their partners obtain vacant or tax-delinquent properties at low cost and access development funds.

▼ CASES IN POINT

Chicago, Sacramento Programs Offer No- or Low-Cost Land

The New Homes program run by Chicago's Department of Housing offers city-owned land for as little as $1 to developers of condominiums, single-family homes, and two flats in targeted neighborhoods. The program also provides purchase subsidies up to $40,000 in the form of low-cost second mortgages. Qualified buyers earn between 60 percent and 120 percent of area median income. In general, the lower the borrower's income, the higher the subsidy. As of the end of 2006, the program had approved over 65 developments for more than 1,600 new affordable homeownership units.

The Sacramento Housing and Redevelopment Agency purchases inner-city infill lots and essentially gives them to nonprofits such as Habitat for Humanity, stipulating that the homes must be sold to low- and very low-income families.

Hartford Closes the "Appraisal Gap" to Encourage Investment In Distressed Neighborhoods

In 1998, Hartford's New Property Acquisition and Disposition Department began to systematically foreclose on tax-delinquent and abandoned properties, making the sites available to nonprofit and for-profit developers primarily for for-sale homes. The program, which began with CDBG funds and eventually secured $25 million in state bond money, turned around several distressed neighborhoods. Under the program, developers can obtain bridge loans that make up the difference between the cost to redevelop a site and the final appraised value.

Suffolk County Bond Issue Funds Land Acquisition

In 2003, Suffolk County, New York authorized the issue of $20 million in general obligation bonds for a land acquisition program. Under the Workforce Housing Program, developers of affordable for-sale or rental housing can apply for acquisition loans. Because of rising home costs, the projects can benefit people who make up to 120 percent of area median income. As of the end of 2006, more than 150 workforce housing units had been built.

LA's Forward Commitment Program Supports Workforce Homes

To expand the workforce housing supply, the Los Angeles Housing Department (LAHD) created a forward commitment program for developers of townhouses and condominiums. The LAHD guarantees provision of purchase assistance through soft second mortgages to units earmarked for moderate-income buyers, better equipping developers in emerging markets to secure financing. The program requires that homebuilders set aside at least 15 homeownership units for moderate-income households (earning 80–150 percent of area median income). The city views the forward commitment program as one tool for preserving opportunities for moderate-income families in the denser, mixed-use communities being developed near transit routes.

Richmond's Targeted Funding Provides More Bang for the Buck

Local governments often spread CDBG and HOME resources across many areas, making it hard to generate sustained private investment. The City of Richmond partnered with Richmond LISC to invest a total of $21 million in seven targeted neighborhoods over five years. For its $14.8 million investment, the city got improved neighborhoods, many new homeowners, and an expected $14.7 million in tax revenues over 20 years—even before accounting for spillover effects.

8 Partner with Intermediaries to Leverage Production Resources

National intermediaries such as the Local Initiatives Support Corporation (LISC) and Enterprise Community Partners, Inc. engage local governments, lenders, and foundations in supporting the work of local nonprofits that build affordable housing, assist homebuyers, and conduct other community development activities. LISC and Enterprise offer various financial, technical assistance, and training resources to ensure that the nonprofits have sufficient managerial, organizational, and financial capacity. Among other things, the intermediaries offer loans for activities that conventional lenders are unable or unwilling to finance, such as predevelopment legal and accounting work. They also make subordinate loans to projects so that conventional lenders can profitably underwrite larger loans for the developments. In addition, intermediaries help nonprofits move projects forward by packaging the financing and working with local public officials to secure approvals.

Intermediaries operating on a local or regional level also offer training, financing, and deal-making support to local affordable homeownership nonprofits and programs. Regional intermediaries include such organizations as the Boston Community Loan Fund, Enterprise Corporation of the Delta, Florida Community Loan Fund, the New Jersey Community Loan Fund, the Reinvestment Fund, Rural Community Assistance Corporation, Self-Help, Shorebank Enterprise Cascadia, and Southern Development Bank Corporation.

Some cities help local nonprofit developers produce affordable housing by providing funds to cover staffing and other core operations. Cities and states also partner with intermediaries, banks, and foundations to fund collaboratives that provide operating support and development funds to local nonprofit developers meeting certain performance criteria. For example, an operating support collaborative run by Cleveland's Neighborhood Progress, Inc.,[15] in concert with LISC and Enterprise offices, has granted millions of dollars to more than a dozen community development corporations to help strengthen their operational and managerial capacities.

9 Consider Land Trusts and Other Tools For Permanent Affordability

At some point, the assistance provided to developers to bring homeownership within reach of working families gets so deep that governments should consider putting their subsidies into a form of ownership that ensures permanent affordability. Otherwise, homeownership units do not stay affordable very long. Community land trusts, limited equity cooperatives, and homes with ongoing resale restrictions can provide a needed middle ground between standard rental and homeownership models. These shared-equity tools allow lower-income families to build some wealth while avoiding mortgages that consume huge shares of their incomes.[16]

Local governments have used several mechanisms and resale formulas to keep units affordable. One common practice is to link the resale price of the units to an index.[17] Boulder, Colorado, for example, ties the resale price of homes it subsidizes to either the change in area median income or the Consumer Price Index, whichever is less. Other communities tie resale prices to changes in the area median income alone. Once a unit is made affordable to the target income level through public subsidies, indexed affordability systems help keep the unit affordable in perpetuity. While indexed affordability does not offer the same asset-building opportunities as ordinary fee-simple homeownership, it still provides opportunities for wealth creation.[18] Whatever the model, the benefits must be sufficient to appeal to homebuyers despite the limitations on equity.

▼ CASES IN POINT

Community Land Trusts Remove Land from Home Sale Costs

Community land trusts (CLTs) are an increasingly popular tool for keeping homes permanently affordable by removing the cost of land from the equation. These nonprofit corporations acquire and hold land on which affordable homes are built, leasing the land on a long-term, renewable basis to the homeowner under terms that limit resale prices. For condominiums, the resale formula is set forth in a long-term deed restriction, which works like a ground lease. CLTs can negotiate with developers for deed restrictions and covenants on existing affordable housing at risk of converting to market rates. Research has shown that it costs less to subsidize home purchases through community land trusts than conventional assistance programs.[19] The Community Land Trust Network reports that trusts in 35 states and the District of Columbia have created more than 6,000 units of affordable housing valued at more than $1 billion.

Local governments should consider creating trusts or partnering with builders and existing CLTs to build homes on trust lands under terms providing development and service fees that help trusts become self-sustaining. Resale formulas should be designed to balance a fair return on investment for homeowners with the need to keep units affordable for future generations.

In Irvine, California, the mayor and city council created a community land trust to provide permanent affordability for roughly 5,000 of the 9,700 homes the town plans to create by 2025. Housing managed under the auspices of the Irvine Community Land Trust will be a mix of owned and rental units. Chicago's citywide community land trust, launched in 2006 with seed funding from the John D. and Catherine T. MacArthur Foundation, hopes to bring at least 300 for-sale units into its portfolio in the first three years. The Portland Community Land Trust, which receives support from the Portland Development Commission, operates on a "buyer-initiated land trust" model that allows eligible homebuyers to purchase an existing home anywhere in the city and bring it into the land trust model of ownership.[20]

Longer Time Periods, Tracking Enhance Effectiveness of Deed Restrictions

Governments and private entities that subsidize construction of for-sale homes often attach deed restrictions that limit the resale price and equity returned to buyers when they sell. A 2006 National Housing Institute report notes that governments are primarily using deed restrictions to enforce the affordability requirements of local inclusionary housing programs.[21] To avoid the loss of thousands of units built under such programs, the report suggests governments extend deed restrictions to at least 30 years (ideally longer) and assign a public agency or nonprofit contractor to enforcement. Jurisdictions requiring 30 years or more of affordability include Boston, Chicago, and Montgomery, Maryland. Jurisdictions doing a particularly good job of enforcement include Boulder, Colorado and municipalities in King County, Washington.

10 Apply Self-Help Models to Urban, Mixed-Income And Rural Projects

Some nonprofit developers specialize in the self-help model, under which families help build the homes they buy. In programs like those run by local Habitat for Humanity affiliates, volunteers from the community also contribute labor. This "sweat equity" contribution serves as or is combined with the downpayment to reduce the new homeowner's up-front costs. Although the model is most prevalent in rural areas, a small but growing number of policymakers are looking at self-help as an affordable housing strategy for urban areas.

▼ CASE IN POINT

Habitat Partnerships Help Lower-Income Families Buy Homes

With more than 1,650 independent affiliates nationwide, Habitat for Humanity International builds and rehabilitates affordable homes with the help of homeowners and their families and, often, community volunteers. Habitat reduces construction costs through volunteer labor and tax-deductible donations of money and materials. Local governments can use federal HOME and CDBG funds to help Habitat affiliates acquire sites and install sewer lines, roads, utilities, and other infrastructure. Local jurisdictions can also provide zoning variances or construction subsidies.

Habitat has traditionally focused on scattered-site single-family homes but is increasingly developing subdivisions as well as mixed-income and condominium projects with partners. Habitat affiliates are often good partners for private developers required to include affordable housing in their mixed-income projects. Habitat houses are financed with affordable, no-interest loans from a locally administered Fund for Humanity. Families who buy a Habitat home are generally required to give the affiliate the first opportunity to buy back the homes at the original construction cost if they decide to sell during the term of their mortgages.

1 Support Homeownership with Counseling Programs

State housing finance agencies can support housing counseling programs by making grants to local counselors, attaching counseling requirements to their loans (particularly those with high loan-to-value ratios), and operating their own homeownership education networks. For instance, the Virginia Housing Development Authority's Homeownership Education Program replaced HUD's Head for Home curriculum in 1994. Through a statewide network of more than 1,300 certified instructors, the program explains the homebuying process and prepares consumers for the long-term responsibilities of homeownership. Partners include numerous local and regional mortgage banker associations, REALTOR® associations, Habitat for Humanity, local and state governments, public housing authorities, United Way agencies, and others. According to the authority, loan recipients who have taken the course have a lower delinquency rate than those who do not participate in pre-purchase counseling.

2 Coordinate Resources with Local Efforts

Coordinating resources is critical to leveraging limited local funds. The Virginia Housing Development Authority (VHDA) aggressively pursues partnerships with localities through its Sponsoring Partnerships and Revitalizing Communities (SPARC) program. Localities with specific outreach or revitalization proposals can apply for below-market-rate loans for first-time homebuyers from a special set-aside of mortgage revenue bond proceeds. SPARC loan rates are 0.5–1.0 percentage point below VHDA's standard first-time homebuyer rates.

The competitively awarded funds are flexible, allowing local partners to use the financing to fill gaps and stretch their resources. For example, the City of Alexandria combines SPARC funding with HOME and CDBG funds to offer loans of up to $50,000 to assist first-time homebuyers making less than 60 percent of area median income. Since 2002, SPARC has allocated more than $500 million to 130 local governments, nonprofits, for-profits, and other partners, supporting about 2,200 new homeowners.

3 Better Serve the Needs of Minority Markets

States can be valuable players in local efforts to expand homeownership in underserved minority markets. For example, Wisconsin's housing finance agency is focusing its Partnership Neighborhood Initiative on African-American borrowers living in Beloit, Madison, Milwaukee, and Racine. Applicants who demonstrate 12 months of good credit can qualify for an interest rate below the authority's already discounted rate, plus $5,000 for downpayment and closing costs.

The Minnesota housing finance agency is also spearheading efforts to expand minority homeownership by working with nonprofit and lender partners. At the behest of Governor Tim Pawlenty, a real estate industry coalition convened by the Minnesota Housing Finance Agency (MHFA), Fannie Mae, and the Federal Reserve Bank of Minneapolis launched a plan to create 40,000 new minority homeowners between 2005 and 2012. The long-term goal of the Minnesota Emerging Markets Homeownership Initiative is to erase the 32 percentage-point gap between white and minority homeownership rates in the state. The initiative has engaged industry partners and begun work on the plan's 12 strategies, which include encouraging real estate agencies to hire bilingual agents, certifying industry professionals in cultural competency, and creating culturally sensitive homebuyer education and marketing materials. Philanthropic partners have pledged funds to support pilot projects and the MHFA has committed $200,000 as well as staff time to launch the homeownership initiative as a separate nonprofit.

The Virginia Housing Development Authority's Genesis Project also seeks to increase homeownership and wealth-creation opportunities for African-Americans. VHDA's partner in the program is Vision Integration Services, which works with the Baptist General Convention of Virginia, the largest African-American Baptist association in the Commonwealth. The project director contacts member churches to schedule homeownership rallies, free homeownership classes, one-on-one counseling, and homebuyer clubs. As of the end of 2006, more than 130 classes serving about 2,000 people had been held, producing at least 300 known homeowners. The program expects to conduct about 30 classes in 2007.

To help ensure that housing finance resources are widely used, states may need to improve their outreach. The Virginia Housing Development Authority operates a web-based "Find a Lender" program that enables homebuyers and real estate professionals to quickly locate lenders that use VHDA loan products.

---

4 Limit the Downside Risk of Investing In Local Homeownership

In many communities, lenders need extra encouragement to lend to borrowers or neighborhoods perceived as risky. The Illinois State Treasurer's office, for example, operates the Our Own Home Program to encourage financial institutions to issue home loans to low- to moderate-income people with low credit scores, high loan-to-value ratios, and other characteristics considered to be risky. When a participating financial institution makes a loan, the state treasurer attaches a 10-percent guarantee good for five years. As of the end of 2006, there was only one loss out of the 304 loans the program made.

5 Support Savings Incentives and Asset-Building Efforts

States should consider establishing Individual Development Account (IDA) programs out of the state treasury or housing departments. According to the Corporation for Enterprise Development's IDA Network, many states have passed laws to support IDAs or run state-supported IDA initiatives. Many have also included IDAs in their welfare reform plans.

The Virginia Housing Development Authority is one of four entities partnering to encourage people to apply for the Earned Income Tax Credit and put the refund into a Virginia Individual Development Account (VIDA), where it is matched 2:1 with state or federal funds.[22] Under the proposals, the federal government would provide every newborn child with an endowed asset account. State governments could set up the savings accounts. Some experts recommend eliminating the asset limits attached to public benefits to encourage asset-building among low-income families.

6 Update Products to Bridge Growing Gaps Between Incomes and Home Prices

In markets with large gaps between incomes and home costs, state housing authorities may need to update and enhance their standard products to meet emerging needs. The California Housing Finance Agency, CalHFA, is using the mortgage revenue bond program and a special general obligation bond issue to support a variety of new financing vehicles. The voter-approved bond, Proposition 46, allocated $117.5 million to the California Home Buyer Down Payment Assistance Program. First-time homebuyers who intend to occupy the homes and who meet certain income limits can receive a deferred-payment second loan of up to three percent of the home sales price or appraised value (whichever is less). The loan may be used to cover a downpayment or closing costs, and can be combined with either a conventional or government first mortgage loan. The agency also offers the High Cost Area Home Purchase Assistance Program, which combines a below-market-rate first mortgage with a deferred-payment, low-interest second loan of up to $12,500 to be used for downpayment assistance.

CalHFA has a popular new mortgage revenue bond-funded first loan that eliminates the need for downpayment assistance. Under the Interest Only PLUS℠ program, homebuyers can obtain 35-year, fixed-rate loans for up to 100 percent of the home's value. Loan payments for the first five years are interest-only. At the sixth year, the borrower begins to pay interest and principal, and the interest rate remains the same for the life of the loan. CalHFA also offers 40-year fixed-rate mortgages.

Several state housing finance agencies—including those in California, Florida, Maryland, Massachusetts, New York, and Pennsylvania—sponsor mortgage insurance funds. These funds, which require state-enabling legislation, provide borrowers with a low-cost alternative to traditional private mortgage insurance and reinvest the profits from the business for the benefit of consumers. MassHousing, the Massachusetts housing finance authority, offers borrowers earning less than 80 percent of the adjusted median household income a 20 percent discount on the premiums charged by private mortgage insurance companies. Since 2004, over 1,500 low-income households have borrowed $280 million and saved almost a half million dollars a year (just under $30 per month per borrower) on the discounted premiums. MassHousing also offers, at no additional cost, up to six months of mortgage payments for borrowers who become qualified under state unemployment programs. All 11 borrowers who received these benefits in 2006 went back to work without going into default.

7 Enable Local Tax Abatement Programs

Through its Homeowner's Property Tax Credit program, Maryland offers low- and moderate-income homeowners a tax reduction on a sliding scale. Under the program, if a tax bill exceeds a certain percentage of income, the state pays the difference.[23] At least five Maryland counties enhance the program by offering their own supplemental credits.

The Oregon Single Family New Construction Limited Tax Abatement (LTA) program, authorized by state law in 1990, allows cities to abate property taxes on the improvement value of newly constructed homes in targeted neighborhoods that are purchased by income-eligible homebuyers. Taxes on the assessed value of the improvements are abated for a period of 10 years, although the owner must still pay taxes on the land. The LTA program enables cities to promote homeownership without a direct general fund allocation or a reduction in tax revenue. In distressed markets, the tax abatement program provides an incentive for buyers to purchase in targeted neighborhoods.

8 Strengthen Developer Capacity to Acquire Sites

Housing finance agencies can provide an important funding stream for nonprofit developers. States such as California have laws that give nonprofit home builders the first right to buy properties through tax lien auctions. State housing finance agencies may also channel end-user home loans to developers as part of the construction financing mix. In addition, states can help capitalize funds by offering acquisition loans to affordable developers. Smaller nonprofits, in particular, need help with predevelopment and acquisition funding.

The Massachusetts housing finance authority offers acquisition and development financing to builders to encourage development of affordable owner-occupied housing when conventional construction financing is unavailable. The two- to four-year loans cannot exceed the lesser of 75 percent of the projected sell-out or 90 percent of the total development costs. The loan is secured by a first mortgage on the land plus improvements. To access the loans, developers ensure that at least 25 percent of the units are affordable to households earning 80 percent of area median income. Since 1992, the program has provided $153 million in financing to assist construction of 1,450 units, 389 of which are affordable.

9 Assist Self-Help Home Providers

The Mississippi Home Corporation (MHC), the state's housing finance agency, created the Habitat Loan Purchase program to provide funding for the Mississippi-based affiliates of Habitat for Humanity. The program is funded with corporate reserves and designed as a revolving loan fund. Habitat constructs and finances single-family or town homes, and MHC provides the permanent funding by purchasing the loans from Habitat. Habitat affiliates are responsible for servicing the loans. Some of the affiliates using the program are among the biggest Habitat producers in the state. As of December 2006, the Mississippi Home Corporation had purchased 160 loans, totaling $4.9 million, from 25 Habitat affiliates.

Several other state housing finance agencies have developed relationships with Habitat affiliates to support home building efforts. For example, the Colorado Housing and Finance Agency, Montana State Board of Housing, and New Mexico Finance Authority are among the state authorities that purchase Habitat mortgages to free up local capital. Through the Texas Bootstrap Program, Habitat homeowners receive no-interest mortgage loans of up to $30,000 to help make their homes even more affordable. The Virginia Housing Development Authority operates a loan fund of $1 million at three-percent interest for Habitat affiliates, sponsors an annual Habitat house, and services more than 800 affiliate mortgages. Virginia Habitat homebuyers also receive about $750,000 per year in downpayment and closing cost assistance from the Virginia Department of Housing and Community Development.

CalHFA's Self-Help Builder Assistance Program (SHBAP) provides development loans of up to $750,000 to nonprofits engaged in construction. Recipients tend to be in urban areas where US Department of Agriculture funding is unavailable. Since most of the nonprofits accessing the loans also have primary lenders, the state loan can serve as a bridge or gap loan. As the homes are built and acquired by their new owners, the mortgage loans help pay off the development loan. The Housing

Assistance Council also partners with CalHFA to offer downpayment assistance to homebuyers. As of December 2006, CalHFA had made 21 SHBAP development loans totaling $6.4 million and benefiting 1,234 families.

10 Support Community Development Financial Institutions

A 2006 report from the Opportunity Finance Network outlines state legislative initiatives to support community development financial institutions (CDFIs), many of which are essential to local homeownership programs.[24] According to the report, 14 states currently provide grants or loans to CDFIs, tax credits for investments in CDFIs, or guarantees for CDFI loans. In some cases, building CDFI capacity is the goal, while in others the support is part of a broader initiative such as boosting homeownership or local business development. For example, the Pennsylvania Community Development Bank, administered by the Pennsylvania Economic Development Financing Authority, offers grants to build and strengthen CDFIs' technical assistance and capitalization. The bank's loan pool is seeded by state appropriation and supplemented with private sector investment.

RESOURCES

CENTER FOR HOUSING POLICY
www.nhc.org/housing/chp-index

Research affiliate of the National Housing Conference that works to broaden understanding of America's affordable housing challenges and examines the impact of policies and programs developed to address these needs. Among the many homeownership resources the center provides is an interactive database, Paycheck to Paycheck, presenting wage information for more than 60 occupations and home prices and rents for nearly 200 metropolitan areas.

CFED
www.cfed.org

Nonprofit that works to expand economic opportunity. CFED operates the IDA Network and offers technical assistance to entities seeking to establish IDA programs.

CLEVELAND HOUSING NETWORK
www.chnnet.com/members.html

Network of community developers producing affordable homes. The network provides training and counseling services to enable families to escape poverty, build wealth, and become homeowners.

ENTERPRISE COMMUNITY PARTNERS
www.enterprisecommunity.org

National intermediary that helps provides financing and expertise to community and housing developers. With offices in 24 cities nationwide, Enterprise has worked with community development partners in 49 states.

HOUSING PARTNERSHIP NETWORK
www.housingpartnership.net

Peer network and business cooperative that includes 87 affordable housing nonprofits operating on a citywide or regional basis.

KNOWLEDGEPLEX® WEEK IN REVIEW
www.knowledgeplex.org

Newsletter summarizing housing-related articles from newspapers nationwide, including regular coverage of local and state homeownership programs.

LINCOLN INSTITUTE OF LAND POLICY
www.lincolninst.edu

Nonprofit educational institution that seeks to improve the quality of public debate and decisions in the areas of land policy and land-related taxation. Its quarterly newsletter, *Land Lines*, has explored connections between land use policy and affordable housing.

LOCAL INITIATIVES SUPPORT CORPORATION (LISC)
www.lisc.org

National intermediary that provides capital, technical expertise, training, and information to help community-based developers create affordable housing and commercial, industrial and community facilities. LISC has offices in 30 cities and urban areas across the country and a rural program that services communities in 37 states.

NATIONAL ASSOCIATION OF REALTORS®
www.realtor.org

Operates an "Ambassadors for Cities" program encouraging members to partner with their city governments to promote housing. The association has also created the Housing Opportunity Program, a state-by-state database of all REALTOR®-sponsored programs promoting affordable housing.

NATIONAL CONFERENCE OF STATE LEGISLATURES
www.ncsl.org

Bipartisan organization providing research, technical assistance, and opportunities for policymakers to exchange ideas on state issues. A recent report, "Individual Development Accounts: How Legislators Can Use IDAs as a Tool to Increase Homeownership and Promote Asset Development," compiles data on public funding sources for state IDA programs.

NATIONAL COUNCIL OF STATE HOUSING AGENCIES
www.ncsha.org

Resource for innovative programs run by state housing finance agencies.

NATIONAL HOUSING CONFERENCE
www.nhc.org

Public policy and affordable housing advocacy organization. Its paper, "Strengthening the Ladder to Sustainable Homeownership for Very Low-Income Families," contains good descriptions of FSS and Section 8 homeownership programs, as well as discussion of alternative tenure strategies, the importance of homeownership education and counseling, and the need for better downpayment and homeownership retention policies.

RESOURCES

RESOURCES

NATIONAL HOUSING INSTITUTE
www.nhi.org

Tracks key issues affecting affordable housing and community development practitioners and their supporters. NHI publishes *Shelterforce, the Journal of Affordable Housing and Community Building* and has produced a comprehensive study of shared-equity homeownership entitled, "Shared Equity Homeownership: The Changing Landscape of Resale-Restricted, Owner-Occupied Housing."

NEIGHBORWORKS® AMERICA
www.nw.org

National network of 236 community-based organizations offering homeownership and other services to localities nationwide. Its website features primers and studies on IDAs, home equity protection in weak markets, and minority homeownership. The NeighborWorks Winning Strategies database highlights programs operating under the NeighborWorks Campaign for Home Ownership, Multifamily, Rural, Insurance Alliance, and Community Building and Organizing initiatives. The NeighborWorks Center for Homeownership Education and Counseling works to establish a national curriculum and certification standards for homeownership education and counseling.

RESEARCH INSTITUTE FOR HOUSING AMERICA
www.housingamerica.org

National organization devoted to independent research on expanding housing and mortgage markets. Among its publications are, "Bridging the Gap Between Supply and Demand: The Evolution of the Homeownership, Education, and Counseling Industry" and "The Social Benefits and Costs of Homeownership: A Critical Assessment of the Research."

US CONFERENCE OF MAYORS
www.usmayors.org

Nonpartisan organization providing a forum for mayors to share ideas and information. Among other activities, USCM helps local leaders develop outreach campaigns to increase use of the Earned Income Tax Credit.

ENDNOTES CHAPTER 5

1. In their report, "Millions to the Middle: Three Strategies to Expand the Middle Class," researchers for Demos point out that "widely shared middle-class prosperity is a signature strength of American society," and that homeownership is "a historical steppingstone into the middle class."

2. "Prepared Remarks of Dick Syron, Chairman and Chief Executive Officer, Freddie Mac," Commonwealth Club of California, San Francisco, October 18, 2006, **www.freddiemac.com/speeches/syron/ds101806.html**.

3. Center for Housing Policy, *Paycheck to Paycheck* online database, **www.nhc.org/chp/p2p/**.

4. Education providers assess potential buyers' income and credit histories to determine if they can buy homes and how much they can afford, help applicants establish or repair credit histories, describe all aspects of the homebuying process, and connect clients with lenders and other service providers. Some providers also offer post-purchase counseling.

5. NeighborWorks® Center for Homeownership Education and Counseling Facts and Figures, August 2004, **www.nw.org/network/training/homeownership/pdf/NCHECFactSheet.pdf**.

6. Under an agreement between the city and the Charlotte-Mecklenburg Housing Partnership, homebuyers obtaining a CMHP second mortgage can also receive a House Charlotte loan, which can take third position. This arrangement has helped public housing residents buying homes in CMHP's HOPE VI redevelopment projects.

7. The 23 participating lenders purchase shares of NHS mortgage-backed certificates collateralized by the loans that NHS originates. In the first round, certificates were sold at 105 percent of face value, with 1.25 percent of the premium going into the loss reserve. In the new program, only two lenders opted for the loss reserve. NHS now sells certificates at a 3 percent premium, and those lenders choosing the loss reserve option pay an additional 1.25 percent.

8. The homes sell for far less than the appraised value because the equity generated by the tax credits greatly reduces the amount of debt remaining by year 15.

9. Individual Development Accounts are matched savings accounts implemented by community-based organizations or government agencies in partnership with a financial institution that holds the deposits. As with 401(k) plans, the account holder makes a monthly contribution that funders match 1:1, 2:1, or even more. Account holders can use their accumulated funds only for specific wealth-generating assets, such as homeownership, education and/or vocational training, and business development.

10. The EITC is a refundable tax credit for low- and moderate-income workers that increases with earnings up to a certain level and offers greater benefits to families with children.

11. Tim Flacke and Tiana Wertheim, "Delivering a Local EITC: Lessons from the San Francisco Working Families Credit," The Brookings Institution Metropolitan Program in collaboration with SFWorks, May 2006.

12. For more details on the program, go to **www.thebenefitbank.com**.

13. Borrower debt-to-income ratios have to be within FHA guidelines. For more information on the program, go to **www.ci.visalia.ca.us**.

14. Jason C. Booza, Jackie Cutsinger, and George Galster, "Where Did They Go? The Decline of Middle-Income Neighborhoods in Metropolitan America," The Brookings Institution Living Cities Census Series, June 2006.

15. Created in the late 1980s with support from the City of Cleveland, local businesses, and two major Cleveland-based foundations, NPI serves as a local intermediary and operates wa subsidiary CDFI.

16. John Emmeus Davis, "Shared Equity Homeownership: The Changing Landscape of Resale-Restricted, Owner-Occupied Housing," National Housing Institute, **www.nhi.org/pdf/SharedEquityHome.pdf**.

17. Jeffrey Lubell, "Increasing the Availability of Affordable Homes: An Analysis of High-Impact State and Local Solutions," Center for Housing Policy and Homes for Working Families, 2007, **www.nhc.org/index/chp-research-publications**.

18. For an analysis of the relative effectiveness of different resale formulas in maintaining affordability and generating individual asset accumulation, see Rick Jacobus, "Shared Equity, Powerful Results: Helping One Generation of Homeowners After Another," Center for Housing Policy, 2007, **www.nhc.org/housing/sharedequity**.

19. Rosalind Greenstein and Yesim Sungu-Eryilmaz, "Community Land Trusts: A Solution for Permanently Affordable Housing," *Land Lines*, Lincoln Institute of Land Policy, January 2007. In their 2003 study, "Permanently Affordable Homeownership: Does the Community Land Trust Deliver on Its Promises?" (**www.burlingtonassociates.net/resources/archives/resale%20 complete.pdf**), John Emmeus Davis and Amy Demetrowitz found that the total value of public subsidies put into 259 Burlington Community Land Trust homes increased from about $1.5 million on the initial sale to over $2 million on resale.

20. At purchase, ownership of the land is transferred to the land trust using Portland Development Commission resources. Ownership of the improvements are transferred to the homebuyer who leases the land from the land trust for a period of 99 years. When the home is sold, the owner's share of the appreciation is limited to 25 percent to ensure the unit remains affordable.

21. Davis, "Shared Equity Homeownership," **www.nhi.org/pdf/SharedEquityHome.pdf**.

22. The Virginia Individual Development Account program is managed by the Virginia Department of Housing and Community Development and supported by the Virginia Department of Social Services. EITC outreach efforts are coordinated through the Virginia Community Action Partnership. The Virginia Housing Development Authority serves as a clearinghouse for inquiries about the opportunity and provides the matching funds to the Assets for Independence federal grant when VIDA is used for homeownership.

23. Susan Gvozdas, "Leopold Pushes Tax Relief: Senior Homeowners Would See Savings Under New Legislation," *The Baltimore Sun*, February 21, 2007.

24. Opportunity Finance Network, "State Legislative Initiatives to Support Community Development Financial Institutions," 2006, **www.opportunityfinance.net/groupmail/state_legislation.pdf**.

Homeownership Preservation Program
Saves Chicago Grandmother from Foreclosure

Like many older Americans on fixed incomes, Deborah Daniels got into trouble when she needed repairs done on her house. The South Chicago resident, who had been in her home for more than 20 years, relied on disability payments, a small pension, and contributions from her children to get by. Daniels was offered what she thought was a fixed-rate refinance deal through the contractor. She found out at closing that the rate was fixed for only the first year and then became adjustable every six months.

Her payments went up sharply after that first year. At the same time, her washing machine broke down, her furnace went out, and her daughter, who had been living with her and paying rent, lost her job. Soon Daniels had to choose between making mortgage payments or having the electricity turned off and the gas disconnected. She had grandchildren living with her, so the choice made itself.

Then, late one night in August 2005, Daniels was presented with a legal notice that she had to come up with $76,000 or lose her home. She told her family to prepare to relocate. But then she spotted an ad in her community newspaper about help available through Chicago's Home Ownership Preservation Initiative. Upon contacting the program's administrator, Neighborhood Housing Services of Chicago, she found she was eligible for assistance.

Through the program, Daniels was refinanced into a 30-year mortgage with a fixed rate of 6.0 percent—three percentage points below her existing loan. She also received a deferred, forgivable loan for electrical upgrades, new windows and doors, and other much-needed repairs on her 100 year-old home.

"NHS was a God-send," Daniels said. "I was fortunate that I had assistance and some help from my family. I've read about other people who were targeted by these bad actors and don't have that kind of support."

CRACKS IN THE FOUNDATION

Eliminating Threats to Sustained Homeownership

6

For most Americans, buying a home is the single biggest investment they will ever make. It is the asset upon which they depend to build wealth, finance education and new business ventures, and ensure a secure retirement.

Low interest rates and innovations in mortgage lending have helped to raise homeownership in the United States to a record 69 percent. While the increased market flexibility has been good for many buyers, the competitiveness of the mortgage marketplace has also had a painful downside. Many buyers have assumed unsuitably risky or high-cost loans that leave them vulnerable to losing their homes and any equity they may have accumulated.

In debt over their heads, with little or no equity cushion against unexpected job losses or expenses, more Americans are losing their homes. In 2006, more than 1.2 million foreclosure filings were reported nationwide, equaling one foreclosure filing for every 92 households. Indeed, foreclosure filings were up 42 percent over 2005.[1]

Many experts predict further spikes in foreclosures as more adjustable-rate mortgages (ARMs) reset to higher rates and stable or falling home values limit owners' ability to sell or refinance their way out of trouble. The Mortgage Bankers Association estimates that ARMs amounting to $1.1–1.5 trillion may reset their rates in 2007.

Analysts are particularly worried about foreclosures in the subprime market, where lenders charge higher rates and fees than on prime loans to compensate for the elevated credit risk. In December 2006, the Mortgage Bankers Association reported that the delinquency rate for subprime loans was more than five times that for prime loans.[2] As of early 2007, reports of higher than expected losses in some subprime portfolios were dragging down shares of bigger subprime lenders. A study from the Center for Responsible Lending has predicted that as many as one in five subprime borrowers who obtained loans in 2005 and 2006 will lose their homes.

Foreclosures impose great costs on families and communities. Properties left vacant after foreclosure may attract crime, lower nearby property values, and lead to neighborhood decline.[3] In addition to lost property tax revenues, foreclosures cost municipalities anywhere from a few hundred dollars to over $30,000 per case for various judicial proceedings, demolition, fire protection, and other services.[4] Excessively high foreclosure rates can even damage state bond ratings and thus reduce the state's ability to raise money.

The concentration of subprime loans in low-income minority neighborhoods puts some of these communities particularly at risk of widespread foreclosure. However, foreclosures are also hitting more affluent suburban areas. Indeed, in certain high-cost markets, upper-income families have the majority of high-cost loans.[5]

Families and communities may suffer even when foreclosures are averted. Often, distressed homeowners live in struggling neighborhoods that need investment. But families paying too much in rates and fees to build any wealth are not in a position to contribute to or benefit from neighborhood revitalization.

Some vulnerable homeowners are senior citizens on fixed incomes lured into punitive refinance loans to pay for unexpected home repairs or medical expenses. Others are low-income or minority families shouldering excessively costly loans that preclude wealth-building because they believed that their credit history prevented them from qualifying for more affordable loans. Still others are immigrants with cultural and language barriers that make them easy targets of scam artists.

Of increasing worry is the expanding number of lower- and middle-class house-holds stretched beyond their means with so-called "alternative" or "nontraditional" mortgages. These products, which include interest-only and payment-option adjustable-rate mortgages, are structured so that borrowers may never pay down principal. Some have very low teaser rates that increase after the first month and keep rising. Although the minimum required payment only changes once a year, the rates increase more frequently—a fact many borrowers don't realize.

Hybrid adjustable-rate mortgages, which are very common in the subprime sector, carry fixed rates (often low teaser rates) for the first two or three years and then start to adjust as often as every six months. Housing advocates call them "exploding ARMs" because of the potential payment shock.

People who obtain nontraditional loans with the belief that prices will continue to rise have no equity to draw on when the shift in loan terms saddles them with sharply higher payments. Many experience "sticker shock" when their rates go up. Such products become even riskier if issued without a downpayment or income documentation. Indeed, enforcement officials in many communities report cases where loan documents overstate the buyer's income.

Sustaining homeownership in today's mortgage marketplace requires not only educating borrowers about loan products and loan terms that increase their risk of default, but also expanding their options. In addition, it requires curbing the use of aggressive and even fraudulent practices that push buyers and current homeowners into loans that they do not understand and cannot manage.

To prevent lending abuses, dozens of states and some municipalities have passed laws to regulate loan terms and the mortgage broker business.[6] To provide a more uniform approach, Congress is considering a national standard for regulating high-cost loans. State and federal regulators have also issued new guidance on nontraditional mortgages.

In their efforts to preserve homeownership, local leaders should draw upon the resources of organizations that focus on promoting wider access to and responsible use of credit. At the national level, such organizations include the Center for Responsible Lending, NeighborWorks® America and its network, the National Community Reinvestment Coalition, and the National Consumer Law Center. National entities disseminate research and best practices and engage in policy advocacy. Real estate trade associations have also been active in efforts to combat abusive practices and broaden access to credit.

Coalitions and nonprofit legal organizations operating at the state and regional levels can mobilize local resources to address local challenges. For example, two of the active players in California on this issue are the California Reinvestment Coalition and Housing and Economic Rights Advocates, an Oakland-based nonprofit legal group with a statewide focus. At the local level, partners may include fair housing centers, legal aid groups, and housing counseling organizations.

RECOMMENDATIONS FOR LOCAL ACTION

1 Strengthen Local Counseling Organizations Working To Preserve Homeownership

Housing counseling organizations serve as the first line of defense against predatory lending and risky borrower behavior. These nonprofit agencies, which operate in most metropolitan areas as well as many smaller cities and rural areas, help potential borrowers understand the complex process of homebuying, ways to repair their credit, and how to access public and private downpayment and mortgage assistance programs. Studies have shown that one-on-one pre-purchase homebuyer education reduces loan delinquencies and defaults.[7]

These agencies are also the first to notice when lending practices start to cause problems. Housing counseling groups can help to prevent foreclosures by negotiating repayment plans with lenders and servicers, a strategy that can significantly reduce the probability of home loss.[8] They can also work with lenders to help borrowers refinance out of troubled loans. Some counseling agencies aid enforcement by brokering relationships among legal services, fair housing, and other local community groups.

Local governments should help housing counseling agencies reach more homeowners at risk or in distress and work with partners to create such agencies where none exists. Communities that lack an effective housing counseling organization should create one, perhaps by calling upon local lenders, developers, and the real estate community for support.

Although many housing counseling agencies get funding from HUD, foundations, and lenders, local public support in the form of CDBG and HOME dollars is crucial to ensure homeowner access to a full array of services—particularly default counseling and other post-purchase services. Given the limited pool of resources, municipalities may need to restructure their grants to support a smaller number of the most effective housing counseling organizations.

In their funding relationships, local governments must understand that success is measured not just by how many new homeowners are produced, but also by whether citizens are matched with appropriate loans and services that preserve their homeownership. Government funders should also encourage or require agencies that lack predatory lending prevention and delinquency and foreclosure counseling to develop these services by using the resources of such national and regional networks as NeighborWorks® America, the National Foundation for Credit Counseling, the National Urban League, the National Council of La Raza, and the National Community Reinvestment Coalition.

2 Require Counseling for Government Homebuyer Assistance

Local governments should offer face-to-face or web-based financial education to their own employees. They should also make counseling a requirement for any government-sponsored downpayment and mortgage assistance program, ensuring that such education also includes counseling against predatory refinance loans. When governments fund second mortgages, they should attach provisions that homeowners must undergo counseling before they can refinance.

3 Offer Rehabilitation, Weatherization, Utility, and Tax Assistance, Particularly to Older Homeowners

Rehabilitation assistance and other supports are a second line defense against high-cost loans. Low-income (particularly elderly) homeowners, who can't afford needed repairs are apt to end up with risky or abusive improvement loans. In some cases, predatory lenders work with contractors to target vulnerable homeowners.

While many governments offer rehabilitation assistance and weatherization programs, they do not adequately publicize them. They could take a page from the playbook in Boston and Los Angeles, where officials have used information from code enforcement programs to get rehabilitation money to homeowners of distressed properties. Through its Handy Worker program, Los Angeles provides $5,000 home repair grants to 1,500–2,000 low-income seniors or disabled households annually. The city's Mom & Pop Program also offers deferred loans to low-income owner-occupants for exterior improvements to their small rental properties.

According to an AARP study, almost half of older homeowners cited their ability to pay property taxes as a potential major barrier to remaining in their homes. Almost half of older homeowners and renters said utility bills were also a major concern.[9] Local jurisdictions should consider property tax abatements or deferments for low-income seniors. Some jurisdictions address the issue by placing liens on properties with overdue tax bills, deferring collection during the owner's lifetime or until the home is sold.

Government programs that provide grants and loans for home modifications with universal design features can also help seniors stay in their homes safely. Universal design includes such features as an entry with no steps, bedrooms and bathrooms on the first floor, wide doorways and hallways, thresholds that are flush with the floor, handrails on stairs, and grab bars in bathrooms.[10]

4 Launch Targeted Campaigns to Raise Awareness of Lending Perils

Public awareness campaigns can help counter the widespread misinformation that leads people to accept high-cost or inappropriate loans. Such campaigns are essential to get critical messages out to a broad audience of seniors, long-time homeowners, and others at risk of lending abuses.

"A Practitioner's Guide to Combating Predatory Lending," published by LISC and NeighborWorks, suggests getting the word out through entities that share an affiliation with the target audience, such as faith-based institutions, neighborhood associations, schools, employers, senior citizen groups, and ethnic organizations. Campaigns should refer people who want more information or think they have been victimized to homebuyer counseling organizations or to local affiliates of ACORN, AARP, the National Council of LaRaza, the National Training and Information Center/ National People's Action, and the Urban League. People who want to file a complaint should be referred to enforcement agencies.

▼ CASES IN POINT

"Don't Borrow Trouble" Campaigns Curb Foreclosures

Don't Borrow Trouble campaigns now operate in more than 40 communities nationwide. Pioneered in Boston in 1999 in response to a spike in foreclosures, Mayor Thomas Menino and the Massachusetts Community and Banking Council led an effort to create a series of posters, billboards, flyers, ads in bus shelters, inserts in tax and water bills, letters from the mayor, and public service announcements—all seeking to educate homeowners about the risks of refinance and home equity mortgages. People were directed to the Boston Home Center, a one-stop housing services operation run by the city Department of Neighborhood Development. The center in turn referred callers to bank lending partners, credit counselors, legal entities, or city home repair programs.

Freddie Mac worked with Boston and the Massachusetts Community and Banking Council to create a bilingual Don't Borrow Trouble toolkit to help other jurisdictions launch similar campaigns. As of 2006, 46 local and state campaigns had been launched, including in Cuyahoga County, Ohio. Some campaigns have expanded to encompass legal and financial assistance to homeowners and advocacy. Boston, for example, has established a $100 million lender consortium offering refinance products to homeowners at risk of foreclosure. Mayor Menino has also proposed legislation to require mortgage originator licensing and to create a statewide foreclosure intervention program modeled after Pennsylvania's Homeownership Emergency Mortgage Assistance Program.

Faith-Based Campaign Protects Denver Seniors

The Clergy Against Senior Exploitation (CASE) Partnership engages 400 church-based partners in Greater Denver in combating foreclosure scams as well as other consumer abuses targeting the elderly. The initiative is funded by a US Department of Justice grant through the Denver District Attorney's office.[11] The program uses several mechanisms to alert senior citizens about consumer scams. The DA's office faxes or emails monthly "fraud alerts" to churches so that religious leaders can include the message in their announcements. The DA's office also sponsors seminars for clergy and lay leaders about ways to spot and prevent common types of financial exploitation of older adults.

5 Use Economic Clout to Shape Local Lending Practices And Provide Alternatives to High-Cost or Risky Loans

Local governments can use their economic clout to encourage positive local lending practices and send a strong signal to financial institutions in the community. Public leaders should foster a network of high-quality lenders who can offer competitive or more suitable products to people normally served by subprime lenders.

Studies have found subprime or high-cost loans are much more common in neighborhoods and among populations traditionally underserved by mainstream financial institutions. Reducing the dependence on subprime loans tackles predatory lending practices while also helping underserved communities build assets.[12] According to Freddie Mac, between 10 percent and 35 percent of subprime borrowers would have been able to qualify for prime loans.

Local programs aimed at providing borrowers with more suitable loans must address some of the market shortfalls that lead people to poor choices. Some lenders set minimum loan amounts or reward originators based on loan size, which encourages "up-selling" or pushing up the loan amount. In some areas of the country where homes are affordable—including some minority neighborhoods—borrowers buying less costly homes must pay higher rates for borrowing "too little." In certain areas, homeowners who need just $5,000 to $10,000 for home repairs and maintenance can't get a five-year second mortgage (or home equity loan) for that amount and are persuaded to do a more costly cash-out refinancing.

Poor credit ratings are another issue. Over a fifth of Latinos have little or no credit history, resulting in a credit score of 0.[13] Increasingly, community-based organizations and government agencies are tackling the credit piece of the equation with programs that either work to boost applicants' scores or encourage lenders to use alternative scoring systems. Many homeowner education and counseling organizations focus on helping prospective homebuyers enhance their credit profiles by paying off debts, correcting credit report errors, and collecting alternative forms of credit history.

▼ CASES IN POINT

Municipal Investment Laws in Chicago and Buffalo Set Lending Standards

In August 2000, Chicago passed the nation's first ordinance requiring that any financial institution or contractor doing business with the city must sign a pledge stating that neither it nor any of its affiliates engages in predatory lending. The ordinance also precludes home repair contractors from receiving payments directly from lenders, allowing homeowners to withhold payment for substandard or nonexistent work.[14] For its part, the Buffalo Urban Renewal Agency prohibits homes built with city subsidies to be purchased with what it defines as predatory loans.[15]

Philadelphia Partners with Banks to Serve Credit-Challenged Homeowners

The Philadelphia Mayor's Office worked with the Greater Philadelphia Urban Affairs Coalition and eight banks to create loan products for lower-income homeowners with weak credit.[16] The Mini-PHIL Home Improvement Loan program offers homeowners with less than perfect credit 10-year, fixed-rate loans of up to $10,000 for emergency repairs or small projects, allowing leftover funds to be used to pay off debt. The PHIL-Plus Home Improvement Loan program provides 20-year loans of up to $25,000 for larger home repairs or major improvements. Borrowers can apply for a one-percentage point rate reduction after 24 consecutive months of on-time payments. Neither program requires equity in the property, and both offer free inspections of completed work.

National Lending Platform Offers Responsible Mortgage Alternatives

The Opportunity Finance Network, a network of community development financial institutions (CDFIs), is launching a residential mortgage platform to offer responsible alternatives to predatory and high-cost mortgage products. In essence, the network is creating a mortgage system that contracts with mainstream mortgage lenders to originate and service loans through its members and others. The Opportunity Finance Network plans to pilot the system in 2007, generating about $50–100 million in originations in the first year and scaling up to $1 billion annually within a few years.

Initiative Helps Bring Customers into Financial Mainstream

Credit unions and banks can use outreach, combined with product innovations, to help put lower-income, minority, and immigrant households on a path to suitable home purchase or refinance loans. The Retail Financial Services Initiative, a three-year project organized by the National Community Investment Fund, convened a group of banks and credit unions to develop, test, and implement sustainable strategies for bringing the "unbanked" into the financial mainstream and onto an asset-building track.[17]

6 Establish Comprehensive Foreclosure Interventions Combining Education, Enforcement, and Rescue Assistance

While public awareness campaigns are critical to the prevention of lending abuses, foreclosure interventions may also be necessary. Such actions can assist homeowners who are in bad loans or behind in their payments because of a loss of income, health problems, or other issues. Interventions may require legal assistance to reduce pay-off amounts inflated by such predatory practices as charging points for serial refinancings or property appraisals.

Effective interventions engage lenders as partners to restructure or refinance loans. While people who are delinquent on their mortgage payments may shun contact with lenders, contact can in fact lead to workout options that could save their homes.[18] Indeed, lenders themselves would rather avoid costly foreclosures.

▼ CASES IN POINT

Chicago's HOPI Program Engages Lenders, Disseminates Best Practices

By one estimate, Chicago's Home Ownership Preservation Initiative (HOPI) has saved lenders as much as $77 million and saved the city $9 million in police, legal, and other costs of dealing with vacant, foreclosed properties.[19] Launched in 2003 by the city and Neighborhood Housing Services (NHS), the initiative works with lenders and servicers to mitigate losses while offering assistance to families at risk of foreclosure. Billboards, advertisements on city buses, mailings to hot-spot zipcodes, and outreach through block clubs, churches, and other organizations instruct distressed homeowners to call the city's 24-hour hotline or visit one of the eight NHS offices throughout the city.

NHS helps borrowers explore all the options, which may include working with lenders to redo loan terms, undergoing loss mitigation,[20] or accessing home repair services or job training. In some cases, lenders offer refinancing to customers at risk of foreclosure, often with a subordinate loan from NHS.

When foreclosure can't be avoided, the program prevents long-term vacancies by getting new owners quickly into the homes using such strategies such as deep discounts, market-rate sales, and assignments. Through its Redevelopment Corporation, NHS has been able to rehabilitate foreclosed homes, sometimes with city subsidy, and sell them to low- and moderate-income homebuyers.

As of July 2006, HOPI had provided counseling and education to more than 4,300 homeowners in distress or in foreclosure, helped about 1,300 families avoid foreclosure, and rehabilitated 330 vacant properties for affordable housing. Countless other homeowners have also avoided trouble by accessing the NHS homebuyer classes and post-purchase workshops.

New York Scales Up Promising Intervention Program

New York City's Preserve Assets and Community Equity (PACE) program is a good example of how city resources can be used to scale up community-based foreclosure interventions. The PACE program was launched in October 2005 with $1.35 million in operating funds from foundations, banks, and the city council, plus several million dollars in in-kind financing and loans from the city's Department of Housing Preservation and Development (HPD) and nonprofit partners. PACE targets its intensive education, financial counseling, legal assistance, and loan remediation to first-time homebuyers and homeowners in three neighborhoods with unusually high foreclosure rates. HPD plans to expand PACE first to other hard-hit neighborhoods and then citywide.

The program is modeled on the Community Equity Protection Project (CEPP), a Ford Foundation-funded partnership among South Brooklyn Legal Services, the Parodneck Foundation, and the Neighborhood Economic Development Advocacy Project. Callers to the city's "Don't Borrow Trouble" hotline, staffed by HPD, are referred to South Brooklyn Legal Services or Queens Legal Aid if they have predatory loans or are in foreclosure. Using the threat of litigation, the lawyers try to get the lender to either restructure the loan terms or agree to a reduced payout. The Parodneck Foundation works through a consortium of lending partners to provide victims of predatory loans who are near or in foreclosure with affordable prime or below-prime refinancing.[21]

National Groups Offer Turnkey Programs for Foreclosure Prevention

The Homeownership Preservation Foundation works in partnership with such organizations as the National Urban League and NeighborWorks® America to launch foreclosure prevention programs. Like the HOPI model, these initiatives center around hotlines. Counselors refer homeowners who need additional assistance to the Urban League or to NeighborWorks affiliates.

Community-based organizations in select states can essentially outsource their foreclosure intervention services to the National Community Reinvestment Coalition's National Anti-Predatory Lending Consumer Rescue Fund. Community groups do the intake and rescue fund staff mediate with the lender or servicer to eliminate abusive terms. If loan terms can't be revised, the fund's lender partner, HSBC Bank, provides a new low-cost first mortgage to pay off the troubled loan. As of summer 2006, these refinancing services were available in 17 states.

---

7 Support Ongoing Investigation of Problem Lending Patterns

Successful foreclosure intervention programs monitor lending patterns and trends to address new risks as they arise. To support this effort, local leaders can direct resources to the housing counseling, fair housing, and other organizations that collaborate on such investigations. A clearer picture of lending patterns enables better targeting of education programs and enhances the enforcement value of lending, consumer protection, and fair housing laws.

Information collected under the Home Mortgage Disclosure Act (HMDA) can reveal lending disparities based on race, ethnicity, and income of borrowers and neighborhoods. Because this resource does not include information on credit scoring, loan-to-value and debt-to-income ratios, and other loan criteria, it cannot in and of itself prove predatory practices. It has, however, been combined with borrower survey data, information on where defaults are occurring, and the minority composition of census tracts to identify reverse redlining—the targeting of unfair lending practices to neighborhoods with a high proportion of minority and elderly households.

As the holders of data on mortgage defaults and census tract composition, local governments can aid these investigations either by providing supplementary information or by funding data collection by local fair housing or legal aid groups. Local governments can also require lending practice assessments as part of their consolidated plans for Community Development Block Grants.

8 Provide Local Enforcement Officials the Resources to Address Predatory Lending and Real Estate Fraud

When predatory lending or mortgage scams threaten the fabric of communities, local law enforcement officials must have sufficient staff and time to conduct investigations. These officials include city attorneys and county district attorneys charged with curbing elder abuse.

▼ CASES IN POINT

High Foreclosures Lead to Enforcement Hiring in Ohio

In 2006, the Cleveland metro area faced one foreclosure filing for every 40 households—more than double the national average and the 14th highest rate among the 100 largest metropolitan areas.[22] In Cuyahoga County, which is part of the metro area, the ratio of foreclosure auctions to sales in black neighborhoods was more than twice that in white neighborhoods. Of the 50 sheriffs departments surveyed, 31 ranked predatory lending as the top factor contributing to foreclosures.[23] The county has responded to this troubling trend by cracking down on suspected real estate scams, such as overstating home values or buyers' wealth. The county has also hired an assistant county prosecutor to focus on mortgage fraud and predatory lending in those neighborhoods, established a foreclosure-prevention program with a $1 million annual budget, and partnered with the FBI and city and state officials to go after predatory lenders.

Baltimore Task Force Curbs Property Flipping

When property flipping and mortgage fraud were destabilizing city neighborhoods, the Baltimore City Flipping and Predatory Lending Task Force was formed in 2000 to pursue criminal charges against those involved in the schemes. Part of a $5 million Neighborhood Initiative Grant from HUD allowed the Community Law Center, Baltimore's legal services organization focused on neighborhood revitalization, to staff and coordinate the task force and launch an emergency loan fund for victims. The Community Law Center provided the initial research for enforcement actions. Convicted defendants were ordered to pay restitution and/or serve jail time. By the end of 2005, property-flipping cases in the city had dropped 77 percent.[24] Enforcement actions led to the conviction of more than 100 appraisers, attorneys, settlement officers, and phony homebuyers. The effort also spawned several other initiatives aimed at stabilizing neighborhoods, including a partnership of banks, government agencies, Fannie Mae, and foundations set up to help victims refinance predatory loans.

Buffalo, New York has established an Anti-Flipping Task Force modeled on Baltimore's. The task force began by tightening the rules on city foreclosure auctions. Winning bidders must sign an affidavit stating they will not sell the property for more than 120 percent of the bid price for at least six months, and that they will fix all housing code violations within six months.

OPPORTUNITIES FOR STATE ACTION

1 Enhance Disclosure and Counseling Requirements

States must do what they can to provide consumers with timely and comprehensible information about the terms of the loan products they are considering. States should enhance disclosure and counseling requirements in their consumer sales practices laws and consider imposing special counseling for borrowers applying for high-cost loans. Enhanced disclosure requirements are critical because many borrowers accept loans with low initial rates, not understanding that the rates will increase drastically and potentially leave them unable to pay their mortgages. Disclosures required under federal laws have in some cases not kept pace with market practices.

States should require that contracts and mortgage documents be translated into the borrowers' languages. Loans are often marketed to non-English speakers in their native language but then closed with English-only documents that borrowers are sometimes pressured into signing. California Civil Code section 1632 provides a good model for disclosure requirements. The code requires the party negotiating a loan in the Chinese, Korean, Spanish, Tagalog, or Vietnamese language to provide loan documents in that same language.

2 Launch Statewide Awareness Campaigns and Interventions

States with high foreclosure rates should launch awareness campaigns, sponsor foreclosure hotlines, and consider operating statewide foreclosure prevention programs. For example, the New York State Banking Department has created bilingual educational materials, held public forums to teach consumers and practitioners how to avoid predatory loans, and used funds from settlement agreements with alleged violators of state and federal laws to support financial education and train-the-trainer programs for community organizations serving populations most at risk. The department also operates a hotline for advice and referrals, as well as a speakers bureau providing experts to address community organizations, schools, nonprofits, and the business community on a variety of topics.

North Carolina's foreclosure prevention program and loan fund offers $20,000 or 18 months of mortgage payments (whichever is less) to homeowners who have lost their jobs due to plant closings or other external circumstances. Pennsylvania's model Homeowners' Emergency Mortgage Assistance Program, enacted in 1983, also targets homeowners who are about to lose their homes because of a job loss or other temporary financial hardship beyond their control.[26] As of November 2006, the program had disbursed more than $388 million, helping more than 37,000 distressed homeowners catch up on their mortgage payments and avert potential foreclosure.[27]

3 Reach Underserved Markets

Like local governments, states can use their economic clout to help guide lending practices and launch programs to provide residents with competitive alternatives to risky or unsuitable loans. The Banking Development Districts program at the New York State Banking Department provides incentives to financial institutions to locate in traditionally underserved communities. Banks that open branches and offer such services as multilingual staff and financial management seminars in the designated districts may receive state and/or municipal deposits at below-market interest rates, property tax exemptions, and Community Reinvestment Act credit.

MassHousing, the Massachusetts state housing finance agency, has adopted First American Corp.'s Anthem score as its credit measure. In contrast to the loan payment records used to compute FICO scores, Anthem bases its scores on a person's record of rent, utility, insurance, and car loan payments. MassHousing also conducted a major ad campaign to market its products to minority borrowers who might turn to subprime lenders.

Through the Illinois Opportunity I-Loan program, the Illinois Housing Development Authority offers 30-year fixed-rate home loans for up to 97 percent of a home's value to borrowers lacking credit histories. The program, launched in 2006 and funded through tax-exempt bonds, enables borrowers who have lived in the state and filed tax returns for at least two years to use pay stubs, rent receipts, and bills to prove their income. The program also serves people who do not have a Social Security number but do have an individual taxpayer identification number (ITIN) from the IRS.[28] Some buyers can get an additional forgivable loan for closing and downpayment costs as well.

The Illinois State Treasurer's Office also has a loan program encouraging conventional lenders to review their underwriting so that credit-challenged homebuyers can qualify for a conventional rather than a subprime or predatory loan. The "Our Own Home" program also serves current homeowners at risk of foreclosure due to circumstances beyond their control. Households earning below $75,000 can apply for loans to purchase homes that cost up to the median county home value. Under the program, the state deposits up to 10 percent of the loan amount in the participating financial institution, to be held for up to five years. If the borrower defaults during that time, the lender can draw on the deposit. The deposit serves as a "first loss," essentially reducing the lender's exposure by 10 percent of the purchase price and improving the loan-to-value ratio. At the end of 2006, 304 loans had been made under the program with only one loss.

4 Adopt Guidance on Nontraditional Mortgage Products

In November 2006, the Conference of State Bank Supervisors (CSBS) issued new guidance on nontraditional products such as interest-only mortgages and payment-option adjustable-rate mortgages. The guidance, which applies to state-licensed mortgage brokers and companies, follows the Interagency Guidance on Nontraditional Mortgage Products issued by federal banking regulators in September 2006. The guidance directs management of insured financial institutions and credit unions, including state-chartered banks, to assess a borrower's ability to repay the loan, strengthen risk management standards (as well as appropriate capital and loan loss reserves) when making nontraditional loans, and ensure that borrowers have sufficient information to understand the terms and risks before taking out such loans.

The guidance developed by CSBS and the American Association of Residential Mortgage Regulators closely parallels the interagency guidance but does not include the portfolio management provisions, which are not applicable to mortgage brokers and providers. State regulators should adopt this guidance for financial institutions under their jurisdiction.

5 Enhance State Regulation of Mortgage Brokers And Other Industry Practitioners

While federal regulators claim the authority to govern loan terms, states generally maintain the authority to regulate many financial services practitioners. Strong state licensing and conduct requirements for brokers, appraisers, and independent mortgage companies can do much to curb lending abuses.

Most national lenders sell their products through independent mortgage brokers, who can comparison shop and offer better rates than lenders may quote directly.

Brokers who are rewarded for getting their customers into the highest-cost loans possible, however, are behind many predatory lending situations. Brokers have also been found to include undisclosed fees in loan costs.

Brokers should be bonded and required to have a license, acquired only after a criminal background check and attainment of certain educational and professional standards. States should set out mandatory standards of conduct requiring brokers to provide borrowers with loans reasonably advantageous given the circumstances and prohibit such activities as pressuring appraisers to inflate home values.

Although most states place mortgage brokers under their unfair and deceptive trade practices laws, some of these laws either do not cover the kinds of abuses that brokers engage in or include provisions that the courts have interpreted as exempting banking, insurance, and mortgage lending.[29] Regulating mortgage brokers, in addition to mortgage companies, helps to address the problems that arise when companies sanctioned for making bad loans go out of business but later reopen under a different name.

States should also work with the National Association of Real Estate Appraisers to enact standards that professionalize the appraisal industry. An appraiser's role is to provide an independent assessment of a home's value. But as a recent Demos report concludes, appraisers pressured to meet numbers knowingly inflate the value of residential properties, leaving homeowners with overvalued homes at risk of foreclosure.[30] Inadequate government oversight of the appraisal process is compounded by insufficient resources for enforcement.

The Demos report's principal recommendations are sound: create new rules that reduce contact between appraisers and lenders or brokers, prohibit and punish the pressuring of appraisers, impose tougher sanctions on dishonest appraisers, streamline complaint processes, invest more in the enforcement activities of currently understaffed state licensing boards, and educate consumers.

The Conference of State Bank Supervisors and the American Association of Residential Mortgage Regulators have contracted with the National Association of Securities Dealers to design a national application system to streamline the mortgage licensing process, enhance consumer protection, and reduce fraud. Regulators—and to a lesser extent, consumers—will have access to a national database of licensee information, including criminal and administrative sanctions. As of mid-2006, the program was being piloted in Idaho, Massachusetts, New Hampshire, and Washington. State regulators should opt into this system as a good baseline.

In 2006, Ohio's alarmingly high foreclosure rates brought leaders from both sides of the political aisle together to enact precedent-setting requirements for mortgage brokers as part of the Home Buyers Protection Act. This predatory lending law sets out requirements for certain high-cost loans, expands the state Consumer Sales Practices Act to cover mortgage brokers, loan officers, and nonbank lenders, and amends licensing laws to add a comprehensive standard of customer care that mortgage brokers and nonbank lenders must follow. Under the new standard, brokers must make a reasonable effort to secure products that are advantageous to the customer and may not unduly influence the appraisal process. Under the law, Ohio is also instituting the nation's first mandatory state licensing requirement for appraisers.

North Carolina, Illinois, Ohio, and Washington are among the states that have enacted tougher licensing regimes in the last several years. The 2001 North Carolina Mortgage Lending Act, for example, requires that brokers make a reasonable effort to secure for their customers loans that are "reasonably advantageous to the borrower."[31] Some of the discussions surrounding a potential federal law have promoted such a "suitability" standard.

6 Enforce Existing Laws and Protections

It is time for federal legislation to clearly define predatory lending and impose strict penalties on those who engage in these harmful practices, while also preserving access to subprime credit for underserved borrowers. Our 2004 publication, *Opportunity and Progress,* spells out what such federal legislation must encompass.

A national lending law should provide fundamental protections for American consumers against well-documented abusive practices without unduly curtailing subprime lending or the ability of states to target the violations peculiar to their region. In the meantime, states must focus their homeownership preservation efforts on activities less likely to be preempted by a new national law. This includes enhancing disclosure and counseling, launching statewide awareness campaigns and foreclosure intervention programs, reaching underserved markets, enforcing existing laws and regulations, regulating real estate industry players, and targeting perpetrators of foreclosure scams.

Federal action still leaves room for states to strengthen the application of existing laws. To help deter real estate practices that can lead to home loss, state attorneys general and oversight agencies should enforce current lending laws and regulations. In many states, this requires more resources to increase monitoring and enforcement staff. It is also likely to require improved communication among the offices that regulate industry participants such as mortgage brokers and real estate agents.

Abusive lending practices may violate a number of federal laws including but not limited to HOEPA, the Real Estate Settlement Procedures Act,[32] the Fair Credit Reporting Act,[33] and the Fair Housing Act.[34] Many states also have laws regulating loan terms, requiring disclosures, and regulating the mortgage broker business, with authority for enforcement falling to the state agencies that have oversight of the real estate industry.

Furthermore, the federal government and all states have unfair and deceptive trade practices laws—commonly referred to as consumer sales practices laws—that protect consumers from misconduct. These laws are monitored and enforced by the Federal Trade Commission at the federal level and by attorneys general at the state level. The laws prohibit specific practices such as false advertising or misrepresenting the price of a product or service, as well as undelineated practices found to be unfair or deceptive. The laws typically provide both for enforcement by the government to stop the practice and the award of damages to consumers hurt by the practices. Some of these laws, however, may exclude some or all kinds of credit providers.

Strong state consumer sales practices laws are a critical tool for curbing real estate industry abuses because they apply a less stringent standard for conviction than the beyond-a-reasonable-doubt standard set for criminal cases. The potential recovery of damages encourages lawyers to participate.

While all states except Alaska subject mortgage brokers to their unfair trade practices laws, many do not subject lenders to the laws. In addition, some laws are stronger than others. For example, bipartisan legislation enacted in Ohio in 2006 applied the state's consumer protection law to lenders, brokers, and appraisers and detailed specific violations, such as lending without regard to the borrower's ability to repay, improperly influencing an appraiser, and refinancing mortgages without a tangible net benefit to the borrower.

In recent years state attorneys general, working with federal regulators, have used strong consumer sales practices laws to target patterns of conduct associated with predatory lending, filing civil actions that seek penalties for each violation that a company commits. Cases involving alleged violations by First Alliance Mortgage Company, Household Financial, Ameriquest and others have resulted in multi-million dollar settlements that include reforms of lending operations. Iowa, California, New York, Illinois, and Minnesota have been particularly active in enforcing their unfair trade practices laws.

California allows counties to authorize a surcharge of up to $2.00 on recording refinance documents and then use the funds to prosecute real estate fraud, particularly cases where homeowners could lose their homes. Alameda County is one of the more than 10 counties that have created funds and used them to launch mortgage fraud units in the district attorney's office. The system provides substantial resources for pursuing fraudulent practices. For example, Alameda County's fee generated about $759,000 for 2005, and as much as $1.2 million annually in prior years. The funds accrue. Dedicated staff have been able to win some significant convictions, including many cases involving defrauding the elderly, sending a signal that prosecutors are taking fraud seriously. Following California's lead, Washington State enacted a law in 2003 allowing counties to impose a $1.00 surcharge on deed recording fees for purposes of funding fraud prosecution efforts.

State banking departments and agencies that regulate mortgage brokers, real estate agents, appraisers, and other players should also expand their staffs to strengthen enforcement and protect consumers, perhaps working in partnership with attorneys general. This is particularly important in states where brokers and other professionals are exempt from the state's deceptive trade practices laws and are instead regulated solely by a state agency.

7 Enact Protections from Foreclosure Scams

States should take legal and legislative action to address the alarming rise in foreclosure rescue scams. Though some rescuers are legitimate, many are essentially thieves who rob victims of their equity and often their homes.

A recent National Consumer Law Center report describes a variety of foreclosure rescue scams. Under the more egregious "bailout" schemes, homeowners remain in their homes as renters and surrender title to investors who supposedly make payments while the homeowners get back on their feet. The terms of these deals are usually so onerous that owners are unable to repurchase their homes and lose most —if not all— of their equity.

The report also outlines some sensible preventive measures that stop short of banning such services outright. These measures would require foreclosure specialists to obtain licenses, limit their practice to a set of defined activities, and to assess whether homeowners who turn over their deeds in a buy-back arrangement have the capacity to fulfill the deal.

Minnesota's 2004 foreclosure bailout law permits rescue services but provides several important protections, such as the unconditional right to cancel a contract within five days of signing and the assurance that owners unable to repurchase their homes receive at least 82 percent of the home's fair market value, minus the purchaser's investment in the home. Other states with laws targeting foreclosure schemes include California, Georgia, Illinois, Maryland, and Missouri.

RESOURCES

THE BROOKINGS INSTITUTION
www.brookings.edu

Private nonprofit organization devoted to independent research and innovative policy solutions. The Brookings Metropolitan Policy Program has published several reports and briefs on credit issues, including "From Poverty, Opportunity: Putting the Market to Work for Lower Income Families." The Political and Economic Research Council and the Brookings Institute Urban Markets Initiative also published "Give Credit Where Credit is Due: Increasing Access to Affordable Mainstream Credit Using Alternative Data."

CENTER FOR COMMUNITY CAPITALISM
www.kenan-flagler.unc.edu/KI/commCapitalism/index.cfm

Research center at the University of North Carolina–Chapel Hill that engages in multidisciplinary research and outreach activities, exploring ways to apply private sector approaches to revitalizing America's distressed communities.

CENTER FOR FINANCIAL SERVICES INNOVATION
www.cfsinnovation.com/index.php

Affiliate of ShoreBank Corporation that develops market research, overviews of best practices, and industry analysis reports on innovative financial services targeting the unbanked. Among the many resources accessible from CFSI's publications page is the report, "Reaching Deeper: Using Alternative Data Sources to Increase the Efficacy of Credit Scoring."

CENTER FOR RESPONSIBLE LENDING
www.responsiblelending.org

Provides an extensive library of research on strategies and public policies to combat predatory lending, as well as analysis of lending trends and impacts. Resources include "Losing Ground: Foreclosures in the Subprime Market and Their Costs to Homeowners," "Unfair Lending: The Effect of Race and Ethnicity on the Price of Subprime Mortgages," "The Best Value in the Subprime Market: State Predatory Lending Reforms," and "Rural Borrowers More Likely to be Penalized for Refinancing Subprime Home Loans."

CONFERENCE OF STATE BANK SUPERVISORS
www.csbs.org

Represents and serves state bank regulatory agencies. CSBS is working with the American Association of Residential Mortgage Regulators to develop a national licensing system for the residential mortgage industry.

DEMOS

www.demos.org

Nonpartisan public policy research and advocacy organization focusing on democracy reform, expanding economic opportunity, restoring trust in government, and promoting new ideas in the public debate. Among the organization's many Economic Opportunity Program publications is "A House of Cards: Refinancing the American Dream."

FREDDIE MAC

www.freddiemac.com/index.html

Buys mortgages from lenders to keep money flowing in support of homeownership and rental housing, as well as initiates and supports community development projects. Don't Borrow Trouble® is a comprehensive consumer awareness campaign to help homeowners avoid lending practices that strip away their equity. CreditSmart® and CreditSmart® Espanol provide credit education curricula offered through organizations committed to helping underserved communities.

HOMEOWNERSHIP PRESERVATION FOUNDATION

www.hpfonline.org

Creates partnerships with local governments, nonprofit organizations, borrowers and lenders to help families overcome obstacles that could result in the loss of their homes.

NATIONAL COMMUNITY INVESTMENT FUND

www.ncif.org

Certified community development financial institution providing equity, debt, and information to banking institution partners nationwide. NCIF organized the Retail Financial Services Initiative, a three-year project to increase the quantity and quality of financial services for unbanked and low- to moderate-income consumers. For more information, see "From the Margins to the Mainstream: A Guide to Building Products and Strategies for Underbanked Markets."

NATIONAL COMMUNITY REINVESTMENT COALITION

www.ncrc.org

National nonprofit membership organization that promotes economic justice and equal access to credit, capital, and financial services to traditionally underserved communities. Among its recent reports are "Predatory Appraisals: Stealing the American Dream" and "Homeownership and Wealth Building Impeded." NCRC also operates a National Anti-Predatory Lending Consumer Rescue Fund to educate consumers and the industry about the issue.

RESOURCES

NATIONAL CONSUMER LAW CENTER
www.consumerlaw.org

Began as a federally funded agency providing backup support and services to Legal Aid lawyers. It now also works with private lawyers, government lawyers, and provides testimony to Congress and agencies on consumer credit issues. The center offers extensive training to housing counselors and advocates on foreclosure prevention and predatory lending, including training for Freddie Mac's "Don't Borrow Trouble" campaign. Among NCLC's lending-related resources is "Stop Predatory Lending: A Guide for Legal Advocates."

NATIONAL COUNCIL OF LA RAZA
www.nclr.org

Largest constituency-based Latino civil rights organization in the US. NCLR operates a Homeownership Network of 38 affiliates providing homeownership counseling to more than 20,000 Latino families in 19 states each year.

NATIONAL URBAN LEAGUE
www.nul.org

Has more than 100 local affiliates in 35 states and the District of Columbia. NUL and the Homeownership Preservation Foundation have joined forces to reduce home foreclosures in African-American communities.

NEIGHBORWORKS®AMERICA
www.nw.org/network/home.asp

Nation's largest trainer and certifier of homeownership and financial education counselors. NeighborWorks has ramped up support for foreclosure interventions through several programs, notably the NeighborWorks Center for Foreclosure Solutions, and has published several helpful guides, including "A Practitioner's Guide to Combating Predatory Lending."

OFFICE OF THE COMPTROLLER OF THE CURRENCY
www.occ.treas.gov

Charters, regulates, and supervises all national banks. The OCC newsletter, *Community Developments,* has covered predatory lending, alternative credit-scoring methods, and other related issues. Articles include "New Tools to Challenge Predatory Lending and Create More Homebuyer-Ready Borrowers," and "'No Credit? No Problem!' Taking the Nontraditional Route to Bring Borrowers into the Prime Mortgage Market."

OPPORTUNITY FINANCE NETWORK

www.opportunityfinance.net

Group of private-sector community development financial institutions that plans to launch a new residential mortgage system to provide alternatives to high-cost or predatory loans.

POLICYLAB CONSULTING GROUP, LLC

www.policylabconsulting.com

Conducts policy research and analysis on such issues as homeownership, mortgage default and foreclosure, financial literacy, and capital markets. One resource of particular note is "Analyzing Elements of Leading Nonprofit Default Intervention Programs."

WOODSTOCK INSTITUTE

www.woodstockinst.org

Chicago-based policy and advocacy nonprofit that promotes community reinvestment and economic development in lower-income and minority communities. The institute has a strong focus on predatory lending and has published several related reports, including "There Goes the Neighborhood: The Effect of Single-Family Mortgage Foreclosures on Property Values."

ENDNOTES CHAPTER 6

1. RealtyTrac, "More Than 1.2 Million Foreclosures Reported in 2006," press release, January 25, 2007.

2. Bob Tedeschi, "Storm Clouds Over Risky Loans," *The New York Times,* January 7, 2007.

3. Dan Immergluck and Geoff Smith, "The External Costs of Foreclosure: The Impact of Single-Family Mortgage Foreclosures on Property Values," *Housing Policy Debate* 17:1, 2006, **www.fanniemaefoundation.org/programs/hpd/pdf/hpd_1701_immergluck.pdf**. William C, Apgar, Mark Duda, and Rochelle Nawrocki Gorey, "The Municipal Cost of Foreclosures: A Chicago Case Study," report prepared for the Homeownership Preservation Foundation, **www.hpfonline.org/PDF/Apgar-Duda_Study_Full_Version.pdf**.

4. William C. Apgar and Mark Duda, "Collateral Damage: The Municipal Impact of Today's Mortgage Foreclosure Boom," May 2005, **www.hpfonline.org/PDF/Apgar_Duda_Study_Final.pdf**.

5. Matt Fellowes, "From Poverty, Opportunity: Putting the Market to Work for Lower Income Families," The Brookings Institution Metropolitan Policy Program, July 2006.

6. Although a few jurisdictions have enacted laws regulating loan terms and attaching requirements to certain loans, they have been challenged in the courts—often successfully— for unlawfully usurping state or federal authority.

7. Abdighani Hirad and Peter M. Zorn, "A Little Knowledge Is a Good Thing: Empirical Evidence of the Effectiveness of Pre-Purchase Homeownership Counseling," Freddie Mac, May 2001, **www.chicagofed.org/cedric/files/2003_conf_paper_session1_zorn.pdf**.

8. Amy Crews Cutts and Richard Green, "Innovative Servicing Technology: Smart Enough to Keep People In Their Houses?" Freddie Mac Working Paper #4-03, July 2004, **www.freddiemac.com/news/pdf/fmwp_0403_servicing.pdf**. Lender repayment plans lower the probability of home loss by 80 percent among all borrowers and by 68 percent among low- to moderate-income borrowers.

9. AARP, "The State of 50+ America 2006," **www.aarp.org**.

10. For more information on universal design, visit **www.aarp.org/families/home_design/universaldesign/a2004-03-23-whatis_univdesign.html**.

11. Steve Tripoli and Elizabeth Renuart, "Dreams Foreclosed: The Rampant Theft of Americans' Homes Through Equity-Stripping Foreclosure 'Rescue' Scams," National Consumer Law Center, June 2005.

12. Janis Bowdler, "Jeopardizing Hispanic Homeownership: Predatory Practices in the Homebuying Market," **www.nclr.org/content/publications/download/31596**. Over a five-year period, subprime borrowers paying interest rates three to four percentage points above prime will build about half the home equity accumulated by prime borrowers.

13. ———, "Informed Consumer Choice in the Subprime Market: Overview of Oral Testimony," remarks presented before Governor Olsen and representatives from the Federal Reserve in Philadelphia, Pennsylvania, June 9, 2006, **www.nclr.org/content/publications/download/41340**.

14. US Conference of Mayors Best Practices Center, "The Partnership for Working Families: Successful City Initiatives," presented at the Annual Meeting of the US Conference of Mayors, June 2003, **usmayors.org/uscm/news/publications/workingfamilies03.pdf**.

15. Jonathan D. Epstein, "City Agency Due to Block Predatory Home Loans," *Buffalo News*, June 22, 2006. Ineligible loans have interest rates more than three percentage points above the rate on Federal Housing Administration loans or 9.99 percent, total fees that exceed six percent of the loan, balloon payments, or single-premium credit insurance.

16. Fellowes, "From Poverty, Opportunity."

17. The RFSI Strategy Guide, "From the Margins to the Mainstream: A Guide to Building Products and Strategies for Underbanked Markets," is available at **www.ncif.org/services.php?mainid=3&id=41**.

18. A 2005 survey of homeowner workshop participants by Neighborhood Housing Services of Chicago, Inc. found that 33 percent of those making late payments had never spoken with their servicers. Fifty-one percent didn't know that their lender might be able to reduce their payments in the event of job loss or health problems. A 2005 survey by Freddie Mac and Roper Public Affairs and Media found that 61 percent of late-paying borrowers said they were unaware of the existence of workout options that could help them.

19. Neighborhood Housing Services of Chicago, Inc., "Home Ownership Preservation Initiative Partnership Lessons & Results: Three Year Final Report," July 17, 2006, **www.nhschicago.org/downloads/82HOPI3YearReport_Jul17-06.pdf**.

20. Loss mitigation entails working with the lender or loan servicer to bring the loan current. Participating lenders designate their own loss mitigation staff to work with NHS staff.

21. At minimum, clients must submit evidence that demonstrates a causal relationship between poor credit, bankruptcy, and foreclosure, as well as predatory lending incidences or patterns. Refinanced loans are used to pay off existing first mortgages, delinquent taxes and municipal obligations, and property-related expenses. Any payoff of consumer debt must be justified on the basis of necessity and not due to credit abuse.

22. RealtyTrac, January 25, 2007.

23. Zach Schiller, "Foreclosure Growth in Ohio 2006," Policy Matters Ohio, July 2006, **www.policymattersohio.org/pdf/foreclosure_growth_ohio_2006.pdf**.

24. Community Law Center, "Baltimore City Flipping and Predatory Lending Task Force, 2005 Final Report," **www.communitylaw.org**.

25. According to a 2005 study by the North Carolina-based Center for Responsible Lending, "The Best Value in the Subprime Market: State Predatory Lending Reforms" **(www.responsiblelending.org/pdfs/rr010-State_Effects-0206.pdf)**, laws regulating high-cost lending in 28 states are helping prevent consumer abuses without eliminating credit for those who need it. The study found that the number of loans with terms considered predatory declined the most in states with the toughest restrictions. In 26 of the states, subprime mortgage lending activity remained even with or outpaced that in states without such protections. The states identified as having the toughest laws are Massachusetts, New Jersey, New Mexico, New York, North Carolina, and West Virginia.

26. To qualify, homeowners must be at least 60 days delinquent and demonstrate that their financial inability to make mortgage payments is not the result of overspending or other factors within their control. They must also show that the difficulty is temporary and that they can resume mortgage payments once circumstances change through such activities as securing another job or paying off medical expenses.

27. Under the program, participants can receive loans to pay off up to three months' worth of overdue mortgage loan balances or up to two years of assistance to help cover monthly loan payments, not to exceed $60,000. The loans must be repaid once the crisis is averted.

The Pennsylvania Housing Finance Agency administers the program through a network of nonprofit housing counseling agencies. Until the mid-1990s, the program received general fund appropriations but provisions enacted in 1998 transformed the program into a revolving loan fund that has become increasingly self-sufficient, in part by restricting program eligibility to the profile outlined here.

28. Many ITIN holders are in the country legally but cannot get a Social Security number because they are under a work visa or some other legal residency program. Workers whose parents entered the country illegally but who themselves grew up in the US use ITIN numbers to pay taxes and file federal income tax returns. Many private lenders and credit unions have made loans to ITIN holders for years, providing very good performance for their portfolio.

29. According to Uriah King of the Center for Responsible Lending, state unfair and deceptive trade practices laws that contain exemptions for "acts regulated by government entities" have been interpreted broadly by some courts to exempt banking, insurance, and mortgage lending. Other exemptions may be found "back door" in other statutes, he said. Chapter 2 of the National Consumer Law Center's "Unfair and Deceptive Acts and Practices" covers the limits to the scope of some state laws. For example, Oregon mortgage brokers may not misrepresent their own services or costs but misrepresentations about the loans they are selling are not covered.

30. David Callahan, "Home Insecurity: How Widespread Appraisal Fraud Puts Homeowners at Risk," Demos, A Borrowing to Make Ends Meet Briefing Paper #4, March 2005, **www.demos.org/pubs/home_insecurity_v3.pdf**.

31. Under the law, mortgage bankers, brokers, and loan officers are prohibited from brokering a loan without a license and certain other activities. The law gives the North Carolina Commissioner of Banks broad enforcement powers to suspend or deny licenses, impose penalties for violations, and conduct examinations. For a more complete summary of North Carolina's mortgage industry licensing law, see **www.responsiblelending.org/pdfs/mbl_summ.PDF**.

32. First enacted in 1974, RESPA seeks to clarify the mortgage settlement process and closing fees to borrowers as well as eliminate kickbacks and unearned referral fees among settlement service providers. Within three days of applying for a mortgage, prospective borrowers must receive a good faith estimate of all closing costs, lender servicing and escrow account practices, and business relationships between closing service providers and other parties to the transaction.

33. FCRA sets uniform standards for the use of and access to consumer credit information. The act guarantees the right of individuals to access their credit reports and dispute inaccurate or incomplete information with credit reporting agencies and information providers. Credit reporting agencies must follow "reasonable procedures" to protect the accuracy, confidentiality, and relevance of credit information used in consumer reports and take certain actions to safeguard against identify theft.

34. The Fair Housing Act prohibits housing discrimination based on race, color, religion, national origin, sex, disability, or familial status (having or anticipating having children in the household under age 18). It applies to practically all housing-related transactions, including applying for a mortgage. When it specifically targets minorities, predatory lending is a violation of federal fair housing law, which opens up another potential avenue of enforcement. The case can be referred to HUD for prosecution as a civil rights violation.

Boston Commits to Production, Makes it Happen

In 2004, the Asian Community Development Corporation and Edward Fish & Associates cut the ribbon on a 22-story residential high-rise in Boston's Chinatown. It was a proud moment for community leaders and local officials. A mostly vacant and underused site once slated for a parking lot instead became much-needed homes in an urban housing market increasingly out of reach of even middle-income households.

The credit goes to engaged community residents and responsible developers committed to making a difference. By cross-subsidizing the affordable units with market-rate apartments and working with the city and state to find additional subsidies, the partners reduced the "equity gap" that most affordable/workforce housing developers face. Today low-, medium-, and high-income families live side by side in The Metropolitan's 251 apartments and condominiums.

But the complex also owes its existence to the city's efforts to reduce barriers to housing development. Mayor Thomas Menino's campaign to create 17,500 new housing units by mid-2007 directed city departments to sell vacant land for housing development, increase funds by selling surplus city buildings, and find other ways to make projects happen.

Under the gun to meet these highly public housing production goals, the city bureaucracy took action. The Metropolitan is a case in point. The Boston Redevelopment Authority assembled most of the parcels for the project, some of which were owned by a nearby hospital. Land with a market value of roughly $10 million was sold to the developer partners for $1 million and rezoned to allow higher density and taller structures. The city folded some fees and taxes into the land sales cost and covered gaps in the project's multi-layered financing package with about $1.8 million in linkage fees. The funding package enabled the developers to set aside a total of 115 units—nearly half—at costs affordable to households with incomes at or below 60–120 percent of area median income.

Replicated citywide, these efforts are adding up. As of August 2006, nearly 16,000 units had been permitted, about a quarter of which are affordable. In addition to boosting the city's affordable housing stock, the new homes are helping to stabilize neighborhoods and preserve both rental and homeownership opportunities for the city's workforce.

Reducing Barriers to Housing Production

7

Many local governments across the country have costly and exclusionary land use laws, building standards, and permitting processes. Coupled with a shortage of developable land in many locations, the result is that housing prices often exceed the means of even moderate-income families. Indeed, a 2006 Brookings Institution study of the nation's largest metropolitan areas found that the share of middle-income families is shrinking and middle-class neighborhoods are vanishing even faster.[1]

But removing regulatory barriers to affordable housing production is complicated and often difficult to achieve. Communities and local leaders, operating under short-term thinking, often do not want new housing. Barrier removal does, however, have big payoffs. The possibilities are great in part because local and state governments that want to make changes can do so without having to rely on federal or state funding.

A number of mayors recognize that their cities' economic futures depend on increasing the supply of housing for residents at all income levels. Chicago's Richard Daley, New York's Michael Bloomberg, and San Francisco's Gavin Newsom have led highly public campaigns to boost production. Upzoning land, speeding permit approvals, and other barrier reduction efforts are key to these initiatives.

In their efforts to reduce barriers, local governments should take advantage of the resources and leadership provided by the US Department of Housing and Urban Development. As a strong champion of barrier removal, HUD identifies and shares local best practices, rewards innovation, and recognizes local leaders. The department's current efforts grow out of the landmark Report of the Advisory Commission on Regulatory Barriers to Affordable Housing, published in 1991. The report, "Not In My Back Yard: Removing Barriers to Affordable Housing," exposed the regulatory obstacles to housing and fostered ongoing efforts to study solutions. According to the commission, "exclusionary, discriminatory, and unnecessary regulations" raise housing costs by as much as 20–35 percent in some communities.

In a 2005 followup report, "Why Not In Our Community? Removing Barriers to Affordable Housing," HUD considers a policy or procedure a barrier when it prohibits, discourages, or excessively increases the cost of new or rehabilitated affordable housing without sound compensating benefits. The report provides important leadership and outlines ways that some state and local governments are responding to the commission's call to tackle such counterproductive regulations.

The America's Affordable Communities Initiative supports HUD's commitment to barrier reduction by providing technical assistance and model regulatory approaches to governments and housing advocates. As part of the initiative, HUD has commissioned multiple studies on the different types of regulatory barriers, from subdivision rules to obstacles to land assembly.

HUD's Regulatory Barriers Clearinghouse (**www.regbarriers.org**) is a database of state and local strategies, guides, and other publications. To further encourage innovation, the agency has elevated barrier removal to a policy priority in its Notice of Funding Availability processes and is conducting research to develop new regulatory tools and guidance for local governments. Another initiative provides guidance to local partnerships that are also working on aspects of regulatory barrier reduction.

Encouraged by these efforts, a growing number of local and state governments are taking a meaningful look at addressing the factors that drive up production costs. While these are heartening signs of progress, more widespread barrier reduction efforts are necessary. Across the US, local officials who bemoan the lack of housing for even moderate-income residents need to turn their concerns into action by advancing policies that stimulate new construction and reduce prices.

RECOMMENDATIONS FOR LOCAL ACTION

1 Rewrite Zoning Laws to Allow Greater Residential Densities And Uses

Local zoning ordinances commonly include provisions that limit density, raising both per-unit land costs and home prices. In some suburban jurisdictions, zoning laws restrict apartments, condominiums, townhouses, and irregularly shaped or small lots—indeed, any kind of housing that could be affordable.

A 2005 study by the Pioneer Institute for Public Policy Research and the Rappaport Institute for Greater Boston attributes a decades-long decline in residential construction and increases in housing costs in the greater Boston metropolitan area primarily to land use regulations that limit housing density. In particular, more than 80 of the 187 communities studied had zoned between 91 percent and 100 percent of their land for single-family housing.[2]

Some regulations, of course, serve a legitimate purpose. Officials do need to ensure that existing homeowners and local budgets do not suffer inordinately from new development. But overly protective land use controls that constrict housing for lower- to moderate-income workers lead to such problems as traffic congestion, business flight, and other conditions that diminish quality of life.

State and local governments should revise their land use laws to reduce exclusionary zoning and allow greater density and a diversity of housing choices. This includes provisions for multifamily and other affordable housing types, such as accessory dwelling units (also called in-law apartments) and manufactured housing. In-law apartments provide not only affordable homes for tenants but also income streams that help buyers obtain a mortgage. Communities that technically allow such units but effectively preclude their development with off-street parking, large-lot, and other requirements should reconsider making such housing available.

Communities often oppose higher-density housing such as apartments on the grounds that it will decrease nearby property values. However, many studies have shown that higher-density housing does not in and of itself depress property values and, in some instances, may even increase values.[3]

State and local governments should also enact laws prohibiting unequal treatment of manufactured homes in zoning. Manufactured housing on a permanent foundation and underwritten with a conventional mortgage should be allowed in any residential zoning district, as long as it meets standards applicable to other forms of housing. Dramatic improvements in quality and design have made manufactured housing an increasingly attractive option for affordable housing developers, especially in areas with skyrocketing construction costs such as the Gulf Coast region.[4]

Manufactured homes cost less because producers realize economies of scale and because there are no weather delays or construction site theft. Faster construction time also translates into lower carrying costs for developers. Properly sited new manufactured homes are architecturally compatible with stick-built homes, and they are as sound. Research shows that manufactured homes on fee-simple land appreciate reliably, at rates just slightly lower than those for site-built homes.[5]

▼ CASES IN POINT

Portland and Oregon Require All Housing Types

The state-created Metro Housing Rule, which applies to the 24 cities and three counties in the Portland metro area, requires local governments to achieve pre-set average residential densities.[6] The rule also requires jurisdictions other than small cities to designate sufficient buildable land to allow at least half of new residential development to be attached single-family or multifamily housing. Portland Metro, the regional transportation and planning agency, further requires that all jurisdictions achieve an average developed minimum density of 80 percent of their zoned density. Miami-Dade County, Florida, imposes a similar requirement that average approved density must be as least 75 percent of the listed density.

King County Code Changes Increase Densities Almost 40 Percent

King County, Washington adopted a new zoning code for unincorporated areas in 1993, opening previously unusable parcels to housing. By eliminating minimum lot size, the change helped to increase the variety of housing choices by allowing town homes and clustered and zero-lot line development in new subdivisions or short plats.[7] New developments are also required to achieve 65–85 percent of the minimum density established by each jurisdiction in compliance with the King County Countywide Planning Policies. According to county officials, single-family density rose from

3.8 units per acre in 1996–2000 to 5.3 units per acre in 2004. Multifamily density increased from 22.0 to 30.0 units per acre over the same period.

Western Jurisdictions Allow Accessory and Cottage Developments

Santa Cruz, California provides a step-by-step guide, design plans, and low-cost construction loans as part of its highly regarded accessory dwelling unit (ADU) program. Launched in 2003, the program produces about 40 units a year. King County, Washington also permits attached and unattached units on lots exceeding 10,000 square feet. A recently adopted provision of the code allows cottage housing developments—homes of up to 1,200 square feet, clustered on lots at twice the density of single-family neighborhoods. In addition, several King County jurisdictions, including the cities of Seattle, Redmond, Kirkland, Mercer Island, and Shoreline, have made changes to permit ADUs and cottage units. County officials report that about 450 ADUs were developed from 2001 to 2005, and more than 12 new cottage housing projects with close to 100 small homes were completed between 1998 and 2005.

Manufactured Housing Co-op Offers Affordable Homeownership

The nonprofit New Hampshire Community Loan Fund is demonstrating the use of manufactured housing in new affordable developments with a variant of a land-lease community. Its Pepperidge Woods project is a 44-site manufactured home community consisting of three-bedroom, 1,344 sq. ft., EnergyStar-rated manufactured homes placed on four- and eight-foot insulated concrete forms. Because land ownership is critical for asset appreciation, the loan fund has secured approval from the state attorney general to transfer the single parcel of land and improvements to a homeowner cooperative. Since the community will be resident-owned, homeowners have access to high loan-to-value, affordable housing loans from the NH Housing Finance Authority and the USDA's 502 Direct Loan Program.[8]

2 Amend Parking and Other Development Requirements that Consume Land and Construction Dollars

Site development requirements such as minimum street, sidewalk, and lot widths, yard setbacks, and other infrastructure requirements effectively exclude affordable housing by eating up land and boosting construction costs. In a study for HUD, the National Association of Home Builders Research Center found that excessive site development requirements increase housing costs by five percent at minimum and often by much more.[9]

▼ CASE IN POINT

San Francisco, Other Cities Ease Parking Requirements

In 2006, San Francisco eliminated the parking requirement for downtown residential development and set an "as of right" maximum of one parking space per four dwelling units. Developers can apply for conditional use permits allowing up to 0.75 spaces for each one-bedroom or smaller unit, and up to one space for each two-bedroom or larger unit. The city also prohibits downtown residential developers from requiring buyers to purchase a parking space. Spaces must instead be leased or sold separately from the housing unit.[10]

These policies are being proposed for many other San Francisco neighborhoods, particularly areas well-served by transit or with services within walking distance. The legislation was promoted by the nonprofit advocacy group Livable City, which cites a University of California Berkeley study concluding that housing without parking sold for 12 percent less than comparable units with parking.[11] Several other cities, including Coral Gables and Fort Myers, Florida; Milwaukee, Wisconsin; Portland, Oregon; and Seattle and Spokane, Washington have also abolished residential parking requirements for certain downtown neighborhoods.[12]

3 Help Developers Find and Assemble Usable Land

The lack of developable sites and difficulty of assembling large tracts drive up costs considerably in many communities. Local public officials should ease land pressures by identifying parcels available for development and streamlining the process for getting parcels into developers' hands. In the case of surplus public land, jurisdictions can convey land at lower cost in exchange for commitments to affordability. For land that is not "project-ready," local governments should use tax increment financing (TIF) and other tools to build roads, install sewers, and bring other needed infrastructure and enhancements to the site.

▼ CASES IN POINT

Empowered Redevelopment Agencies Are Key to Land Assembly

In a forthcoming study for HUD's Office of Policy Development and Research, the Urban Land Institute (ULI) reports that agencies with eminent domain and tax-advantaged bonding capabilities are critical to the redevelopment of infill lands.[13] While redevelopment agencies are common, not all communities have them and not all agencies have sufficient powers, ULI asserts.The Boston Redevelopment Authority is one agency with the requisite powers. The 22-story mixed-income high-rise in Chinatown profiled at the beginning of this chapter is but one of many housing projects the agency has spearheaded.

Tax Increment Financing Helps to Create Usable Land

At the behest of local government, redevelopment authorities use tax increment financing (TIF) to encourage investment in blighted but promising neighborhoods. Under the TIF approach, a city government designates the boundaries of a redevelopment district. New tax revenues generated by rising property values flow to the district. Often the redevelopment authority administering the district issues bonds backed by the future revenue stream to finance projects and infrastructure improvements. Cities can and should ensure that some of the investment goes to affordable housing. The Portland Development Commission, for example, sets aside 30 percent of TIF revenues in five urban renewal areas for such purposes. Chicago's TIF program has secured more than $200 million for nearly 8,000 affordable housing units since 1994.

Boston Packages and Conveys Low-Cost Sites

Like many cities, Boston at times conveys city-owned lands to affordable housing developers at a substantial discount or arranges up-front compensation through bond sales. The Boston Redevelopment Authority sells land to developers for $25,000 off the appraisal per affordable unit. In addition, the Boston Department of Neighborhood Development packages 15–20 lots for nonprofit/for-profit partnerships and transfers larger sites for 20–50 units to rental projects that set aside half of the units for affordable housing. These programs help the city transfer vacant, city-owned parcels to affordable housing developers for $100 per lot.

New York, Other Cities Target Surplus Public Lands

New York, San Francisco, and Portland, Oregon are among the cities that have used joint development agreements to ensure that a certain amount of publicly owned surplus land is made available for low-income housing development. New York has been particularly active in collaborations to get publicly owned lands into residential developers' hands. For example, the New York City Department of Housing Preservation and Development (HPD) is working with the New York City Housing Authority to create nearly 6,000 affordable units on NYCHA-owned land. In the meantime, HPD is creating relationships with such agencies as the Department of Transportation, the Health and Hospitals Corporation, and several state agencies that may have surplus property that they would be willing to transfer to HPD for housing development. These partnerships are expected to generate over 20,000 units of new housing by 2013.

Chicago Investment Strategy Cuts through Bond Sale Red Tape

Chicago's HomeStart program puts a unique twist on the practice of issuing bonds to compensate the city for land conveyed to developers. Under HomeStart, the city transfers land to developers at below-market rates in exchange for a share of the proceeds from the sale of homes built on the land. By enabling developers to secure their own financing (with the land as collateral), projects avoid the red tape associated with bond sales and can therefore get under way faster. To date, the program has transferred 500 lots in appreciating neighborhoods to private developers. Typically, some 20–50 percent of the homes built are set aside for households making up to 100 percent of area median income, with the rest selling at market rates.

4 Accelerate Reuse of Vacant and Abandoned Properties

In many jurisdictions, authority over such tasks as reclaiming and reusing vacant and abandoned land is dispersed among many agencies, adding time and cost to the development process. To accelerate the reuse of such properties, jurisdictions—in some cases, working with state government—should update tax foreclosure, condemnation, and title clearing procedures.

▼ CASES IN POINT

Baltimore Expedites Purchase of Abandoned Properties

Baltimore's Project 5,000 is an ambitious effort to return 5,000 vacant and abandoned properties to productive use. The program, launched in 2002, relies on aggressive acquisition of abandoned property to stimulate private investment in redevelopment. An integrated geographic data system enables the city to identify vacant properties with significantly overdue tax bills, making them ripe for acquisition through foreclosure. City officials worked with the courts and other agencies to expedite the processing of foreclosure cases. Law firms, title companies, courts, and the sheriff's office reduced their fees for clearing titles and filing documents. According to Baltimore officials, the city has increased property acquisition fivefold while shrinking the acquisition period from 18 to 8 months. By November 2006, the city had acquired 6,200 properties.

On the development side, the city has speeded up the process for getting properties into developers' hands. It beefed up its dispositions staff and increased capital bond authority from $45 million to $60 million, directing more than a third of the funds to housing and community development. To date, Baltimore has returned over 1,000 properties to productive use (both affordable and market-rate housing) and has identified a development outcome for another 2,000 properties. The city has reaped $5.5 million in sales revenue and $1.8 million in property taxes and fees from the abandoned properties.

Land Banks Address Barriers to Reuse of Vacant Land

Overdue property taxes often exceed the fair market value of abandoned inner-city properties, making them unmarketable. In other cases, the properties have gone through tax foreclosure but the title is defective, so no one will buy them. Local ordinances requiring governments to sell properties at auction to the highest bidder are another barrier to reuse of such properties.

Land banks address these obstacles. The banks can pay off or forgive tax liens, clear title to land, and prepare the parcels for transfer to private developers. According to Emory University law professor Frank Alexander, the banks have the discretion to negotiate the terms of disposition so that properties can be used for affordable housing, green space, or mixed-use development. The five urban land banks Alexander studied were all created in part to avoid the statutory requirements to sell tax-foreclosed properties at sheriffs' auctions.[14]

5 Rezone Land Uses to Create More Developable Sites

To expand the supply of developable land, local governments should consider rezoning parcels from other uses. For example, some communities have rezoned industrial lands and smaller privately owned airports for housing development. Others have helped to alleviate the pressure on home prices by opening former agricultural lands to development. Reclassifying land from one use to another is a good time to consider agreements under which builders with access to the formerly off-limits land must include some affordable housing.

▼ CASES IN POINT

New York City "Upzones" Industrial Lands

To help meet its goal of producing and preserving 165,000 units of low- and moderate-income housing by 2013, New York City has rezoned industrial areas to allow higher housing densities. In exchange, developers working in those areas must set aside a portion of their projects for units at varying levels of affordability. One rezoning project alone will enable production of nearly 11,000 housing units, about a third of which will be affordable.

Minnesota, Connecticut Communities Transform Industrial Sites into Housing

Smaller communities also have rezoning opportunities. Officials in Mahtomedi, a town near the Twin Cities in Minnesota, rezoned an industrial park to allow Pulte Homes to construct 70 town homes selling in the low $200,000s.[15] Landscape buffers separate the business uses from the homes. Many Connecticut communities are also devising ways to convert industrial properties into housing. For example, Shelton and Hartford negotiated home heights and sizes with developers under special overlay zones.[16]

Denver Airport Reuse Plan Mixes Affordable, Market-rate Homes

After demolishing the buildings and runways at its former airport, Denver sold the roughly 2,900 developable acres to Cleveland-based Forest City Enterprises, Inc. for almost $80 million (over a 15-year period).[17] Forest City is funding infrastructure improvements with aid from tax increment financing. When completed in the 2020s, the development is expected to have about 12,000 homes and apartments (10 percent of which will be affordable to low- and moderate-income families), 10 million square feet of office space, and 3 million square feet of retail space. In addition to lower-cost land and tax incentives, the city supported the project with creative financing.

6 Provide Density Bonuses and Other Incentives for Affordable Housing Development

In many markets, removing exclusionary land use laws and assembling land are essential but incomplete tools for enabling affordable housing production. Local governments operating in costlier markets should use density bonuses (permission to build at higher-than-allowed densities), fee waivers, and other incentives to encourage developers to build housing for low- and moderate-income working families. By leveraging market-rate development, such programs allow governments to direct higher-density housing to targeted areas and integrate affordable homes into the community.

▼ CASES IN POINT

Mix of Incentives Spurs Housing Development in Chicago

The City of Chicago's flexible, incentive-based approach has yielded a solid number of quality affordable housing units at different prices for working people, seniors, renters, and the homeless. The Chicago Partnership for Affordable Neighborhoods program allows condominium developers in appreciating neighborhoods to build at higher densities and obtain fee waivers and site improvements in exchange for setting aside at least 10 percent of the units for households making up to 100 percent of the area median income. Under, Chicago's Affordable Requirements Ordinance, developers receiving reduced-priced city land or city financial assistance must set aside 10 percent and 20 percent of the units, respectively, for affordable housing. Between 2002 and January 2007, the two programs created 1,331 affordable units in market-rate developments. Since its inception in 2004, Chicago's Downtown Density Bonus program, offering additional square footage to downtown residential builders, has generated about $24 million in fees for neighborhood housing development and rental subsidies.[18]

Negotiated Bonuses Generate a Third of Boston's Affordable Housing

In Boston, developers seeking zoning variances (de facto density bonuses) must set aside a percentage of the units in their projects for affordable housing or pay a fee. Since its inception, the city has increased the in-lieu fee to encourage on-site development. Affordable homeownership units must target households earning 130–160 percent of the Boston median household income, and rental units must be affordable to people earning 100–125 percent. As of early 2006, the Inclusionary Development Program accounted for about a third of the affordable housing produced in Boston. Moreover, the program is one of the few providing help to residents who earn too much to qualify for traditional government-assisted housing but not enough to afford median-priced homes in the city.

Fast Approvals, Fee Waivers Boost Production in Texas, Florida Communities

The S.M.A.R.T. Housing™ initiative, administered by the Austin Housing Finance Corporation, helped to create more than 8,100 housing units between 2000 and the end of 2006. Nearly three-fourths of the units are affordable to households making up to 80 percent of the area median income. S.M.A.R.T., which stands for Safe, Mixed Income, Accessible, Reasonably Priced and Transit Oriented, provides expedited permitting, fee waivers, and advocacy for developers who include affordable homes in their projects and adhere to green building, accessibility, and transit-oriented standards that exceed building code requirements.

A Manatee County, Florida incentive program increased the proposed number of affordable and workforce homes from 90 in 2004 to more than 1,400 in 2006. The program offers fee rebates, subsidies, and expedited approvals to developers who set aside at least 25 percent of their projects for affordable housing. Builders who set aside at least 10 percent of their projects for more expensive but still moderately priced workforce housing also receive expedited reviews and approvals.

Seattle, Portland Grant Tax Breaks, Other Perks for Affordable Units

In certain neighborhoods, Seattle offers 10-year tax exemptions to projects that set aside at least 20 percent of units for households making up to 70 percent of the area median income. Portland has a program providing an array of property tax exemptions for affordable housing and transit-oriented development. Portland also provides density bonuses for affordable housing in the center city and northwest Portland, as well as for elderly and disabled housing in multifamily and commercial zones.

7 Implement Carefully Designed Inclusionary Zoning As Part of a Broader Affordable Housing Strategy

Inclusionary zoning should not be the first or only approach to providing affordable housing in a community. According to home builders and developers, the laws often amount to a de facto tax on development and constrict supply, increasing housing prices overall while helping only a small number of homebuyers or renters.[19] Inclusionary zoning should therefore be used only as part of a comprehensive strategy that also allows greater density or provides density bonuses, streamlines the building approval process, and modifies building codes to reduce costs. Local officials cannot rely solely on inclusionary zoning to accomplish what can only be achieved through the harder work of the various barrier reduction strategies outlined in this chapter.

▼ CASES IN POINT

Housing Advocates, Builders Craft Joint Principles

The Nonprofit Housing Association of Northern California and the Home Builders Association of Northern California issued a joint policy statement advising that inclusionary zoning laws should allow developers several options for including affordable housing. The alternatives include providing a range of for-sale housing types, such as duplexes, townhouses, or condominiums; providing rental housing; clustering the units on-site; producing the units off-site; donating land; and contributing fees to a housing fund instead of building the affordable units. The groups also recommend allowing two or more market-rate builders working in partnership to satisfy their inclusionary requirement through a single affordable housing project. The joint statement advocates for cost offsets such as density bonuses, impact and processing fee waivers or subsidies, exemptions of the inclusionary units from building permit caps and growth allocation processes, surplus public lands for affordable housing, and help marketing the affordable units.

Flexible Model in Carlsbad Draws Followers

Carlsbad, California's inclusionary zoning ordinance is flexible yet effective, ensuring the long-term affordability of the units it creates. Carlsbad requires that 15 percent of all new residential developments be affordable to low-income households. Rental units must remain affordable for 55 years and for-sale homes for 30 years. The city has the right of first refusal to purchase projects with inclusionary zoning units that go on the market.

For their part, developers can cluster the affordable units for greater efficiency. Developers may also earn credits by rehabilitating affordable units, converting existing market-rate units to affordable units, constructing transitional units or other special needs housing, and building accessory dwelling units. The credit can be transferred, allowing builders to purchase credits in a system. Projects with fewer than seven units may pay an in-lieu fee, or, at the city council's discretion, donate a comparable value of land. The city may also choose to offer cost offsets such as density bonuses.

---

8 Streamline the Building Approval Process

Lengthy, convoluted permitting processes delay construction, adding significant costs to development. In some jurisdictions, reviews take years. The delays come from multiple approval processes, cumbersome decision-making procedures, permitting inconsistencies, local administrative discretion, multiple public hearings, and citizen opposition. In many cities, responsibility for various aspects of a project is dispersed among many agencies, with no one person or agency in charge.

Municipalities serious about producing more housing of any kind must devise more business-friendly approaches. City staff must work with developers to negotiate the regulatory gauntlet rather than stick to hard-and-fast rules. Efforts should be made to cut the number of public hearings required for approvals. In their dealings with developers and community residents, city staff should emphasize conflict reduction and consensus building. Staff should also receive training on how to deal with new types of development.

▼ CASES IN POINT

Coordinated Review Teams in Sacramento, White Plains Speed Approvals

Through its MATRIX initiative, Sacramento eliminates traditional function-based "silos." Staff from all city departments involved in the review process form teams organized around niche development types. Starting at the concept phase, developers work with a team consisting of planners, building inspectors, engineers, landscape architects, and so on. Early engagement of the various experts provides designers and city reviewers time to resolve any code-related issues without delaying the project's start date. The program was piloted in an area of the central district where higher-density developments were increasingly under way. After the pilot's success at significantly shortening project timelines, the city planned to expand MATRIX citywide.

White Plains, New York began a similar coordinated review process in the late 1990s. Applicants who formerly had to visit separate departments for reviews now attend one or more work sessions chaired by the mayor or executive officer and attended by all relevant department heads. Clear and timely direction reduces developers' risks and soft costs. Coupled with other reforms (such as amended building codes and provision of density bonuses), the city permitted more than 150 new affordable units in 2001–2005, representing over 10 percent of all new housing permitted in the city since 1998.

Permit-Ready Designs Ease Infill Development

To accelerate development of vacant lots in older city neighborhoods, Sacramento's Infill House Plan Program offers four plans for homes on the most common-sized lots in the targeted areas. The plans are preapproved through the city's design and building plan review process and are available for purchase. Private developers may also request that their plans be preapproved for repeated use. Portland, Oregon provides permit-ready designs for single-family homes for narrow infill lots, while Santa Cruz, California offers off-the-shelf designs for accessory dwelling units.

---

9 Modify Building Codes to Reduce Housing Costs

Municipal and state governments must examine their building codes to identify unnecessary provisions that increase housing costs. Building codes requiring expensive materials or construction techniques can serve as a barrier to affordable housing. In addition, out-of-date codes may prevent developers from taking advantage of technological advances that can enhance quality and reduce costs. The lack of consistency across jurisdictions is in itself costly, requiring developers to constantly adapt to new rules. According to the National Conference of States on Building Codes & Standards, Inc., regulations governing the design and construction of buildings contribute up to 20 percent of the production costs.

Unless there are special circumstances, local jurisdictions should adopt the International Code Council (ICC) building code without amendments. Given that the amendment process often opens up opportunities for special interest groups to add costly provisions, the ICC should generally do the amending. State and local governments must regularly examine their existing codes for unnecessary, outdated, and costly provisions. They should also subject proposed amendments to a cost/benefit analysis, weighing the safety issues against affordability.

Code Reforms Allow Alternative Methods, Eliminate Costly Provisions

Spokane, Washington amended its building code to allow use of alternative methods and new materials for buildings that contain both residential and nonresidential uses. As part of its regulatory reform process, White Plains, New York removed costly provisions from the plumbing code that provided no health or safety benefits. For its part, the New York City Department of Buildings is working closely with public and private entities to streamline and modernize the building code to incorporate new technologies and practices, including performance criteria for building construction.

New Jersey's Smart Code Cuts Rehabilitation Costs and Boosts Activity

"Smart" building codes make it easier to preserve properties by eliminating the requirement that rehabilitated buildings meet the same standards as modern buildings. Under the New Jersey Smart Code, for example, the regulatory requirements for repair, alteration, addition, and change of use projects are essentially proportional to the amount of work undertaken. The New Jersey Department of Community Affairs claims that the subcode has cut the costs of rehabilitation up to 50 percent in some cases, and 10 percent on average.[20] After the code was adopted, rehabilitation activity in the state increased significantly.[21]

HUD published a more broad-based rehabilitation code that was developed in cooperation with New Jersey.[22] Based upon the New Jersey and HUD models, cities and states have adopted similar codes, including Maryland, Minnesota, New York, North Carolina, and Rhode Island, along with Wilmington, Delaware and Wichita, Kansas. Broad strategic alliances were critical to passing these codes.[23]

10 Review Environmental and Growth Policies for Impacts On Housing Affordability

Regulations imposed to protect the environment rather than primarily limit development serve an important role. Indeed, requirements for open space and trees can make a development more attractive and thus increase the value of the land—potentially offsetting the costs of compliance. Environmental regulations and growth control ordinances do, however, add to the cost of housing by limiting the amount of developable land. Such regulations include building moratoria, permitting caps, conservation and open space requirements, and excessive buffering and setbacks. In cases such as wetlands protection, the regulations may impose burdens that far outweigh the benefits.

Local leaders must review their environmental regulations to ensure they are clear, objective, and reasonable. Much of the time, the most costly piece of environmental compliance is the community approval and litigation processes that drag on when rules are vague. Municipalities should also consider exempting smaller projects from certain review processes. For example, King County, Washington increased the threshold for the State Environmental Policy Act review process from four housing units to 20 in urban areas and eight in rural areas.

11 Consider Impact Fee Alternatives and New Mechanisms For Financing Infrastructure

Impact fees deserve close scrutiny because of the costs they may add to new homes. Many jurisdictions (including counties, cities, special districts and school districts) require developers to pay one-time fees to cover the costs that a new development is presumed to impose on schools, roads, parks, and water and wastewater systems. These fees are increasing. According to a 2006 draft report for HUD, average non-utility impact fees for single-family homes rose from $5,781 in 1998 to $11,012 in 2004.[24]

While impact fees may encourage higher-density development, poorly structured fees discourage workforce housing production by requiring developers to shoulder too much of the burden for infrastructure improvements that benefit the entire community. The costs of the impact fees are then passed on to homebuyers and renters. Whenever possible, local governments should choose alternatives to impact fees that may be more appropriate and more likely to spread the costs of new housing community-wide. Options include general taxes, dedicated taxes, special assessments, and user fees.

Given their political expediency, however, impact fees are likely to remain a source for infrastructure improvements. Municipalities should follow the generally accepted legal standard that any imposed fees directly correspond to the infrastructure that ties only to that development. To tailor residential impact fees as closely as possible, they should be based on size in square feet rather than on housing type (single-family detached, multifamily, etc.). On average, larger homes have more people living in them than smaller homes. A fixed impact fee thus forces smaller, lower-cost homes to subsidize larger ones. It also requires modifying the standard average cost pricing method in which every unit pays the same for the same service, regardless of such differences as how far the unit is from sewer lines. The square footage of the house, the distance from the house to services, and the density of the neighborhood should thus come into play when calculating water and sewer impact fees.

▼ CASE IN POINT

Fort Collins, Others Offset Impact Fees for Affordable Housing

Fort Collins, Colorado provides $2.5 million annually in rebates to affordable housing projects on a competitive basis. The city also delays collection of some fees until the certificate of occupancy is issued. From 1995 to 2000, these programs helped to create 650 new affordable housing units.[25]

A growing number of communities are adopting this approach. Denver, for example, reduces water-related utility fees based on the development's density. Atlanta eliminates or reduces fees for projects targeting lower-income households or located near transit or in certain areas.

While waivers of fees on affordable homes have also been used, their effects on the sales prices of the housing are uncertain. As a result, some jurisdictions, such as Alachua County, Florida, provide forgivable downpayment loans to eligible homebuyers as an indirect way to waive fees.

OPPORTUNITIES FOR STATE ACTION

1 Offer Incentives for Higher-Density And Affordable Development

State land use laws should include provisions encouraging higher-density housing in certain areas, such as near transit (especially in state-funded projects). States should also provide priority funding, technical assistance, and tax incentives to communities that plan higher-density, transit-oriented, and affordable housing.

California has a number of laws and programs encouraging higher-density, lower-cost development. Along with Illinois and Oregon, it requires cities and counties to include "housing elements" in their comprehensive plans. The elements include assessments of future housing needs (including affordable units) and strategies for meeting those needs. California's law is credited in part with the widespread development of local inclusionary housing programs throughout the state.

Under state law, a certain share of housing developments within project areas must be reserved as affordable housing.[26] The state also requires local governments to provide density bonuses to developers who include lower-cost housing in their projects.[27] Funding programs offering incentives include Building Equity and Growth in Neighborhoods (BEGIN), which makes grants to cities and counties that reduce regulatory barriers to the construction of new, affordable ownership housing, and the Workforce Housing Reward Program, which provides financial incentives for issuing building permits for homes affordable to lower-income households.

Massachusetts has reformed its "carrot-and-stick" approach to affordable housing planning. Under the Chapter 40B law, a developer setting aside affordable units can override zoning rules in any community where less than 10 percent of the housing is affordable. The legal framework generally requires that the zoning board of appeals in these communities must approve any development project that includes at least 25-percent affordable, deed-restricted housing unless approval would jeopardize the health and safety of residents. Municipalities recover full control when they reach their 10 percent goals. To count toward the 10 percent, units must carry deed restrictions assuring long-term affordability. The law has resulted in construction of over 35,000 affordable housing units since its inception, bringing low- and moderate-income housing to many communities for the first time.

Nonetheless, it has generated considerable controversy. Local officials feel that it gives developers too much power to override local authority without commensurate cost offsets. The state has responded to these concerns by broadening the definition of what counts as an affordable unit and providing some relief to municipalities that create plans to reach their goals. Lawmakers also enacted two new pieces of legislation to provide more incentives for mixed-income housing construction. Chapter 40R, enacted in 2004, provides cash payments of $10,000 to $600,000 to communities that create new higher-density zoning overlay districts near transit stops, town/commercial centers, and other areas especially suitable for such development, including major brownfields. Every unit permitted in such districts generates a $3,000 bonus from state funds. Chapter 40S addresses the cost impact of development, reimbursing qualified communities for the net increase in costs of educating students living in housing developed under the smart growth overlay zoning.

2 Enact Prohibitions on Exclusionary Zoning

States should amend their zoning-enabling legislation to require localities to accept all housing types. For example, the Oregon Commission on Land Conservation and Development requires that jurisdictions zone residential land for a full array of housing types and price ranges, and forbids prohibitions on apartment buildings, manufactured housing, and government-assisted housing.

State law should require equal treatment of manufactured housing and accessory dwelling units (ADUs) as long as conditions of safety and soundness are met. California's model law says that manufactured housing is a by-right use in any residential district.[28] It goes further than many states in also prohibiting deed restrictions from discriminating against manufactured housing. In addition, California prohibits municipalities from barring accessory dwelling units. Although limits on lot coverage, setback requirements, and other local regulations essentially prevent ADU developments in some communities, localities such as Santa Cruz have successfully promoted the units.

States should also ensure that manufactured homes attached to permanent foundations and on owned land can be titled as real estate. Without a real estate title, manufactured-home owners must finance their purchase with personal property or "chattel" loans. These loans require larger downpayments and typically carry higher interest rates and fewer consumer protections than home mortgages.[29]

3 Help Communities Identify Available Land

California has promoted development of vacant or underused urban properties by improving the information on potential sites. The California Business, Transportation, and Housing Agency commissioned the Institute for Urban and Regional Development at the University of California Berkeley to canvass urban neighborhoods for sites that are either vacant or have structures with extremely low valuations relative to the land. The study found nearly 500,000 potential infill parcels that could be used for new homes and apartments. The findings formed the basis of the California Infill Parcel Locator (**www.infill.org**), a statewide inventory of potentially developable sites.

Florida now requires that local jurisdictions inventory sites that could be used for affordable housing development. The law is prompting local governments to consider developing policies to govern the disposition of surplus properties.

4 Enact Tax Foreclosure and Related Reforms

Outdated state laws governing ownership transfers for properties with tax liens or code violations can thwart local land reclamation efforts. As just one example, most state laws require that bidders at tax sales pay at least the amount due in delinquent taxes, interest, and penalties. In weaker markets, this requirement makes it difficult to buy properties with delinquent bills that exceed fair market value. Potential limits to eminent domain powers require states to enhance tax delinquency procedures and provide other vehicles for transferring vacant and abandoned properties to cities and developers.

Pennsylvania and New York have both worked to improve their foreclosure processes. The Pennsylvania legislature has eliminated the two-year redemption period on sheriff's sales of vacant properties, streamlined procedures so that cities can use en masse filing of tax foreclosures, and allowed credit bureaus to report tax liens, which may discourage owners from walking away from their properties. The Housing Alliance of Pennsylvania is advocating for reforms modeled after New York's judicial foreclosure law. In New York, vacant and abandoned properties do not have to go through a sheriff's sale, which prevents local governments from controlling who gets the property. Applicants go before a judge who can order the property's transfer to a responsible owner.

New Jersey's receivership program also expedites processing. The Abandoned Properties Rehabilitation Act clearly defines what constitutes an abandoned property, restructures tax foreclosure procedures, allows for vacant property receivership (where the courts appoint guardians for vacant property), and makes it easier to use eminent domain in cases of spot blight.

5 Reform State Code and Permitting Systems

The Montana Department of Housing Working Group and the Montana Building Industry Association conducted a review of the building code and assisted the Department of Commerce in identifying changes that would enhance housing affordability. The project resulted in code changes that will potentially save $4,802 in costs per home.[30]

As noted earlier, some states have enacted special codes that encourage rehabilitation by lowering costs. According to a National Governors Association brief, "Integrating Affordable Housing with State Development Policy," Maine, Maryland, Michigan, New Jersey, New York, and Rhode Island all have such codes.

On the permitting side, Florida has instituted a unique process for developments that incorporate affordable housing components. According to 1000 Friends of Florida, expedited permitting is required for all affordable housing land use decisions in every county. Fast-track permitting for affordable housing is also required from local governments that receive support through the State Housing Incentives Partnership (SHIP) program.[31]

6 Limit Reviews and Litigation

Much of the cost arising from environmental and other regulations comes from lengthy reviews and court appeals. Potential litigation can also deter development of affordable housing. States should enact laws limiting the time allowed for building code, zoning, and other approvals. They should also reform the land use appeals process to ensure that formal actions occur on the record and are subject to state housing affordability policy.

In most states, appeals of land use decisions to local courts are "de novo." As a result, developers and opponents alike can challenge local decisions in low-level state courts, then progress gradually through appeal processes to a superior court. The problem is that all of the parties hold their best arguments for the higher court, explains Arthur C. Nelson, professor and director of urban affairs and planning at Virginia Tech's Alexandria Center. As a result, local decision-making is delegated to state courts where judges are not experts in either land use or affordable housing. Oregon and Washington are among the few states that require the courts to review land use cases based on the record, preventing all parties from introducing new evidence on de novo appeals.

States should also limit the potential for litigation by clarifying the responsibilities of parties, creating mediation procedures to resolve conflicts between developers and local governments, requiring clear and objective standards, and imposing strict timeframes for decisions. For example, Oregon law requires clear and objective land use regulations and sets deadlines for appeals. Most contested cases are in and out of the process within a year, while cases in many parts of the country can drag on for much longer.

RESOURCES

AMERICAN PLANNING ASSOCIATION
www.planning.org

Nonprofit public interest and research organization committed to urban, suburban, regional, and rural planning. The APA's "Growing Smart Legislative Guidebook: Model Statutes for Planning and the Management of Change" and accompanying User Manual are the culmination of a seven-year project to draft the next generation of model planning and zoning legislation for the US.

CFED
www.cfed.org

Nonprofit organization that administers the Innovations in Manufactured Homes (I'M HOME) initiative, providing grants for demonstration projects in such areas as using manufactured homes in infill development, converting manufactured home parks to resident-owned parks, and policy development. The I'M HOME website features a variety of publications, data, best practices, and links to other resources.

LOCAL INITIATIVES SUPPORT CORPORATION
www.lisc.org

Helps community-based development organizations transform distressed communities and neighborhoods by providing capital, technical expertise, training, and information. LISC's Online Resource Library includes such publications as "Renewing Public Assets for Community Development," describing how municipalities deal with tax-delinquent and publicly owned properties and reforms that can help convert these properties into productive community assets.

METRO PORTLAND
www.metro-region.org

Regional planning agency for Portland, Oregon. Chapter 4 of its "Regional Affordable Housing Strategy" includes numerous recommendations for increasing and preserving the supply of affordable housing, including land use and regulatory reforms.

MIT CENTER FOR REAL ESTATE
Housing Affordability Initiative
web.mit.edu/cre/research/hai

Program operating in conjunction with MIT's Department of Urban Studies and Planning that focuses on housing affordability issues in the Boston metropolitan area.

NATIONAL ASSOCIATION OF HOME BUILDERS
www.nahb.org

Trade association with a mission to enhance the climate for housing and the building industry. The Resources section of the NAHB website provides a "Smart Codes" checklist that offers guidance for jurisdictions on ways to pursue smart growth without overly impeding housing development.

NATIONAL CONFERENCE OF STATE LEGISLATURES
www.ncsl.org

Bipartisan organization that serves the legislators and staffs of the US states, commonwealths, and territories. NCSL maintains a web feature, "Manufactured Housing: Not What You Think," which addresses issues related to manufactured housing, including a chart of states with nondiscriminatory statutes for manufactured housing.

NATIONAL CONFERENCE OF STATES ON BUILDING CODES AND STANDARDS
www.ncsbcs.org

Organization of state chief building regulatory officials, local code officials, construction industry associations, and others interested in building codes and the public safety system. The website presents the "Final Report on the NCSBCS/Alliance Survey on Savings from the Application of Information Technology to Building Code Administration and Enforcement Processes," February–April 2005.

NATIONAL GOVERNORS ASSOCIATION
Center for Best Practices
www.nga.org

Supports governors in responding to policy challenges through technical assistance and policy research. The center has published several briefs on affordable housing-related topics, including "Integrating Affordable Housing with State Development Policy" and "Coordinating Resources to Grow More Efficiently—The Massachusetts Approach."

NATIONAL MULTI HOUSING COUNCIL
www.nmhc.org

Trade association representing apartment owners, managers, developers, lenders, and service providers. NMHC offers tools to help advocates transform NIMBY sentiments into support for affordable housing, including a PowerPoint presentation called "A Plan for Tomorrow: Rethinking Density to Create Stronger, Healthier Communities." The council has also published a white paper, "From NIMBY to Good Neighbor," summarizing reports that indicate that apartments (even affordable apartments) pose no threat to local property values and can in fact help raise nearby values in certain neighborhoods.

RESOURCES

NATIONAL VACANT PROPERTIES CAMPAIGN
www.vacantproperties.org

Provides technical assistance and support to vacant land reuse programs in multiple cities. The website includes a variety of related news articles, presentations, and reports, such as "Vacant Properties: The True Costs to Communities."

NEWPORT PARTNERS LLC
www.newportpartnersllc.com

Provides analytical, technical, and market strategy services to the housing industry and public sector. Among the group's reports on housing development barriers is "Housing Impact Analysis," a guide to assessing the effects that new regulations might have on housing costs, supply, and affordability.

NONPROFIT HOUSING ASSOCIATION OF NORTHERN CALIFORNIA
www.nonprofithousing.org

Association of nonprofit developers, local governments, financial institutions, and others promoting affordable housing in the Bay Area. The association partnered with the Home Builders Association of Northern California to produce "On Common Ground: Joint Principles on Inclusionary Housing Policies."

POLICYLINK
www.policylink.org

National research institute focused on economic and social equity, including the fair distribution of affordable housing. PolicyLink has a web feature on inclusionary zoning that links to several local and state ordinances. Its report, "Shared Prosperity, Stronger Regions: An Agenda for Rebuilding America's Older Core Cities," includes a chapter on reclaiming vacant and abandoned properties.

URBAN LAND INSTITUTE
www.uli.org

Nonprofit research and education organization whose members represent the spectrum of land use and real estate development disciplines. Among ULI's numerous relevant reports is "Higher-Density Development: Myth and Fact."

US CONFERENCE OF MAYORS
www.usmayors.org

Nonpartisan organization of cities with populations of 30,000 or more. The conference recently commissioned the report, "Combating Problems of Vacant and Abandoned Properties: Best Practices in 27 Cities."

US DEPARTMENT OF HOUSING AND URBAN DEVELOPMENT
America's Affordable Communities Initiative
www.hud.gov/affordablecommunities

Provides technical assistance and model regulatory approaches to governments and housing advocates who want to reduce barriers in their communities and states. The website features links to numerous resources, including "Why Not In Our Community? Removing Barriers to Affordable Housing."

US DEPARTMENT OF HOUSING AND URBAN DEVELOPMENT
Regulatory Barriers Clearinghouse
www.regbarriers.org

Database of state and local strategies for reducing regulatory barriers to affordable housing. The Relevant Publications web page provides links to HUD-commissioned and other studies that focus on regulatory barriers.

1. Jason C. Booza, Jackie Cutsinger, and George Galster, "Where Did They Go? The Decline of Middle-Income Neighborhoods in Metropolitan America," The Brookings Institution Metropolitan Policy Program, June 2006. The study found that the proportion of metro-area families earning middle incomes fell from 28 percent in 1970 to 22 percent in 2000, while the share of all metropolitan neighborhoods that were middle income declined from 58 percent to 41 percent.

2. Edward L. Glaeser, Jenny Schuetz, and Bryce Ward, "Regulation and the Rise of Housing Prices in Greater Boston," Kennedy School of Government, Harvard University, January 5, 2006, **www.ksg.harvard.edu/rappaport/downloads/housing_regulations/regulation_housingprices.pdf**. The study looks at 187 communities within 50 miles of Boston, but not Boston itself. The report states that there were roughly 50 percent fewer housing units permitted in the 1990s than in the 1960s. Tracking the impact of lower housing densities, the authors found that as minimum lot size increases by one acre, the share of affordable homes drops by 8–20 percent.

3. See, for example, Alexander von Hoffman et al., "America's Working Communities and the Impact of Multifamily Housing," Neighborhood Reinvestment Corporation and the Joint Center for Housing Studies of Harvard University, 2004, **www.jchs.harvard.edu/publications/communitydevelopment/w04-5.pdf**; and Henry O. Pollakowski, David Ritchay, and Zoe Weinrobe, "Effects of Mixed-Income, Multi-Family Rental Housing Developments on Single-Family Housing Values," Center for Real Estate, Massachusetts Institute of Technology, April 2005, **web.mit.edu/CRE/research/hai/pdf/40B_report_HAI_0405.pdf**.

4. Manufactured homes are built at a factory and installed and assembled on site. They meet the National Manufactured Home Construction and Safety Standards (HUD code), a national preemptive code eliminating the need for certification by local inspectors. According to HUD, the homes cost 25 percent to 55 percent less to construct than site-built homes of comparable size.

5. Reggie James, Kevin Jewell, and Kathy Mitchell, "Manufactured Housing Appreciation: Stereotypes and Data," Consumers Union Southwest Regional Office, April 2003, **www.consumersunion.org/pdf/mh/Appreciation.pdf**.

6. The so-called 6-8-10 rule was adopted in the 1980s by the Oregon Commission on Land Conservation and Development. Under the rule, large cities such as Portland must have an overall density of 10 units per net developable acre. Smaller towns must achieve an average net density of six units per developable acre. Jurisdictions in the middle must reach eight units per net developable acre. It is important to note, however, that Portland does have a growth boundary that prohibits residential development outside the boundary. Thus, although Portland does a great job of allowing for different housing types within the growth boundary, some of those benefits are offset by the detrimental effects of putting so much land off limits to housing.

7. Under zero-lot line development, homes can be placed on one side of the lot to allow greater usable yard space on the site. Because each home's location is determined before subdivision approval, developers have more flexibility in site development while also assuring a single-family detached character.

8. For details on the New Hampshire Community Loan Fund program, go to **www.nhclf.org/programs/housing/mhpp/newprod_pepperidge.html**.

9. National Association of Home Builders Research Center, "Study of Subdivision Requirements as a Regulatory Barrier," draft report for HUD's Office of Policy Development and Research, forthcoming.

10. The same ordinance also requires that projects seeking parking above the by-right allowances store excess vehicles in mechanical stackers, valet facilities, or other non-independently accessible means, and that projects with more than 50 units provide free parking spaces for car-sharing companies such as Flexcar, Zipcar, and City Car Share.

11. Livable City, "Residential Parking Reform for Downtown San Francisco," **www.livablecity.org/campaigns/c3.html**.

12. For another look at parking's impact on housing, see Donald Shoup, "The High Cost of Free Parking," American Planning Association, 2005.

13. The report is expected to be published in summer 2007 and posted on HUD's website.

14. Frank S. Alexander, "Land Bank Authorities: A Guide for the Creation and Operation of Local Land Banks," Local Initiatives Support Corporation, April 2005, **www.lisc.org/content/publications/detail/793/**. The five urban land banks Alexander studied (in Atlanta, Cleveland, Flint, Louisville, and St. Louis) were created in tandem with changes to state laws that included shortening foreclosure timelines, providing more advance notice to owners and other interested parties, and making it easier for local governments to acquire properties with overdue taxes exceeding the property's value.

15. Alex Friederich, "City OKs Homes In Industrial Park," *Pioneer Press,* April 14, 2006, B6.

16. Bill Cummings, "Old Factories Eyed to Ease Housing Load," *Connecticut Post Online,* February 26, 2006.

17. Urban Land Institute, "Solving America's Shortage of Homes Working Families Can Afford: Fifteen Success Stories," March 2006, **content.knowledgeplex.org/kp2/cache/documents/154821.pdf**.

18. Builders seeking the downtown density bonus have the option of including affordable units in their projects or making a contribution to the city's Affordable Housing Opportunity Fund. The fund supports the city's New Homes for Chicago program and other initiatives.

19. An emerging issue related to inclusionary zoning is whether communities should be able to require affordable uses without providing density bonuses commensurate to the added cost. If there is true cost offset through density bonuses, inclusionary zoning can serve as an incentive for affordable housing. Without greater density allowances, however, inclusionary zoning may provide lower-cost housing for a few but also add barriers and limit growth. In fiscal 2007, HUD plans to commission a large-scale study of the effectiveness and fairness of inclusionary zoning programs.

20. Ben Forest, "New Jersey Revs Up Its Rehabs," *Planning,* August 1999.

21. Raymond J. Burby, David Salvesen, and Michael Creed, "Encouraging Residential Rehabilitation with Building Codes: New Jersey's Experience," *Journal of the American Planning Association* 72:2, Spring 2006.

22. See Nationally Applicable Recommended Rehabilitation Provisions, **www.huduser.org/publications/destech/narrp.html**.

23. Sara C. Galvan, "Rehabilitating Rehab Through State Building Codes," *Yale Law Journal* 115:7, May 2006.

24. Newport Partners, LLC, "Impact Fees and Housing Affordability: A Guidebook for Practice," draft prepared for the US Department of Housing and Urban Development, February 2006. The final report is expected in spring 2007.

25. City of Fort Collins, Community Planning and Environmental Services Advance Planning Department, 2005 Affordable Communities Awards Application.

26. Thirty percent of housing developed or rehabilitated by the redevelopment agency itself and 15 percent of housing developed or rehabilitated by private entities must be offered at affordable costs. The obligation may be met on a project-by-project basis or in the aggregate over a 10-year period.

27. The density bonus must be at least 25 percent for housing developers that set aside at least 20 percent of units for low-income households, 10 percent of units for very low-income households, or 50 percent of units for seniors. The state law also requires additional incentives for these developers, such as reduced parking requirements, reduced setbacks, and fee waivers.

28. State laws have not, however, achieved as much as anticipated, given that local governments have used design and material restrictions to keep out manufactured homes.

29. Fannie Mae provides state-specific requirements for titling manufactured housing as real property at **www.efanniemae.com/sf/guides/ssg/relatedsellinginfo/manufachousing/index.jsp?from=hp.**

30. HUD's Regulatory Barriers Clearinghouse, **www.huduser.org/rbc/search/rbcdetails.asp?DocId=38**.

31. The SHIP program was created when the state passed a law allocating a portion of the documentary stamp tax to affordable housing. About two-thirds of the revenues go to SHIP, which distributes funds to local governments to develop and implement local affordable housing strategies.

Black Foster Father Asserts Equal Right To Housing Choice

Those who say housing discrimination no longer exists should consider the case of Harold Adams III, an African-American foster parent who rented an apartment in Largo, Florida. In April 2004, Adams filed a fair housing complaint with the Pinellas County Office of Human Rights, claiming that he was charged higher rent than other tenants because he had two foster children residing with him. The complaint also alleged that the landlord refused to make requested repairs on his unit while making repairs to apartments occupied by white tenants. And, after vacating the apartment, Adams was unable to obtain his security deposit.

The office of human rights launched an investigation that included witness statements that the landlord made derogatory statements about Adams, using a common racial epithet. After subsequent efforts to reach a settlement between the parties failed, the human rights agency contacted the county attorney's office. A lawsuit was filed, and both the investigator from the office of human rights and the professional who had attempted mediation testified.

The jury found in favor of Mr. Adams and awarded him $450 for out-of-pocket expenses and $2,000 in punitive damages. Justice was served and the message was sent—it is unacceptable to discriminate in housing on the basis of race or family status.

ON FAIR AND EQUAL TERMS

Protecting Housing Choice And Opportunity

8

Not all Americans enjoy the same opportunity to live where they choose. Although federal, state, and local fair housing laws have significantly changed housing market practices,[1] deeply rooted patterns of discrimination remain.

A recent National Urban League report found that black wealth significantly lags white wealth, with much of the disparity traceable to racial segregation in housing.[2] The report argues that many black middle-class homeowners live in communities that are overwhelmingly black, where poverty rates are higher, and where amenities and services are lower than in white neighborhoods. As a result, blacks have less opportunity to build equity in their homes and create wealth.

Minorities are more affected by the "jobs-housing mismatch"—the disparity between where jobs are being created and where housing is affordable to low- to moderate-income families. In a comparison of the racial composition of the Chicago region's high-opportunity areas (with good-quality schools, access to jobs, and other benefits) with low-opportunity areas, just three percent of households in high-opportunity areas were African-American. Between 1995 and 2000, the highest-opportunity communities created 34 times as many jobs as the lowest-opportunity communities.[3]

"Segregation in our neighborhoods and communities weakens the overall infrastructure, results in a drain on the tax base, and minimizes the capacity of local officials to provide essential services to their community," notes the National Fair Housing Alliance in its 2006 Fair Housing Trends report.[4] Georgetown University law professor Sheryll Cashin issues an even more forceful warning in her book, *The Failures of Integration: How Race and Class Are Undermining the American Dream:* "The majority-minority America that is to come cannot prosper with a system of public education that relegates most minority public school children to schools disadvantaged by high degrees of poverty and often inadequate resources."

Segregation is too costly to ignore. State and local governments must step up and speak out, leading the challenge against patterns of segregation that repeat unless checked. Local governments must create and strengthen the public and private agencies that are the backbone of the fair housing enforcement system. Local and state civil rights commissions that investigate cases need adequate and ongoing financial support from the local general fund to keep up with caseloads and train staff to take on complex investigations. The local fair housing enforcement system also consists of a number of critical nongovernmental organizations that are key players in raising public awareness through outreach and education.

No community can ensure fair housing through litigation alone. Significant, systemic change will occur only by educating citizens and enlisting real estate industry partners as advocates for fair housing. Finally, local and state governments must make fair housing principles of poverty deconcentration and racial integration a part of ordinary operations. This includes ensuring that staff and grant recipients comply with fair housing laws, that subsidy policies do not concentrate low-income housing in high-poverty, high-minority neighborhoods, and that zoning laws and practices do not discriminate against minorities or people with disabilities.

RECOMMENDATIONS FOR STATE AND LOCAL ACTION

1 Strengthen Enforcement by Enacting or Broadening Fair Housing Laws

The Fair Housing Act prohibits housing discrimination based on race, color, religion, national origin, sex, disability, or familial status (having or anticipating having children in the household under age 18). People protected against discrimination by the fair housing laws belong to a "protected class." The laws apply to practically all housing-related transactions, including applying for a mortgage, being shown for-sale homes, applying for rental housing, and policies for tenant conduct.

Several other federal laws relate to fair housing, particularly for units funded with federal assistance and with enforcement by HUD's Office of Fair Housing and Equal Opportunity.[5] Together, these laws prohibit taking any of the following actions against someone in a protected class solely because that person is a member of that class:

- Refusing to rent, sell, or negotiate for housing.

- Falsely denying that housing is available for inspection, sale, or rental.

- Making housing unavailable or setting different terms, conditions, or privileges for sale or rental.

- Providing different housing services or facilities (such as having policies that make families with children unwelcome).

- Denying anyone access to or membership in a facility or service related to the sale or rental of housing.

- Refusing to make a mortgage loan or provide information on a loan.

- Imposing different terms on mortgage loans such as higher interest rates or points and fees.

- Advertising or making any statements indicating a preference based on race, color, national origin, religion, sex, familial status, or disability.

In addition, there are fair housing and disability laws that protect people with disabilities. Under the Fair Housing Act, it is illegal to refuse to adjust rules that inhibit people with disabilities from using their housing successfully (to make reasonable accommodations) or refuse to allow people with disabilities to make their housing physically accessible (reasonable modifications at a cost to the resident). The act requires that all buildings with four or more units designed and constructed for first occupancy after March 13, 1991 meet certain requirements.[6] In addition, all housing funded in whole or in part by federal funds must meet certain design standards.[7] The property owner must pay for any reasonable accommodations and reasonable modifications.

At the behest of Congress, the US Department of Housing and Urban Development is charged with enforcing the Fair Housing Act and its implementing regulations. People who believe that they have experienced housing discrimination may file a complaint in person at a local HUD office, by telephone, online, or through the mail. But HUD cannot single-handedly ensure fair housing. State and local ordinances that are substantially equivalent to the Fair Housing Act allow jurisdictions to enforce fair housing in the same manner as the federal government. Thirty-six states as well as Washington, DC have substantially equivalent laws to the Fair Housing Act. Local civil rights commissions operating in states with these laws can enter into worksharing agreements with HUD. This puts "more cops on the beat" and allows for quicker investigation and punishment of violators. In addition, victims can go to state courts for redress, which is much less expensive than going to federal court.

States and localities that do not have such a law should enact one. States and localities that do have these laws should consider broadening their reach by adding protected classes or limiting exemptions.

▼ CASES IN POINT

California Expands Protected Classes, Covers More Housing

California is one of several jurisdictions to add sexual orientation to its categories of protected classes. State code also includes source of income as a protected class and covers a wider range of housing providers. While both federal and state laws exempt small housing providers,[8] California defines "small provider" more narrowly as single-family residences that rent rooms to one person.

"Source of Income" Protections May Target Hidden Discrimination

Source of income provisions make it illegal to reject prospective tenants solely because they receive public assistance. Adding source of income as a protected class helps to enhance the effectiveness of rental subsidy programs, particularly those with mobility components that seek to desegregate subsidized renters.

Adding source of income may also help prevent more hidden forms of discrimination. According to some fair housing advocates, discrimination based on income such as welfare or disability may reflect a desire to exclude minorities, people with children, or people with disabilities. Jurisdictions with some form of source of income laws include

Chicago, Los Angeles, Montgomery County (Maryland), and San Francisco. More than a dozen states have such provisions, including California, Maine, Oregon, and Utah.[9]

2 Create and Strengthen Local Fair Housing Agencies

Local governments must create and strengthen the public and private agencies that are the backbone of the enforcement system. Most states and some localities have human rights commissions or other public agencies charged with enforcing civil rights laws. Under the Fair Housing Assistance Program, HUD provides funding to these state and local agencies to further fair housing within their jurisdictions.

Research has shown that local and state civil rights commissions can often process and investigate cases more effectively and win bigger settlements than HUD, in part because they are closer to the community. But to do so, the agencies need adequate and ongoing support from the local general fund. Although HUD provides startup funding and supplemental grants for education and other activities, local funds must support enough investigators to keep up with caseloads and train staff to take on complex investigations. Political support from local leaders is also crucial. Local leaders must set the clear expectation that the agency's mission is to pursue justice.

Governments should monitor the performance of their civil rights commissions to ensure that they resolve cases in a timely manner and litigate when necessary. A review of agency performance should include a comparison of complaints filed with those in cities of similar size and demographics as well as with national standards. The reviews should also look at whether the conciliation agreements or settlements lead to changes in policies and practices, as well as to proactive steps such as expanding community reinvestment or housing opportunities and providing affirmative, class-action, and monetary relief when applicable.

The local fair housing enforcement system consists of a number of critical nongovernmental organizations—nonprofit fair housing councils, legal aid societies, university task forces, private attorneys, and protection and advocacy agencies that serve people with disabilities and receive federal funds.[10] Roughly 100 of the private, nonprofit fair housing organizations receive some funding under HUD's Fair Housing Initiatives Program.

Local and state governments should commit CDBG funds and other resources to these private fair housing organizations, perhaps by sponsoring a testing program to uncover the extent and nature of housing discrimination.[11] While HUD and public fair housing agencies are required to pursue conciliation where possible and remain neutral, private fair housing groups may act as advocates for complainants. By sending testers out into the field, private groups have exposed such practices as racial "steering" by real estate agents or discrimination against minority rental applicants. Testing can aid enforcement by providing corroborative evidence in cases that otherwise amount to one person's word against another's. There are many examples of private fair housing groups uncovering egregious violations of fair housing laws that were damaging entire communities by eroding the tax base or leading to poor school performance and other effects of segregation.[12]

Enforcement is strongest when a full-service private fair housing center and government human rights commission work together.

Top Performers in Ohio and Florida Partner, Have Strong Mediation Programs

To improve the effectiveness of their human or civil rights commissions, public leaders should look to states and localities with strong programs. Among the leaders is the Ohio Civil Rights Commission, which handled 540 housing cases in 2005. Agency leaders attribute their success in part to strong committed leadership within the regional offices, as well as to investigators who specialize only in housing rather than handle the whole range of civil rights cases. In addition, the state has historically had strong local private fair housing organizations with which to partner. Moreover, the agency has an excellent mediation program that resolves 70 percent of cases.

The Pinellas, Florida County Office of Human Rights has also been cited as a local leader. The office handles 50–60 cases a year. About 10 percent result in findings of cause, compared with 2–3 percent nationwide. The agency credits its success to partnerships with other local education and enforcement agencies, a solid mediation program, and strong financial support from local government, which allocates more than $1 million annually to agency operations.

Testing Partner Boosts Milwaukee Enforcement Performance

In the early 1980s, Wisconsin's enforcement agency—the Equal Rights Division of the Department of Workforce Development—entered into a worksharing agreement with the Metropolitan Milwaukee Fair Housing Council that significantly boosted performance. Under the agreement, the state agency referred cases of alleged discrimination in the fair housing council's region to the council for investigation through testing. The state agency provided funds for the testing and used the results to determine probable cause, i.e., whether the alleged victim could pursue redress through the administrative or legal system.

Before the state agency incorporated testing as part of enforcement, 19 percent of cases resulted in findings of probable cause. After incorporating testing, the incidence of such findings increased to over 85 percent of cases. Attesting to the value of such services, the State of Wisconsin has provided financial support to the Metropolitan Milwaukee Fair Housing Council for most of the past 24 years. The council also receives CDBG allotments from multiple cities and counties.

Fair Housing Groups Build Capacity to Investigate Discriminatory Lending

Discriminatory lending practices tend to get short shrift in the private enforcement system because few HUD offices or fair housing agencies have the resources to focus on this very complex issue. A few private fair housing groups have, however, developed the in-house capacity to investigate mortgage lending practices. In communities where unfair lending is an issue, local leaders should hire fair housing groups or engage universities to look at lending patterns in Home Mortgage Disclosure Act (HMDA) data, to be followed by testing. Although they cannot prove discrimination, HMDA statistics can reveal occurrences of redlining (intentionally withholding services from certain neighborhoods) or reverse redlining (targeting certain neighborhoods with certain practices or products such as high-cost loans).

3 Educate Renters and Homebuyers on Their Legal Rights And Remedies

Many people who experience discrimination either do not recognize it or do nothing about it because they do not know where to turn. Victims of discrimination may also fail to act because they feel they will not be supported. In addition to ensuring that the fair housing groups they fund conduct outreach and training, public leaders should support educational campaigns in partnership with state associations of Realtors®, property management groups, and other real estate industry organizations.

If city, county, and state homebuyer programs incorporate fair housing training, they would go far to ensure fair housing. For example, a person who uses a wheelchair and participates in a publicly funded homebuyer program would be able to identify violations when househunting. In particular, he or she would know that a new condominium development must have an accessible first floor. Similarly, an African-American who has participated in the program might be suspicious when an owner announces that a home that he or she has an appointment to see has suddenly been taken off the market.

▼ CASE IN POINT

Partnership Develops Campaign Ready-Made for Local Markets

The Leadership Conference on Civil Rights Education Fund, National Fair Housing Alliance, Ad Council, and HUD have partnered on a nationwide awareness campaign featuring radio and television public service announcements, posters, and print ads in multiple languages. The ads target people most likely to run into problems when they rent or buy property or apply for a mortgage. The spots close with the tagline, "Fair Housing. It's not an option. It's the law." and direct people to call a toll-free hotline or visit **www.fairhousinglaw.org**. Organizations can ask their local radio and television stations to run the ads.[13] State and local governments can customize a national spot by adding an endorsement from the mayor or governor at the end of the message.

4 Partner with the Real Estate Industry to Promote Fair Housing

Recent research, together with some high-profile lawsuit settlements, suggests that landlords and real estate agents need ongoing education about fair housing laws. According to a recent report by the National Fair Housing Alliance (NFHA), real estate brokers still steer black and Hispanic homebuyers away from white neighborhoods and white buyers away from minority neighborhoods.[14]

Discrimination against renters is even more of a problem. The NFHA report lists various forms of rental discrimination, including denial of available units; refusal to make a reasonable accommodation for a disabled individual; higher rents or security deposits for minorities and individuals in other protected classes; segregation of African-Americans, Latinos, and Asian-Americans; segregation of families with children to certain parts of a building or complex; restriction of access to rental property amenities such as swimming pools or community rooms; and initiation of eviction proceedings against white tenants who have African-American, Latino, or Asian-American visitors.

Landlords appear particularly in need of training on disability access requirements. Most of the complaints filed at HUD and Fair Housing Assistance Program agencies involve disability discrimination, which has now surpassed race discrimination as the most common allegation.[15]

Failure to make reasonable accommodation to disabled tenants has cost property owners across the country anywhere from thousands to millions of dollars. In 2005, California's Department of Fair Employment and Housing won a $1 million disability discrimination settlement against a San Francisco landlord who refused a tenant's request for an accessible parking space.

No local leaders should want businesses in their jurisdictions to run afoul of fair housing laws. Unfortunately, very few hotline resources exist for landlords who have questions on civil rights or landlord/tenant laws. In addition, landlords who don't belong to rental property owner associations do not have access to comprehensive printed information. Landlords and managers operating in communities without licensing requirements do not have to attend fair housing training.

Real estate brokers, real estate management companies, and other members of the housing industry should be required to maintain written rental and sales policies that conform to fair housing laws as a condition for an operating license. Licensing requirements should also include demonstrated knowledge of fair housing laws. Alabama, California, the District of Columbia, Georgia, Maine, Massachusetts, and Missouri require that applicants for a real estate license undergo training. Some states have also approved fair housing courses for continuing education credit.

Local leaders should partner with rental industry groups to sponsor fair housing training or education campaigns, encourage real estate agencies to hire minority and bilingual agents, and advocate for affirmative marketing programs that encourage minority households to move to desirable areas where they are underrepresented.

▼ CASES IN POINT

Milwaukee Training Reaches Over 16,000 Landlords

Between 1993 and mid-2006, the Milwaukee Department of Neighborhood Services trained more than 16,000 landlords, representing close to 270,000 housing units. The CDBG-funded program, originally intended to teach landlords how to keep illegal activities out of their properties, now encompasses training in bookkeeping, maintenance, building codes, and fair housing.[16] Free sessions in English, Spanish, and Hmong are held twice a month at various locations around the city. Training videos and DVDs are also available at public libraries.

About a dozen banks require that people who obtain mortgages for income properties participate in the training. Property owners who receive rehabilitation money from the city or first-time homebuyer assistance for purchasing duplexes are also required to attend. In addition, large property management companies send their staff to the trainings. The Metropolitan Milwaukee Fair Housing Council provides the fair housing component of the sessions. The council also provides training under contracts with private management companies.

Virginia Program Certifies Fair Housing Knowledge

Virginia's Fair Housing Board, which is responsible for enforcing fair housing laws, administers a certification program for individuals involved in selling or renting dwellings. The state established the program in 2003 to provide property managers, property management companies, and small landlords a way to demonstrate their knowledge of fair housing. The two-hour course is offered free of charge to any company willing to host the session. Certificate applicants do, however, pay a $25 fee. The course meets continuing education requirements for real estate licensees.

To make the classes readily accessible, the Fair Housing Board partners with the Richmond Apartment Management Association to host the course at RAMA offices every month. The arrangement provides the multifamily housing industry a regularly offered fair housing course for training new hires. Since the partnership was launched in spring 2005, the courses have consistently sold out. As of April 2006, 1,899 individuals had obtained Fair Housing Board certification.

Michigan Partnership Conducts Tests for Realtors®

A partnership among the Michigan Association of Realtors®, Michigan Department of Civil Rights, and the state's fair housing centers seeks to address discriminatory real estate practices by testing one out of every 10 Realtors® between 2007 and 2011. Under the agreement, the fair housing centers conduct the tests. While the centers cannot use the test results to file a complaint, the Michigan Association of Realtors® pledges to take appropriate action against any real estate professionals failing the tests. The contract allows the fair housing groups to pursue complaints that come in during the testing period. The partners are designing a formal training program eligible for continuing education credits. The National Association of Realtors® hopes the partnership will serve as a national model.

Partnerships Introduce Toledo Real Estate Agents to Inner-City Neighborhoods

The Toledo Fair Housing Center partners with the city, a local community development corporation, and the Toledo Board of Realtors® to offer an annual tour to increase agents' familiarity with inner-city neighborhoods. In addition, the Toledo and Columbus boards of realtors have adopted a Certified Affordable Housing Realtor® program to recognize realtors who commit their time and obtain experience working in the affordable housing market. To qualify for certification, participants must sell a certain number of affordable housing units per year.

5 Help Builders and Developers Comply with Accessibility Requirements

Many local officials and real estate development professionals apparently do not understand or are unaware of the Fair Housing Act's design and construction requirements. In the last several years, regional and national apartment developers have spent millions of dollars to settle lawsuits alleging violations of federal accessibility requirements.

In some jurisdictions, it is far too easy for inspectors to approve projects that fail to meet accessibility standards. Designers, architects, builders, and developers often blame one another if violations are found. To ensure a more seamless compliance process, states and localities should adopt a standard that requires at least as much accessibility as one of the eight standards HUD recognizes as "safe harbors." A safe harbor document is a manual or code that meets or exceeds the requirements in the Fair Housing Act. Builders in compliance with a safe harbor document are therefore automatically in compliance with the Fair Housing Act.

Local and state governments should consider partnering with real estate industry groups to sponsor training on design and construction requirements for builders working in their jurisdictions. Fair Housing Accessibility FIRST is a HUD initiative to promote compliance with requirements for multifamily housing. The program conducts workshops for all members of the design community, provides training modules online for reference and download, and operates a toll-free information line for technical guidance and support. As of May 2006, the program had trained over 6,000 people who were constructing, or advising clients on the construction of, more than 750,000 accessible units.[17]

The International Code Council and United Spinal Association also provide free workshops on FHA accessible design features and how the FHA and the International Building Code work together.[18]

6 Ensure that Government Housing Programs Promote Integration

Under the implementation regulations of the Fair Housing Act, state and local agencies must "affirmatively further fair housing" in their administration of HUD programs and the Low-Income Housing Tax Credit program.[19] This requirement extends beyond enforcing compliance with fair housing laws to ensuring that subsidy policies do not concentrate low-income housing in neighborhoods with large minority or poor populations.

The placement of federally funded housing can make a big difference in patterns of segregation. In many communities, affordable housing and assisted housing projects serve primarily minorities or people with disabilities. Communities that do a good job of creating new affordable housing but do not pay attention to its location may simply perpetuate segregation.

Local officials should provide more integrated housing for people with disabilities by using local trust fund dollars or tax-credit programs to set aside units for people with disabilities in new multifamily complexes, using CDBG or HOME dollars for additional support or housing subsidies. Congregate housing precludes opportunities for community integration and economic self-sufficiency.[20]

Jurisdictions should also enlist fair housing centers in conducting training for legal staff, housing inspectors, zoning and planning departments, assisted housing staff, homeless programs, police departments, and community and economic development agencies. Alternatively, they can send key staff members to law school clinics or national trainings. For example, the City of Milwaukee has its housing authority and Section 8 staff trained by the Metropolitan Milwaukee Fair Housing Council on fair housing law provisions and remedies available to their clients.

▼ CASES IN POINT

Boston Requires Developers to Affirmatively Market Projects

Boston administers an Affirmative Fair Housing Marketing Program that promotes equal access to government-assisted and inclusionary housing. Developers of projects with five or more units must prepare plans detailing how they intend to affirmatively market the units. The plans include outreach through newspapers and multilingual services to households with certain demographic characteristics who, given the project's location, would be least likely to apply for the housing. Plans are reviewed to ensure that the selection process does not unduly disadvantage any demographic group. During Boston's first Leading the Way affordable housing plan, the Boston Fair Housing Commission reviewed and monitored 100 affirmative marketing plans. It also provided low- and moderate-income families information about housing opportunities in more than 100 communities via the Metropolitan Housing Opportunity Clearing Center.

Boston, Chicago Require High Accessibility in City-Assisted Projects

As part of their affordable housing production campaigns, both Boston and Chicago have adopted aggressive standards for city-assisted single-family and multifamily construction and rehabilitation projects. Boston strives to incorporate universal design in all of its programs. Chicago requires all two-flats and 40 percent of single-family homes to have one-step entry.

City/County Partnership Fosters Integrated Housing for Disabled People

The Community Residential Siting Program—operated by a partnership of Portland, Gresham, and Multnomah County, Oregon—demonstrates best practices in fostering integration. The program provides citizens, neighborhood associations, social service providers, and service recipients information related to the siting of special needs housing, which includes 24-hour on-site services for adults and children requiring assistance or supervision. Program staff and volunteer mediators facilitate resolution of specific issues arising before, during, and after the siting process, as well as offer community relations services such as education and information.[21]

Portland's program radically revised regulations, procedures, philosophies, and public attitudes about siting of mass shelters for the homeless, transitional housing, and longer-term housing for those with special needs. Where previous regulations discriminated against people because of their conditions or ability to pay, the new regulations increase housing options, neighborhood diversity, and equity. The new regulations also allow all types of housing—including mass shelters—by right in some zones.

Rigorous Standards Set for Ohio Entitlement Communities

Ohio requires that all jurisdictions receiving CDBG and HOME funds through the state operate a fair housing program that meets or exceeds a rigorous standard. The Ohio Department of Development's Office of Housing and Community Partnerships administers the program, which applies to approximately 80 counties and 60 small cities. Each community must have a general information contact for residents to call regarding fair housing issues, a fair housing complaint intake and referral system, and education and outreach on fair housing rights. Fair housing materials must be available in at least 10 different locations, and presentations must be made to residents of CDBG and HOME target areas, as well as school classes and civics groups. Non-entitlement communities must also conduct an impediments analysis.[22]

7 Analyze and Address Impediments to Fair Housing Choice

Jurisdictions that receive $50,000 or more in CDBG funds are required, as part of their consolidated plan, to complete an Analysis of Impediments to Fair Housing Choice. An impediment to fair housing is anything that may hinder or prevent a person from having equal access to housing because of membership in a protected class under fair housing laws. An effective analysis includes a comprehensive review of laws, regulations, administrative policies, housing market conditions, and housing practices to determine how they affect the location, availability, and accessibility of housing.[23]

Such an analysis should seek to uncover whether some market players are perpetuating segregation in a way that erodes the tax base. The review should serve as a starting point to design a comprehensive strategy to eliminate factors that impede fair access to housing. An effective fair housing plan should also include benchmarks that the community can use to measure its progress.

---

8 Provide for More Equitable Patterns of Development

Jurisdictions must ensure that zoning laws and practices do not adversely affect protected classes under fair housing laws. Under the theory of "disparate impact," housing providers and civil rights groups have successfully sued local governments for land use laws or decisions that do not appear discriminatory but are found to disproportionately affect members of a protected class. Such a case might occur if a community denies an affordable housing developer a zoning variance similar to those provided to market-rate developers. If a disproportionate share of the community's African-American or Hispanic residents live in affordable housing, the denial could be challenged on the grounds that it effectively limits housing opportunities for minority households.

Disability rights advocates have successfully challenged city ordinances that prohibit group homes from operating within a certain distance of one another. Similarly, a density requirement that effectively prohibits new affordable housing projects could also be found unconstitutional.

Land use policies vulnerable to such "disparate impact" challenges include limits on units per acre or number of units; prohibition of multifamily housing, tax-credit housing, or Section 8 housing; mandated design and other criteria that result in extremely high per-unit costs; and a limit of four unrelated adults in each unit.[24] Jurisdictions should also revise potentially discriminatory zoning ordinances regarding group homes for people with disabilities.

Civil rights advocates have used fair housing laws to challenge municipal housing and zoning laws that they consider discriminatory. The US Department of Justice has authority to challenge discriminatory land use practices.[25]

Local and state governments should also support public awareness campaigns on the importance of affordable and workforce housing.[26] A campaign might include information countering widely held myths and provide images of well-designed affordable housing projects[27] and of the range of people who live in such housing. Housing Minnesota and Housing Illinois have led highly regarded public awareness campaigns. Homes for Working Families, Inc., based in Washington, DC, also seeks to change outdated perceptions of workforce housing in part by creating new communications strategies through local coalitions.

9 Monitor Tax-Credit Properties for Discriminatory Practices

Given their relationships with developers and lenders, state housing finance agencies have a special role to play in ensuring fair housing. They must carefully evaluate whether the people they do business with meet fair housing requirements. In particular, state housing finance agencies must closely monitor tax credit properties for discriminatory practices and assess the effects of tax-credit allocation policies on racial concentration.

The Poverty & Race Research Action Council and the Lawyers Committee for Civil Rights have published a guide on best practices in administration of the Low-Income Housing Tax Credit program.[28] The guide highlights state allocation policies that favor developments proposed for high-opportunity areas, limit the authority of local jurisdictions to veto projects, encourage outreach and supportive services to those with the lowest incomes and the disabled, and encourage the construction of units suitable for large and extended families.

For example, North Carolina's Qualified Allocation Plan prohibits siting projects in areas with a high concentration of minorities and low-income households. In addition to provisions ensuring access to LIHTC units by Section 8 voucher holders, North Carolina's plan gives extra points to applicants that pledge to serve people on waiting lists for public housing.

Texas requires developers receiving tax credits to affirmatively market their units to promote integration. Several states require developers receiving tax credits to affirmatively market the units to low-income households. A few states also require reporting of racial composition of residents in tax-credit projects.

State housing finance agencies can take additional steps to further fair housing. For example, in the 1990s the Wisconsin Housing and Economic Development Authority awarded $1 million in low-income tax credits to the Metropolitan Milwaukee Fair Housing Council to develop five affordable housing complexes in low-poverty suburban communities.

RESOURCES

BUILDING BETTER COMMUNITIES NETWORK
www.bettercommunities.org

Web-based clearinghouse and communication forum dedicated to building inclusive communities and successfully siting affordable housing and community services. The success stories page links to examples of what local governments are doing to promote fair housing. Michael Allen, former co-director, outlines specific steps for local planning commissioners in "Why Not in Our Back Yard?"

FAIR HOUSING ACCESSIBILITY FIRST
www.fairhousingfirst.org

Website sponsored by the US Department of Housing and Urban Development offering extensive resources that include a list of common violations of the Fair Housing Act design and construction requirements and links to HUD-certified "safe harbors" for compliance.

HOMES FOR WORKING FAMILIES
www.homesforworkingfamilies.org

Nonprofit, charitable organization that seeks to increase the availability of quality homes within reach of America's working families. The organization spotlights policies and programs that help meet the need for workforce housing.

HOUSING ALLIANCE OF PENNSYLVANIA
www.housingalliancepa.org

Statewide membership organization that seeks to ensure housing for all Pennsylvanians through policy work, research, and education.

INTERNATIONAL CODE COUNCIL
www.iccsafe.org

Membership association that develops the codes used to construct residential and commercial buildings, including homes and schools. ICC's website features an array of fact sheets about the codes, standards, and laws that address accessibility.

LAWYERS' COMMITTEE FOR CIVIL RIGHTS UNDER LAW
www.lawyerscomm.org

Nonpartisan, nonprofit organization that involves the private bar in providing legal services to address racial discrimination. The committee and its affiliates have been key players in numerous housing discrimination cases.

LEADERSHIP CONFERENCE ON CIVIL RIGHTS
www.civilrights.org

Coalition that has coordinated the national legislative campaign on behalf of every major civil rights law since 1957. Its education and research arm, the Leadership Conference on Civil Rights Education Fund, sponsors a website providing links to federal fair housing laws and other resources.

NATIONAL ACCESSIBLE APARTMENT CLEARINGHOUSE
www.accessibleapartments.org

National database of accessible apartments, cosponsored by the National Apartment Association, the Multi Family Housing Council, and the Virginia Housing Development Authority.

NATIONAL ASSOCIATION OF REALTORS®
www.realtor.org

Offers a comprehensive training program on diversity, an orientation program on fair housing laws and regulations, and a grant program that works to extend the benefits of homeownership to more Americans.

NATIONAL COUNCIL ON INDEPENDENT LIVING
www.ncil.org

Membership organization that advances independent living and the rights of people with disabilities through consumer-driven advocacy.

NATIONAL FAIR HOUSING ADVOCATE ONLINE
www.fairhousing.com

Website operated by the Tennessee Fair Housing Council featuring news items and links to legal research, discussion forums, and other resources.

NATIONAL FAIR HOUSING ALLIANCE
www.nationalfairhousing.org

Consortium of nonprofit fair housing organizations, state and local civil rights agencies, and individuals throughout the US. Through education, advocacy, and enforcement programs, NFHA provides equal access to apartments, houses, mortgage loans, and insurance policies. The website includes many resources for state and local leaders seeking to enhance fair housing, such as the "2006 Fair Housing Trends Report: Unequal Opportunity—Perpetuating Housing Segregation in America."

RESOURCES

NATIONAL HOUSING LAW PROJECT
www.nhlp.org

Housing law and advocacy center providing legal assistance, advocacy advice, and housing expertise to legal services and other attorneys, low-income housing advocacy groups, and others who serve the poor. NHLP monitors jurisdictions with laws prohibiting housing discrimination based on source of income.

NATIONAL MULTI HOUSING COUNCIL
www.nmhc.org

Represents the interests of the nation's largest multifamily rental housing development and management firms. With the National Apartment Association, the NMHC published a guide for members, "Understanding Your Obligations: Accessibility Under the Fair Housing and Americans With Disabilities Acts."

NATIONAL URBAN LEAGUE
www.nul.org

Nation's oldest and largest community-based movement devoted to empowering African-Americans to enter the economic and social mainstream. NUL publishes an annual report, "The State of Black America," examining black progress in education, homeownership, entrepreneurship, health, and other areas.

POVERTY & RACE RESEARCH ACTION COUNCIL
www.prrac.org

Civil rights policy organization that helps connect social scientists with advocates working on race and poverty issues, and to promote a research-based advocacy strategy on issues of structural racial inequality.

URBAN INSTITUTE
www.urbaninstitute.org

National research and public policy organization. Among its reports on fair housing are "Discrimination in Metropolitan Housing Markets: National Results from Phase I HDS 2000" and "Discrimination Against Persons With Disabilities: Barriers at Every Step."

US DEPARTMENT OF HOUSING AND URBAN DEVELOPMENT
Office of Fair Housing and Equal Opportunity
www.hud.gov/offices/fheo

Enforces federal fair housing laws and administers the Fair Housing Assistance and Fair Housing Initiatives Programs. The office publishes "The State of Fair Housing: Annual Report on Fair Housing."

RESOURCES

ENDNOTES CHAPTER 8

1. Margery Austin Turner et al., "Discrimination in Metropolitan Housing Markets: National Results from Phase I HDS 2000," Urban Institute, November 2002. The third national paired-testing study sponsored by HUD to measure patterns of racial and ethnic discrimination in urban housing markets found that "The nation is making real progress in combating housing market discrimination. New estimates...indicate that while discrimination persists against African Americans and Hispanics searching for homes in major metropolitan areas, its incidence has generally declined since 1989."

2. National Urban League, "The State of Black America 2006: The Opportunity Compact," March 2006.

3. Leadership Council for Metropolitan Open Communities, "The Segregation of Opportunities: The Structure of Advantage and Disadvantage in the Chicago Region," May 2005, **www.irpumn.org/uls/resources/**.

4. National Fair Housing Alliance, "Unequal Opportunity—Perpetuating Housing Segregation in America," April 5, 2006, **www.nationalfairhousing.org/resources/**.

5. Section 109 of the Housing and Community Development Act of 1974, as amended, prohibits discrimination in activities funded by HUD, such as CDBG. The Age Discrimination Act of 1975 makes it illegal to discriminate based on age in programs or activities receiving federal financial assistance.

6. Specifically, all dwelling units in buildings containing four or more units with one or more elevators, and all ground floor units in buildings containing four or more units without an elevator, must be accessible to and usable by people with disabilities, meeting seven requirements: public and common areas must be accessible to people with disabilities, and doors and hallways must be wide enough for wheelchairs; all units must have an accessible route into and through the unit; light switches, electrical outlets, thermostats and other environmental controls must be accessible; bathroom walls must be reinforced to allow installation of grab bars; and kitchens and bathrooms must be usable by people in wheelchairs.

7. Under Section 504 of the 1973 Rehabilitation Act, buildings are required to have a certain number of accessible units, based on percentages. Units must meet a higher level of accessibility than required under the Fair Housing Act. For example, Fair Housing Act units must have walls strong enough to install grab bars; Section 504 requires grab bars. Under HUD implementing regulations, however, Section 504 does not apply to landlords who accept tenants with Section 8 rental vouchers.

8. Under federal law, owner-occupants of multifamily housing with four or fewer units are exempt.

9. National Housing Law Project, "Source of Income Protections in the US," 2005. While most such statutes seek to protect Section 8 voucher holders from discrimination, some are unclear about their coverage or have been challenged on the scope of their protection. For an updated list of jurisdictions with source of income statutes, see "State, Local, and Federal Statutes Against Source of Income Discrimination," **www.prrac.org/pdf/Source_of_Income_Summary.pdf**.

10. For a list of Fair Housing Assistance Programs and private fair housing enforcement groups, see **www.fairhousing.com/index.cfm?method=agency.search**. For a list of federally funded legal services groups, see **www.rin.lsc.gov/scripts/LSC/PD/PDList7.asp**. For a list of protection and advocacy agencies, see **www.ndrn.org/aboutus/PA_CAP.htm**.

11. Testing programs send investigators disguised as potential renters or buyers to landlords and real estate agents. Testing is a very effective tool for enforcing, detecting, and documenting discrimination in local housing markets. Cases often come down to the complainant's word against the alleged violator's, and testing can provide the evidence that breaks the tie.

12. As one example, Housing Opportunities Made Equal of Richmond, Virginia settled a lawsuit in 2000 alleging that Nationwide Insurance Company had redlined the city by refusing to underwrite homeowner insurance within city limits while underwriting insurance just outside the perimeter for comparable homes. The settlement required the company to change its underwriting guidelines. Once-blighted city neighborhoods are now thriving in part because of the more competitive homeowners' insurance market. Nationwide is now credited with some of the best industry practices, and the precedent-setting lawsuit helped make quality homeowner insurance available in urban areas throughout the country.

13. For more information on campaign materials, go to www.fairhousinglaw.org/the_campaign/index.html.

14. NFHA, "2006 Fair Housing Trends Report." Over three years, the alliance sent teams of testers posing as homebuyers to contact 73 real estate sales offices in 12 metropolitan areas. Almost 20 percent of the time, African-American and Latino testers were refused appointments or offered very limited service, the report said. Testers who were given the opportunity to see homes were steered to neighborhoods on the basis of race and/or national origin 87 percent of the time. Furthermore, the testers noted such practices as using comments about the quality of schools as a proxy for the racial composition of a neighborhood.

15. Office of Fair Housing and Equal Opportunity, "The State of Fair Housing: FY 2005 Annual Report on Fair Housing," www.hud.gov/offices/fheo/library/FY2005_Annual_Report.pdf. According to the report, disability discrimination accounted for about 41 percent of complaints.

16. John Campbell of Campbell DeLong Resources, Inc. developed the Landlord Training Program for the Portland, Oregon Police Bureau in 1989, with funding from the US Justice Department's Bureau of Justice Assistance. Since then, over 400 agencies nationwide and in Canada have adapted the program materials. For more information, go to www.cdri.com/cp_index.htm.

17. While the program offers a limited number of trainer-led conferences each year, all materials are available on the web at www.fairhousingfirst.org/index.asp.

18. The 2003 International Building Code is a HUD "safe harbor" document. Workshop dates are posted at www.accessibility-services.com/fair-housing-act-accessibility-program-registration. ICC's website also provides a compliance guide for local government officials and their staffs at www.iccsafe.org/safety/fairhousing/.

19. CDBG communities, for example, must promote wider housing opportunities for all racial and ethnic groups while maintaining a nondiscriminatory environment in all aspects of the public and private housing markets within their jurisdiction. All jurisdictions receiving HOME funds must also complete the CHAS (Comprehensive Affordability Strategy), one component of which is a certification to affirmatively further fair housing. This duty also applies to the Department of the Treasury and to state housing finance agencies in the administration of the Low-Income Housing Tax Credit program, as well as to owners and managers of tax-credit properties.

20. Michael Allen, "Deconstructing Deconcentration," *The NIMBY Report*, National Low Income Housing Coalition, March 2004.

21. For more information, go to www.portlandonline.com/oni/index.cfm?c=dcebh.

22. For more information on the program, go to **www.odod.state.oh.us/cdd/ohcp/civilrights.htm**.

23. The National Fair Housing Alliance has produced a useful guide on the critical elements of a good Analysis of Impediments, available at **www.nationalfairhousing.org/data/resources/ guideline_for_evaluating_fair_housing_impediments.pdf**.

24. Sara Pratt and Michael Allen, "Addressing Community Opposition to Affordable Housing Development: A Fair Housing Toolkit," Housing Alliance of Pennsylvania, 2004, **www.cacities.org/resource_files/24068.fairhousingtoolkit.pdf**. The toolkit describes ways that Austin, Texas and Portland, Oregon have adopted land use policies that address and contain mechanisms to avoid potential discrimination.

25. For a list of cases where local housing laws were found to be discriminatory, go to **www.usdoj.gov/crt/housing/caselist.htm**.

26. The Non-Profit Housing Association of Northern California website includes a guide on how to organize tours of affordable housing projects, available at **www.nonprofithousing.org/actioncenter/toolbox/acceptance/organizehousingtour.pdf**.

27. Local governments must ensure that any development they fund uses quality design. Examples of well-designed affordable housing projects are abundant. In these efforts, it is crucial to get local permitting officials on board, because quality design may require regulators to waive outdated or unnecessary requirements.

28. Alanna Buchanan et al., "Building Opportunity: Civil Rights Best Practices in the Low-Income Housing Tax Credit Program," Poverty & Race Research Action Council and the Lawyers' Committee for Civil Rights Under Law, October 2006, **www.prrac.org/pdf/BuildingOpportunity.pdf**.

Illinois Employers Become Housing Champions

When community opposition threatened a sorely needed workforce housing development in the Chicago suburb of Arlington Heights, one of the key supporters of the proposal was Northwest Community Healthcare. An executive at this major regional employer told village officials that the mixed-income condominium complex would complement the company's efforts to provide housing assistance to its staff—the nurses, young doctors, medical technicians, and other low- and moderate-income workers increasingly priced out of the village. This healthcare executive and other business and community leaders successfully made the case that appropriately applied density boosts economic development and helps to create walkable communities near jobs. The board approved the new housing development.

Northwest Community Healthcare is no accidental supporter of workforce housing. The institution, among many others, became a corporate champion of workforce housing in part through its involvement in REACH Illinois. REACH is an employer-assisted housing network established in 1999 by the Metropolitan Planning Council. About 60 organizations offer their employees homebuyer education and credit counseling, as well as downpayment assistance and access to low-cost mortgages through the program. Chicago Mayor Richard M. Daley has been an active recruiter for REACH in the city, supported by the Department of Housing. Governor Blagojevich and the Metropolitan Mayors Caucus have promoted it elsewhere in the state, using administrative and financial incentives provided through the Illinois Housing Development Authority and the Department of Commerce and Economic Opportunity.

"These have been very effective programs, not only for the city but the metro area and rural areas as well," Daley said of the drive to convince Greater Chicago employers to help workers buy homes. "You can't put [a price on] how much it's worth. It's basically rebuilding somebody's soul."[1]

Engaging Employers in Local Housing Strategies

9

In some of the nation's highest-priced housing markets, employers are having a difficult time recruiting and retaining employees. At the same time, employees who move farther away from their jobs to find affordable housing end up spending valuable hours stuck in traffic. They may arrive late and stressed, and experience low morale as time on the road supplants time with their families. Employee retention may also suffer in struggling, redeveloping communities as workers use salary advances to seek housing, and then job opportunities, in more favorable locations.

A growing number of employers are tackling these challenges by creating or subsidizing housing for their workers. Top executives with some major companies, such as Tyson Foods, Inc. and Harley-Davidson, have become ardent supporters of employer-assisted housing (EAH). They view such programs as a workforce stabilization tool—both in expensive, high-growth areas where financial support is sorely needed, and in redeveloping communities where employer incentives can help turn the tide on reinvestment.

Schools, hospitals, municipal agencies, and other major employers of low-paid but critical workers are leading the trend. With their vast real estate holdings and human resources, colleges and universities have a special role in rebuilding communities.

Local and state government should encourage and support employers in these efforts. Civic strength depends on a healthy business community, which in turn depends on housing availability. Studies have shown a link between housing supply constraints and economic competitiveness, demonstrating that employment growth is lower in places where the housing supply is constrained.[2]

As they design their strategies, local leaders need to define their objectives. Goals of employer-assisted housing may include boosting homeownership and the associated tax base in distressed or unstable neighborhoods, encouraging more employers to relocate to or remain in the area, reducing traffic congestion and increasing employee quality of life by enabling workers to live closer to their jobs, and fostering positive relations between the surrounding communities and employers whose real estate expansion plans may be viewed as a threat.

A growing body of best practices in employer-assisted housing offers practical steps for implementation. Thanks to the work of such organizations as NeighborWorks® America, the National Housing Conference, the Institute for a Competitive Workforce of the US Chamber of Commerce, Fannie Mae, and Freddie Mac, the steps—and program ideas—are documented in several recent how-to guides.

In communities facing multiple competing demands for scarce public resources, employer homebuyer assistance can be a particularly powerful yet slow-building element of the local housing strategy. Public leaders who engage employers in providing homebuyer assistance and developing housing can significantly leverage their housing investments. For example, under the Illinois REACH program, through 2004, every $1.00 of state matching funds leveraged over $5.00 from employers. As Robin Snyderman of Chicago's Metropolitan Planning Council notes, employer-assisted housing efforts take time due to the "multiple levels of buy-in for corporations to change the way they do business, choose EAH in addition to (or over) other benefit or scholarship programs, and ultimately decide to launch."[3] While some businesses are getting into housing development, most of the activity is among academic or other anchor institutions, agricultural operations, and hospitality businesses in resort towns.

That said, signs of accelerated interest are appearing. From California to Florida and points in between, business leaders are talking about their need to address housing barriers in order to attract and retain the workers they need to succeed. Mayors and governors can do a great deal to expand employer engagement by emphasizing the benefits of affordable workforce housing and supporting employer efforts. In addition to bringing their own resources to the table, employers who care about housing issues are valuable allies in city, suburban, and state efforts to enact policies to expand housing opportunities for all citizens.

RECOMMENDATIONS FOR LOCAL ACTION

---

1   Offer Homebuyer Assistance to Public Sector Employees

Police officers, firefighters, teachers, and emergency response personnel are among the moderately paid workers that some local governments have difficulty recruiting and retaining in the absence of affordable housing options. By offering their own employees assisted housing, local governments can help to ensure their own staffing success while modeling the kinds of programs they would like their business partners to adopt. Some governments are also encouraging employees to purchase homes in certain neighborhoods as a way to stabilize an area.

Most employer-assisted programs consist of downpayment help in the form of grants and forgivable loans or second mortgage loans at below-market rates through supporting lenders.[4] Less common are loan discounts that are negotiated with lenders; mortgage buy-down programs, where employers pay points to reduce the long-term loan rate; and mortgage guarantee programs, where employers agree to cover any lender losses from defaults.

Employers seeking help with designing and implementing an EAH plan can use Freddie Mac's Workforce Home Benefit program. Under this turnkey initiative,

Freddie Mac can help identify community organizations equipped to offer homebuyer counseling, provide the names of lenders that may make home loans to employees, and coordinate with other agencies.

Downpayment Aid Helps Municipal Employees Buy within City Limits

Alexandria, Virginia's Employee Homeownership Incentive Program offers an interest-free, deferred-payment loan of $5,000 for downpayment or closing costs to full-time city and school employees who purchase homes in the city. Homeowners who leave city employment within three years must repay a pro-rated amount. Otherwise, the loan is repayable upon sale of the home. Between its launch in July 2004 and November 2006, the program helped 58 households—including teachers, police officers, firefighters, and other city employees—purchase homes.

Baltimore's City Employee program provides $3,000 forgivable loans toward settlement fees and downpayment costs to employees in good standing who have worked for the city for at least six months. Homes must be inside city limits. Those who purchase in the Mayor's Healthy Neighborhoods get an additional $750. As of June 2005, 160 city employees had bought homes through the program.

Leveraging Helps San Jose, Santa Fe Assist Hundreds of Teachers

San Jose, California started its Teacher Homebuyer Program in 1999. Recipients can get up to $65,000 in zero-interest downpayment loans from the San Jose Housing Department. The city also uses loan and tax credit programs from other local, state, and federal agencies to leverage homebuyer support for teachers. By January 2006, the program had helped more than 500 teachers buy their first homes and the city's funding commitments had leveraged more than $137 million in other public and private funds.

Santa Fe Public School District's Teacherwise program, administered by the nonprofit Homewise Inc., provides district employees with an interest-free loan of up to $10,000 to cover a downpayment. Loans must be repaid upon sale of the home. The program is financed by the school district, city HOME funds, and an investment from the state legislature. As of October 2006, the program had helped 86 employees purchase homes.

Fairfax County Provides Firefighter, EMT Recruits with Low-Cost Rentals

In 2004, Fairfax County, Virginia bought 10 condominiums in the county and offered them at affordable rents to firefighter and EMT recruits for two years as they completed their training. The program was expanded to include police recruits, county employees, and critical area teachers, and the county subsequently purchased an additional 18 units. The program is supported through the county's new affordable housing fund and other county sources. The county plans to set up a similar program to provide approximately 45 affordable apartments and townhouses for hospital staff who currently work, or agree to work, for Inova Health System, a major local employer facing a nursing shortage.

City-Union Partnership Provides Downpayment, Rental Assistance

Boston partially seeded and provides ongoing support to trust funds that help municipal union members handle the high cost of housing in the city. (The city has a residency requirement for municipal employees.) The American Federation of State, County, and Municipal Employees, Council 93 (AFSCME) and Service Employees International Union®, Local 888 (SEIU) housing trust funds each received an initial allocation of $500,000 from the city budget. In addition, the city donates five cents for every hour a municipal union employee works, providing an annual revenue stream of roughly $125,000. The city trust office invests the funds along with other trust monies in its portfolio. The trust funds provide forgivable downpayment loans and rental and emergency housing assistance. As of November 2006, 55 employees had been assisted.

Low-Cost Second Mortgages Make Columbia, SC Homes Affordable

Under Columbia's Employee Loan program, employees who make less than 150 percent of the area median income and purchase homes in targeted city neighborhoods can put only $1,000 down on their homes. Low-interest, 30-year second and third mortgages from the city cover 30 percent of the total loan amount, with the rest covered by a market-rate first mortgage. The blended rate is approximately 1.5 percentage points below the current market rate. Private mortgage insurance is not required, but credit counseling and homeownership training are mandatory. A property must be owner-occupied for the life of the city loan. Thirty-nine loans totaling over $4.4 million had been made as of September 2006. By that same date, a separate program had also helped 17 police officers purchase homes needing extensive repair in low- to moderate-income neighborhoods.

---

2 Match Housing Benefit Programs Sponsored by Area Employers

According to Society for Human Resources Management surveys, the number of employers offering downpayment assistance nearly tripled from 2002 to 2006 (from four percent to 11 percent).[5] Municipalities should join this modest but growing trend by supporting programs with a public match, perhaps drawing on HOME or CDBG funds.

▼ CASES IN POINT

Rochester, NY Program Provides Up to $3,000 Match

Rochester has used its success in providing homebuying assistance for its own employees to implement a matching grants program for area employers. Launched in 2004, the program requires participating employers to provide at least $1,000 of assistance to workers. The city matches up to $3,000 of the employer contribution. Employees must contribute at least $1,500 of their own money toward the purchase of a home, buy within the city, and commit to living in the property for at least five years. City of Rochester employees also receive a $3,000 grant toward a home purchase, following the same guidelines as the local employer programs. To fund the program, the city council approved an initial allocation of $600,000 from HOME funds, American Dream Initiative dollars, and repayments from the now-defunct Urban Development Action Grant program. As of September 2006, there were five participating employers and 44 home purchases made through the program.

Arlington County, VA Negotiates Discounts on Condo Sales

Arlington County negotiates with condominium developers to provide discounts to employees of entities participating in the city's employer-assisted housing program.[6] For example, about 40 city, George Mason University, and Virginia Hospital Center employees have bought condominiums at the IDA Group's new Dominion Terrace Development for $10,000 less than the market rate. To prevent buyers from flipping the units, the county retains the right of first refusal to purchase any condos sold within a year of purchase at the original price.

Baltimore's "Live Near Your Work" Program Encourages Shorter Commutes

Live Near Your Work programs, a variation on public matching of private programs, encourage people to buy homes close to their workplaces. Municipalities offering such programs must work with employers to define the eligible area around the work site. The Transportation Management Association, which seeks to reduce traffic congestion, improve mobility and air quality, and promote transportation alternatives, assists employers in setting up such programs. Participants in Baltimore's Live Near Your Work Program receive a grant of $2,000 or more—half from the city and half from the employer—to help pay settlement and closing costs. As of June 2005, 142 people had bought homes through the program.

---

3 Support Regionwide Employer-Assisted Housing Initiatives

Local governments, perhaps working in partnership with the chamber of commerce or a consortium of nonprofits, can play a leadership role in promoting city- or regionwide EAH programs that continually add new participants.[7] Each employer recruited can help build momentum and attract new participants, reaching a scale beyond that achievable by individual programs.

Once a program is under way, daily administration may be handed to a nonprofit organization. Often, nonprofits with experience in homeownership counseling and established relationships with potential lenders are best equipped to run a program over the long term. Effective EAH initiatives enlist several partners that are responsible for key aspects of the program.[8]

Information about housing affordability and trends, the jobs/housing mismatch, and other conditions can help engage partners while providing a foundation for program design.[9] The Institute for a Competitive Workforce is working on creating new, practical methodologies for identifying and quantifying the bottom-line implications of high housing costs.

Sixty Employers Join Illinois EAH Initiative

Chicago Mayor Richard M. Daley is one of many regional and state leaders working to expand the REACH Illinois employer-assisted housing initiative. The Metropolitan Planning Council (MPC), a Northeastern Illinois business and civic group, launched the Regional Employer-Assisted Collaboration for Housing in 1999. The council recruits employers and helps them design homebuyer benefits programs. Employers provide forgivable loans to workers, which receive a state match of up to $5,000 from the Illinois Housing and Development Authority if the employee makes up to 80 percent of the area median income.[10] In some cases, the county government or another entity provides an additional match.

Nonprofit housing groups handle day-to-day administration, as well as provide confidential credit counseling and homebuyer education services. Employers get a state tax credit equal to half their investment, which they can sell to companies that pay taxes.[11] A new partner, Housing Action Illinois, serves a role similar to MPC in other parts of the state. As of 2006, 60 Illinois employers had signed on with REACH Illinois, helping over 900 workers buy homes.

Milwaukee Brings Employer-Assisted Housing to Scale

Milwaukee nonprofit Select Milwaukee has expanded employer-assisted housing by enabling companies to offer homebuyer benefits without ramping up their human resources staff. Select Milwaukee designs EAH programs for employers, charging an annual fee ranging from $2,500 to $38,000 to administer the programs, which include counseling employees, packaging loans, processing benefit applications, and ongoing marketing. Most of the 10 participating employers (including a community development corporation with multiple members) offer forgivable loans ranging from $1,000 to $5,000 to cover downpayment and closing costs. Partner lenders provide conventional, state housing finance agency, and low-cost fixed-rate portfolio loans. Several other resources are available to offer additional incentives to certain buyers or to purchase in targeted areas of the city.[12] Between 2000 and October 2006, 644 employees with a median household income of $38,480 had purchased homes through the initiative. Fifty-eight percent of the buyers were African-American or Hispanic, helping to close the city's minority homeownership gap.

4 Help Employers Build Housing Affordable to Their Workers

Some employers have responded to serious recruitment challenges by developing new housing for their employees. California's public universities are pioneers in this area, forced by the state's high housing costs to partner with developers on lower-cost housing projects on school campuses. While California State University has been building staff housing for some time, the impending retirement of a large portion of its faculty and staff has made the need to offer lower-cost housing to recruit quality replacements particularly acute. The university serves as the lead developer and finances the construction itself. In other situations, employers invest equity in other projects or donate land or services, such as engineering and accounting.

Given the housing crunch affecting both university staff and critical public service employees, the Cal State Fullerton Housing Authority is looking beyond its own developments to advocacy. Authority officials are urging the city to set aside underutilized city-owned land or to incorporate ground-lease housing into upcoming projects. They should then open these housing opportunities to those in high-demand/modest-income occupations such as teachers, police officers, firefighters, nurses, and others.

▼ CASES IN POINT

With Municipal Support, California Universities Invest Big in Housing

As of August 2006, there were approximately 2,000 faculty and staff housing units completed or under construction on seven of California State University's 23 campuses. Another 2,000 or so units were in some stage of planning or design. The units range from 800 sq.-ft. apartments and condominiums to 3,000 sq.-ft. single-family homes. The vast majority of for-sale units are constructed under land-lease arrangements pioneered by UC-Irvine and quickly adopted by other campuses.

Under such an arrangement, the university retains ownership of the land and uses sales covenants with buyers to preserve affordability in perpetuity. When homes are resold, the price cannot exceed the initial purchase price plus an inflation adjustment and the value of capital improvements. Local governments have supported CSU housing efforts by providing density bonuses to developer partners and by offering home-purchase assistance to buyers.

Cal State Fullerton's University Gables development provided homes at 40–50 percent less than the going market rate by working with local government. In 2001, the county conveyed an eight-acre parcel of surplus land valued at more than $3 million to the university's Housing Authority for $1.00.[13] The housing authority used the donated land to secure $16 million in construction funds. In exchange, the university agreed to preserve the 86 homes as affordable for 30 years. Seventy-five units were set aside for moderate-income buyers earning up to 120 percent of area median income, with the other 11 units reserved for low-income families making up to 80 percent of area median income. The City of Buena Park provided loans up to $30,000 apiece to most of the low-income buyers. By 2003, Cal State Fullerton faculty and staff had bought 80 of the homes, while faculty and staff at neighboring universities purchased the rest.

Riverdale, IL Employers Support New Mixed-Income Community

Three Riverdale, Illinois area employers committed, as part of the developer's application for Low-Income Housing Tax Credits, to providing rent subsidies to employees who choose to lease in a new mixed-income community that was replacing a blighted housing complex. To supplement this investment, participating employers also agreed to match the savings of employees who were putting aside money to buy homes in future phases of the community.

University of Chicago Helps Preserve Rental Housing

After successfully helping over 100 employees access existing housing through the Metropolitan Planning Council and REACH Illinois model (covered earlier in this chapter), the University of Chicago took employer-assisted housing to the next level. To preserve the affordable rental units that are critical to housing university affiliates, the institution invested $1 million with the nonprofit Community Investment Corporation (CIC), which specializes in lending to independent hands-on developers.

5 Engage in University Neighborhood Revitalization Efforts

In some urban areas, the housing and community development efforts of academic and other anchor institutions are helping to revitalize surrounding neighborhoods. Rather than walling themselves off, these institutions are investing in retail and commercial development, engaging staff and students in community research projects, and strengthening local housing markets by developing units and encouraging employees to relocate to distressed neighborhoods.

Local governments should recognize engaged universities as the asset that they are and foster productive partnerships with them. In their efforts, local leaders should note the resources available through HUD's Office of University Partnerships, which supports partnerships between colleges and universities and their communities through grants, conferences, and research. Current grant programs target community development initiatives led by colleges and universities serving African-Americans, Hispanics, Native Americans, and native Alaskans and Hawaiians.

▼ CASES IN POINT

"Granny Flats" Make Duke Homes Affordable

Duke University in Durham, North Carolina spearheaded efforts to stabilize the nearby Trinity Heights neighborhood by increasing the number of owner-occupied homes in the area. Duke engaged Traditional Neighborhood Development Partners to design new housing that matches the area's classical architecture but is sufficiently dense to reduce the per-unit costs to homebuyers. As of summer 2006, the partnership had generated 75 new units of affordable housing.

The new units include 33 new detached, single-family homes, 15 townhouses, and 27 garage apartments or "granny flats" attached to some of the homes. By generating rental income for the homeowners, the rental units increase the affordability of the for-sale homes. Restrictive covenants require that the homes only be sold, or re-sold, to Duke employees and that owners live in the homes. This project, which has helped to increase city property tax revenues, could not have happened without city approvals and permits. To allow for the New Urbanism design, the city had to make multiple exceptions and adopt multiple amendments to the zoning code related to areas such as street widths, setbacks, units per parcel, and other restrictions.

Penn Sets Standard for University-led Revitalization

The University of Pennsylvania's success at jump-starting the rebirth of the distressed West Philadelphia neighborhood demonstrates how universities can be a catalyst for transformation. Stimulating homeownership in the University City neighborhood was a key part of the multi-pronged plan. At the time, the homeownership rate was only 22 percent and the neighborhood's large, once-magnificent homes essentially served as student boarding houses. Crime rates were alarmingly high. The university acquired and renovated 20 abandoned properties in strategic locations and offered employees university-guaranteed mortgages, covering 120 percent of the purchase price and no-interest, forgivable loans of up to $21,000 to fund home improvements. Other programs were also launched to help fund upgrades. Between 1998 and December 2006, these programs helped 1,088 people purchase or improve homes. These investments have spurred nearby homeowners to improve their properties and will ultimately help restore confidence in the local real estate market.

On the rental side, the university created a Neighborhood Housing and Development Fund with additional financing from Fannie Mae, the University of the Sciences in Philadelphia, Commerce Bank, and the Trammell Crow Company. By November 2006, the fund had helped to acquire and renovate 441 units, many of which were highly visible but poorly managed properties prior to renovation. The rental market is now attracting private development.

The university was able to create a vibrant intellectual community, complete with a state-of-the art public school and thriving commercial corridor.[14] As a result of the university's engagement, several hundred thousand square feet of retail space was added to University City between 2000 and 2005—the largest commercial investment in West Philadelphia history. The university also engaged in many activities that helped to reduce crime by 41 percent between 1996 and the end of 2005.

Trinity Alliance Revitalizes Latino Community

The Southside Institutions Neighborhood Alliance (SINA)/Trinity Initiative has invested close to $200 million in education, housing, and economic development in a 15-block area around Trinity College in Hartford, Connecticut.[15] The initiative was launched by SINA and former Trinity president Evan Dobelle in the mid-1990s to help revitalize the mostly Latino community.[16]

One unique program developed both for-sale and rental housing. With acquisition funds and construction financing from Hartford Hospital, the SINA Neighborhood Initiative acquired, rehabilitated, and sold 33 homes to first-time homebuyers making up to 80 percent of area median income. As of fall 2006, another 18 new single-family homes were in development. Designed in cooperation with neighborhood residents, the homes include a rental unit to help owners cover their mortgage payments. Some of the homes have been purchased by Trinity faculty and staff with the aid of Trinity's decades-old employee mortgage assistance program. SINA places covenants that restrict resale costs of homes sold within 15 years.

To address concerns about displacement of renter families, SINA partnered with the Broad Park Development Corporation to transform 12 distressed structures in the Frog Hollow district into 74 rental units, some of which are accessible to people with disabilities. The city has supported these housing efforts by helping to convey blighted and foreclosed properties at favorable costs, providing gap financing for rehabilitation and construction, and offering downpayment assistance to homebuyers. The state housing finance agency has also provided construction assistance and low-cost mortgages to homebuyers.

EAH Program Supports Public Housing Transformation in Chicago

In April 2003, the Illinois Institute of Technology (IIT) announced a new employer-assisted housing initiative intended to transform its notorious neighbor, Stateway Gardens, from high-rise public housing into a mixed-income community. IIT offered employees a $7,500 forgivable loan to buy homes in the new community, known as Park Boulevard. The program includes no income caps, given that its primary goal is to encourage employees of all income levels to invest in the community.

OPPORTUNITIES FOR STATE ACTION

1 Support Local "Live Near Your Work" and Other EAH Programs

State housing finance agencies should offer products that support local employer-assisted housing programs. For example, MassHousing, the housing finance authority for the Commonwealth of Massachusetts, has a municipal employee program providing 100-percent financing at reduced interest rates for police officers, firefighters, and teachers who buy homes in the towns where they work. As of November 2006, 322 mortgage loans totaling $72.7 million had been closed. The program has its highest volume in Boston, which has a residency requirement for city employees.

Mississippi's Housing Assistance for Teachers grant program offers incentives to teachers to work in rural and urban school districts that face teacher shortages. The Mississippi Home Corporation, the state housing finance authority, administers the program with a $250,000 annual appropriation from the legislature. Launched in 1999, the program offers teachers who agree to work in a target school district for at least three years up to $6,000 to cover downpayment, closing costs, mortgage insurance, and prepaid items. As of October 2006, 294 loans had been made under the program. California's Housing Finance Agency has a similar initiative called the

Extra Credit Teacher Home Purchase Program, targeting incentives to teachers working in underachieving or low-income schools.

Illinois and Maryland both match local EAH downpayment assistance programs. The Illinois program, which has been central to the REACH Illinois strategy described earlier, is funded through the Illinois Housing Development Authority and administered by the Metropolitan Planning Council and Housing Action Illinois. Under the program, employer contributions up to $5,000 can be matched for households earning up to 50 percent of area median income, and contributions up to $3,000 can be matched for households earning up to 80 percent of area median income. Employers are required to work with local nonprofit experts to ensure employees receive quality housing counseling services.

Under Maryland's House Keys 4 Employees program, the Department of Housing and Community Development (DHCD) provides a dollar-for-dollar match up to $5,000 for contributions toward downpayment and/or closing costs from participating employers. The match, in the form of a zero-percent deferred loan, can be used with other DHCD products, providing as much as $15,000 toward downpayment and closing costs. As of November 2006, approximately 55 employers were participating in the House Keys 4 Employees program, including the State of Maryland, the City of Annapolis, the College of Notre Dame of Maryland, and both Johns Hopkins University and the Johns Hopkins Health System. Since the launch in September 2005, 292 loans totaling $51 million were reserved under the program.

New Jersey removes mortgage insurance costs from the equation through its Mortgage Finance Agency's Home Ownership for Performing Employees (HOPE) program. HOPE offers 30-year fixed-rate loans for up to 100 percent of the value of the home without requiring mortgage insurance. Employers must submit a plan describing which employees qualify and guarantee up to 20 percent of employee mortgage loans. The loan guarantee allows buyers to roll the downpayment and sometimes closing costs into the mortgage loan. Borrowers must meet certain income and price limits.

2 Create Tax Incentives for Employer-Assisted Housing Programs

The Illinois Affordable Housing Tax Credit provides donors with a $0.50 state income tax credit for every dollar invested in a qualified housing activity. Of the $13 million in credits available annually, $2 million is set aside for employer-assisted housing for households earning up to 120 percent of area median income.

The state's Economic Development for a Growing Economy (EDGE) program, which offers tax credits for job creation and retention, also includes special incentives for employer support of affordable housing. Under the EDGE program, companies that decide to locate or expand operations in Illinois and create at least five new jobs in the state are eligible for credits. The credits equal the amount of state income taxes withheld from the salaries of employees in the newly created jobs.[17] In 2006, the state enacted the Business Location Efficiency Incentive Act to provide additional EDGE credits to qualifying companies that locate in areas with affordable housing and access to public transportation.

Connecticut offers a dollar-for-dollar reduction in state tax liability to employers that create a qualified revolving loan fund providing homeownership and rental assistance to their low- and moderate-income employees. The Connecticut Housing Finance Authority administers the program with a $1 million annual budget. Employers must maintain the funds for at least five years. Homes purchased under the program cannot exceed 150 percent of the purchase price limit established by HUD. Employees must work full time and may make up to 140 percent of area median income.

---

3 Create Incentives for University Partnerships

In December 2005, the Brookings Institution published a paper on the statewide economic impact of Pennsylvania's colleges, universities, and vocational schools.[18] The paper outlines the important role institutions play as trainers of the future workforce, as incubators of firms, and as employers, purchasers, and real estate developers. To expand university engagement in revitalization, the report recommends that the state create a Higher Education Advisory Board to unify ad hoc town-gown partnerships into a set of priorities and actions, expand criteria for preferential awarding of state economic development dollars to include projects carried out in partnership with universities and other anchor institutions, create a new grant program to facilitate university partnerships in community development, consider enacting a state "payment-in-lieu-of-taxes" program similar to Connecticut's,[19] and hold an annual forum on higher education and communities.

RESOURCES

FREDDIE MAC
www.freddiemac.com

Company created by Congress to ensure a reliable supply of funds to mortgage lenders in support of homeownership and rental housing. Freddie Mac's Workforce Home Benefit[SM] Toolkit provides tools and guidance on structuring cost-effective EAH programs. The company also provides turnkey Workforce Home Benefit programs to employers with more than 1,000 workers.

METROPOLITAN PLANNING COUNCIL
www.metroplanning.org

Nonprofit group of business and civic leaders focused on planning and development policies necessary for an economically competitive Chicago. MPC offers technical assistance to those seeking hands-on support implementing employer-assisted housing.

NATIONAL ASSOCIATION OF REALTORS®
www.realtor.org

Represents more than 1.3 million members involved in all aspects of the residential and commercial real estate industries. NAR has launched a Home from Work™ campaign to encourage and train realtors to work with businesses to develop employer-assisted housing benefit plans.

NATIONAL COUNCIL OF STATE HOUSING AGENCIES
www.ncsha.org

Nonprofit organization of state housing finance agencies that coordinates and leverages advocacy for affordable housing, including homeownership programs and in some cases programs directly supporting EAH.

NATIONAL HOUSING CONFERENCE
www.nhc.org

National public policy and affordable housing advocacy organization that draws its membership from across the housing industry. NHC has been an important advocate of EAH and posts several useful resources on its website, including "Employer-Assisted Housing: State by State List," and "Private Sector Partnerships: Investing in Housing and Neighborhood Revitalization." The Center for Housing Policy, NHC's research arm, also published "A Heavy Load: The Combined Housing and Transportation Burdens of Working Families."

RESOURCES

NEIGHORWORKS® NETWORK
National network of more than 240 community-based organizations that has published several guides on employer-assisted housing, including "Employer-Assisted Home Ownership: A Sourcebook for Nonprofit Organizations" and "Start-Up Guide for Employer-Assisted Home Ownership."

REACH ILLINOIS
www.reachillinois.org

Provides extensive information on the Illinois EAH program advanced through the Illinois Housing Development Authority, the Metropolitan Planning Council, and Housing Action Illinois.

US DEPARTMENT OF HOUSING AND URBAN DEVELOPMENT
Office of University Partnerships

www.oup.org

Facilitates campus-community partnerships through information sharing. The office has published many reports on university-community partnerships to revitalize neighborhoods through housing development and other activities.

WINNING WORKPLACES
www.winningworkplaces.org

Nonprofit organization that promotes quality workplaces by providing information, training, ideas, consulting, and easy-to-use tools for small and midsize organizations. The organization has created an online toolkit on EAH.

ENDNOTES CHAPTER 9

1. Emmet Pierce, "A Paycheck and a House: Some Employers Find It's Good Business to Provide Housing Assistance," *San Diego Union Tribune,* May 15 2005, **www.metroplanning.org/press/mpcnews.asp?objectID=2764**.

2. Raven E. Saks, "Job Creation and Housing Construction: Constraints on Employment Growth in Metropolitan Areas," Joint Center for Housing Studies of Harvard University, W04-10, 2004, p. 26, **www.jchs.harvard.edu/publications/markets/w04-10_saks.pdf**. In the long run, an increase in labor demand results in 20 percent less employment in metro areas with a low elasticity of housing supply.

3. Robin Snyderman, "Making the Case for Employer-Assisted Housing," *Shelterforce Online,* May/June 2005, **www.nhi.org/online/issues/141/EAH.html**.

4. Fannie Mae and Freddie Mac offer low-cost, flexible mortgage products through their nationwide networks of lenders and mortgage brokers. For example, Freddie Mac's Home Possible suite of low downpayment products offers flexible terms for firefighters, teachers, healthcare workers, and law enforcement professionals that can increase homebuying power by up to 30 percent. Through its partner offices, Fannie Mae also offers downpayment products that can be part of local EAH programs.

5. Shawn Fegley, "2006 Benefits Survey Report," Society for Human Resource Management, June 2006.

6. County and school board employees who purchase homes under the program may also obtain a Live Near Your Work forgivable loan of $4,500. Employees who move to the county as renters get a $500 grant.

7. The chamber can be a great link to an anchor employer or employers that can serve as local champions for the program, recruiting others through their respected leadership. Another potential source of local leadership may be a hospital, university, or other institution whose fortunes depend in part on the community's economic health.

8. Partners include funders, such as city or state downpayment assistance programs, foundations, and local nonprofits with downpayment assistance funds; nonprofit providers of homebuyer education and counseling; real estate agents who help buyers find homes in the target areas; lenders who provide appropriate, and in some cases, low-cost home purchase loans that take advantage of the EAH financial benefit; and marketing partners such as local faith-based and business groups. The NeighborWorks® "Start-Up Guide for Employer-Assisted Home Ownership" covers the roles and motivations of key partners as well as ways to recruit employers to join an EAH program.

9. A 2005 paper prepared by the Joint Center for Housing Studies of Harvard University and the US Chamber of Commerce's Center for Workforce Preparation (now called The Institute for a Competitive Workforce) covers how to obtain data on local markets and lists useful measures in the appendix. The paper, "Strengthening our Workforce and our Communities Through Housing Solutions," also covers testimony from business leaders as well as references to research on how high workforce housing costs hurt companies and localities and the benefits of EAH programs.

10. The match cannot exceed $5,000 for employees who make less than 50 percent of the area median income, or $3,000 for employees who make 50–80 percent of area median income. Employees must be first-time homebuyers.

11. Most recently, the state legislature approved a third public incentive in Illinois, providing a competitive edge and more dollars to EAH employers through Economic Development for a Growing Economy (EDGE) tax credits for job creation and retention.

12. These include the Chicago Federal Home Loan Bank's Affordable Housing Program, the City of Milwaukee's Targeted Investment Neighborhoods Initiative, HUD's American Dream Downpayment Initiative, and Individual Development Account matching funds. In addition, several members of the local chapter of the American Society of Home Inspectors offer reduced-fee inspections, scope writing, and construction expediting to EAH participants.

13. William Dickerson, "University Gables—from Concept to Reality," National Association of College Auxiliary Services, June 2004, **www.csufasc.org/pdf/universitygables.pdf**.

14. To attract retail, the university developed a 300,000 sq.-ft. mixed-use project that includes a luxury hotel, bookstore, public plazas, and stores and restaurants. Other university-supported projects include a grocery store and movie theater.

15. Significant investment—about $95 million from the state department of education—went into creating a "Learning Corridor" spanning 16 acres between Trinity College and a trio of other anchor institutions. In its 2005 report, "Shared Prosperity, Stronger Regions," PolicyLink describes the corridor as a "one of the most racially and economically diverse campuses in the country." The complex includes four public magnet schools, a performing arts center, support programs for youth, and the Aetna Center for Families. All together, they serve about 1,500 students from more than 40 school districts.

16. SINA is a neighborhood revitalization group founded by Trinity College, Hartford Hospital, and the Institute of Living mental health hospital in the late 1970s. In the mid-1990s, Connecticut Children's Medical Center and Connecticut Public Television and Radio also joined the collaborative. Trinity made a $6.4 million one-time investment in the program, while Hartford Hospital invested $5 million. From 1996 to 2006, Trinity made close to $3 million more in annual investments, leveraging additional funds from various public and private sources.

17. For more information on eligibility and how the credits are calculated, go to **www.commerce.state.il.us/dceo/Bureaus/Business_Development/Tax+Assistance/EDGE.htm**.

18. Jennifer S. Vey, "Higher Education in Pennsylvania: A Competitive Asset for Communities," The Brookings Institution Metropolitan Policy Program, December 2005.

19. According to the report, municipalities with struggling neighborhoods suffer when some of their land is occupied by institutions of higher education, which do not pay taxes. To offset revenue losses from schools' tax-exempt status, Connecticut pays municipalities approximately 77 percent of projected property taxes, based on assessed values if college, university, and hospital property were taxable.

Some residents of Mountain View, California think the line from the song "New York, New York" applies just as well to their situation, with a slight rewording to "if I can get by here, I can get by anywhere." Even many of the steadily employed don't make enough to afford the high rents in this Silicon Valley city. Seniors on fixed incomes, single parents with children, and people with disabilities feel particularly excluded.

That's why hundreds of people applied for a spot in San Antonio Place when it opened in 2006. The complex of 118 efficiency studios, or SROs, fulfilled a long-time dream of local housing advocates and city leaders. The 330-sq. ft. units may be small, but they are a far cry from the substandard or overcrowded living situations many tenants once occupied. The new residents, primarily single adults, earn between $15,000 and $33,000 annually or about 20–45 percent of area median income. In addition to an attractive apartment, residents have access to case management services and weekly educational workshops.

San Antonio Place would not have been possible without assistance from the Housing Trust of Santa Clara County, a regional housing fund that draws substantial support from local government and the business community. As with many projects, trust funds assisted at two crucial stages of the development process. A predevelopment loan of roughly $250,000 enabled developer Charities Housing (an offshoot of Catholic Charities) to finance early-stage needs, such as working with the city to identify a site for the complex and collaborating with neighborhood residents to design a facility that would meet their approval. Another $500,000 loan served as crucial "gap" financing that allowed the developer to complete the complex financing package.

This scenario, in which a local housing trust fills a key role in the affordable housing finance system, plays out in communities nationwide. But as Charities Housing executive director Chris Block explains, housing trusts do more than fund projects. The very act of engaging stakeholders to form a local housing trust creates new constituencies for affordable housing. And when it is time to site a development, that support eases the process.

Taking Advantage of Flexible Funding Resources

10

The decline in federal funding has forced state and municipal governments to seek other revenue sources for programs to preserve and expand affordable housing and homeownership opportunities, as well as support homelessness prevention. This chapter focuses on two general resources—housing trust funds and government-sponsored enterprises (GSEs)—that are key players in local housing strategies because both offer flexible funding to fill gaps in the system.

State and local governments that have not already created housing trust funds with renewable nongeneral fund sources should consider doing so. Local leaders should also make sure that they and their developer partners are using the resources available through the GSEs—Fannie Mae, Freddie Mac, and the Federal Home Loan Banks—to expand the supply of affordable housing and to reach out to moderate-income and minority homebuyers and renters.

1 Housing Trust Funds

Housing trust funds are a critical tool for preserving and developing affordable housing in communities throughout the US. They have weathered tough economic and political climates and their numbers continue to grow. They are increasingly popular because they provide a flexible funding pool for supporting a variety of initiatives. According to the Housing Trust Fund Project of the Center for Community Change, there are nearly 600 housing trust funds in cities, counties, and states around the country that together generate roughly $1.6 billion annually for affordable housing.

In general, housing trust funds receive a dedicated source of public revenues, such as a percentage of the income produced by a particular tax. Creating a permanent funding stream outside the appropriations process provides a stable source of funds for advancing community priorities and makes it possible to plan for the future.

Establishing a successful housing trust fund requires first identifying the most effective revenue sources. Local governments should thoroughly review the various funding options, including single or multiple sources. For local housing trust funds, state-enabling legislation may or may not be necessary or advantageous.[1] In almost all cases, jurisdictions can tap into revenue sources without state legislation.

While the real estate transfer tax is the most common source for funds, states have tapped some two-dozen other sources.[2] Counties most commonly fund their trusts with document recording fees. Cities are more likely to pull from a range of sources, such as linkage programs, fees from inclusionary zoning programs,[3] and other taxes and levies.

Public leaders should evaluate potential funding sources on several criteria: revenue potential, dependability, conceptual connection to housing, tax incidence, and political feasibility. The Sacramento, California Housing Trust Fund, for example, focuses on workforce housing. The city/county fund is administered by the Sacramento Redevelopment Authority and earns income from linkage fees on new development—a revenue source with a clear connection to housing.

Governments should conduct studies to ensure that the proposed revenue source does not impose undue hardship on any one industry. Local leaders should also set priorities for a fund. What makes housing trust funds so popular is the power to design them to meet specific community needs. Unlike CDBG and HOME funds that come with many restrictions, trust funds can be deployed more flexibly.

Trust funds should be targeted to complement existing resources. Funds can assist a specific market segment (such as the homeless) or support affordable housing more broadly. In general, trust funds make loans and grants to both nonprofit and for-profit developers, as well as government entities, Native American tribes, service providers, and housing authorities. Funds may help developers build or rehabilitate rental and for-sale housing or acquire property, make emergency home repairs, retrofit homes to be accessible to the disabled, and assist renters or first-time homeowners.

While the aim of establishing a trust fund is rarely controversial, the revenue source often is. Setting up a housing trust fund thus requires high-level champions, educating the public, and building constituencies. Advocates for the fund must negotiate and compromise with affected organizations and sectors. For example, the Housing Trust of Santa Clara County was capitalized and promoted by Silicon Valley business groups in collaboration with government, advocacy, and civic groups. It now draws on a range of private and public contributors, including private citizens, regional employers, corporate foundations, and county and city governments.

In another example, the coalition that passed the 1992 act establishing Florida's housing trust fund included a bipartisan group of real estate professionals, home builders, growth management advocates, housing groups, and the business community.[4] In both Washington and Vermont, housing advocates joined forces with environmentalists to create the state trust funds. In the case of St. Louis and Washington, DC, the mayors were the driving force.

Once funds are up and running, local leaders and program administrators should coordinate spending with other housing resources. Trust funds are never the sole source of funds for a housing project, but rather part of a financing package that also includes federal funds, bank loans, and perhaps mortgage revenue bonds. Because the model is well-respected, and because the funds are often established to complement HOME, CDBG, tax credit, and bond monies, trust fund investments can usually leverage significant additional funds. Indeed, the Housing Trust Fund Project reports that housing trust funds leverage five to ten dollars for every one dollar committed to housing.

Local and state governments should also follow the lead of New York City, Philadelphia, San Diego, and Washington State, among others, and administer trust fund dollars within a comprehensive housing policy, coordinating trust fund spending with other funds to tackle priorities. The following review of local and state funds across the country shows that many are serving unique local needs and filling critical gaps.

▼ CASES IN POINT

Big City Funds Support Mayoral Production Goals

The Washington, DC, Philadelphia, and New York housing trust funds are helping to support mayoral initiatives to increase housing production. At the urging of the mayor, the District of Columbia City Council dedicated 15 percent of deed recording and transfer taxes to the Housing Production Trust Fund in 2002. Mayor Anthony Williams and housing advocates had wanted a dedicated resource to help preserve housing opportunities for average workers amid the city's real estate boom. Fund revenues began at $5 million in fiscal 2003 and rose to nearly $48 million in fiscal 2006.

Funds committed as of December 2006 will help create more than 3,000 housing units. Under law, at least half of fund allocations must produce or preserve rental housing. At least 40 percent of funds must support projects serving families making up to 30 percent of area median income, and at least 40 percent must go to families making 31–50 percent of AMI. The remaining funds serve households making 51–80 percent of AMI. The city council has authorized using $12 million of trust fund monies annually to secure an estimated $150 million in bond issues for the mayor's "New Communities" initiative, which promotes mixed-income housing developments and other improvements in selected distressed communities.

Philadelphia officials are tapping the city's trust fund to help realize the goals of Mayor John Street's Neighborhood Transformation Initiative (NTI). Unveiled in 2001, NTI aims to clean up blighted neighborhoods and return properties to productive use. Prior to the trust fund, the city lacked sufficient resources to build new housing on land that had been cleared and prepared for redevelopment. Street's administration worked with advocates to push through legislation in 2005 enabling the city and county to double real estate document recording fees to generate revenues for affordable housing.[5]

The fund launched with $1.5 million in seed money from the city and collected about $11 million in fiscal 2006, with expected revenues of $14 million in fiscal 2007. The fund's first Request for Proposal supported gap financing for the rehabilitation or development of 465 housing units. Trust fund monies are also helping low-income residents of targeted neighborhoods repair existing homes. This both protects new investment in the area and allows current residents to enjoy the benefits of neighborhood revitalization. In addition, trust fund resources support Philadelphia's efforts to reduce homelessness by helping to pay for permanent supportive housing and rent subsidies for people who are ready to leave transitional housing but not yet able to shoulder rent payments.

The New York City Housing Trust Fund, established with $130 million in revenues from the Battery Park City Authority,[6] focuses on poor and middle-class families ineligible for most affordable housing (with incomes below 30 percent, and between 60 and 80 percent of area median income). The fund aims to create or preserve 4,300 affordable housing units as part of Mayor Michael Bloomberg's 10-year plan to add 165,000 units of affordable housing by 2012.

Public-Private Partnership Helps Residents of High-Cost Santa Clara

The Housing Trust of Santa Clara County is a true public-private partnership that draws revenues from multiple local governments, private and philanthropic contributions (including from local companies), and citizen donations. The trust began distributing funds in 2001. As of November 2006, it had invested $23.7 million and leveraged nearly $1.1 billion, creating 5,977 housing opportunities. Funds support housing programs for homeless people with special needs, homelessness prevention, first-time homebuyer assistance, and multifamily rental housing. Using the trust's no-interest loans for closing costs and low-cost mortgages, 1,697 families with average incomes of $70,533 have purchased homes in a market where the median cost is over $700,000. The trust has also created 1,258 units of new rental housing in 16 developments in nearly every community in the county. The trust's multifamily grants and loans are often used as crucial financing toward the end of a developer's fundraising cycle or as predevelopment loans to secure the property and for other early-stage needs.

Virginia Communities Preserve Affordable Rental Housing

Fairfax County and the City of Alexandria have housing trust funds that focus on preserving affordable rental housing in one of the nation's highest-cost markets. The Fairfax County Board of Supervisors earmarks an amount equal to one penny of the real estate tax rate for the One Penny for Housing Flexibility Fund. The impetus came in part from ongoing losses of affordable housing countywide. Appropriations to Fairfax's penny fund amounted to about $40 million in the first two years (fiscal 2006–2007). As of December 2006, the fund was well on its way to leveraging other monies and helping to preserve 1,000 units by the end of 2007.

Alexandria's fund also receives one penny on the real property tax rate. In Alexandria, housing, tenant advocacy, and smart growth interests sought to stem displacement due to condominium conversions and escalating rents. Alexandria's One Penny fund generated approximately $2.9 million for affordable housing in fiscal 2006 and is expected to generate $3.3 million in fiscal 2007. To reflect the high priority that the city places on maintaining a supply of affordable housing, the city council authorized the issuance of up to $22.1 million in general obligation bonds, pledging the income stream from the penny-for-housing tax to pay the debt service. The bond funds are expected to preserve 134 rental units.

Boulder, Colorado Trust Assures Permanent Affordability

Boulder is using its housing trust fund, the Community Housing Assistance Program (CHAP), to ensure that 10 percent of the housing stock (4,500 units) is permanently affordable to households at or below 68 percent of area median income (HUD's low-income limit for Boulder). CHAP is funded by property taxes and a tax on new development, called the housing excise tax. These sources generate $1.0–1.5 million annually. The fund is generally used to support the acquisition and maintenance of rental housing for households making 15–60 percent of area median income. In an RFP process administered by the city's Department of Housing and Human Services, CHAP funds are pooled with other fund sources.[7] Covenants attached to the housing assure continued affordability. As of November 2006, there were 2,700 permanently affordable units (2,098 rental and 602 owned) in the City of Boulder.

San Diego Fund Adapts to City's Changing Needs

San Diego's Affordable Housing Fund supports the city's Balanced Communities Policy that seeks to disperse affordable housing throughout the city by funding mixed-income projects. Fund monies are also used to develop and launch programs to meet new needs without requiring additional legislation. For example, the fund created a program offering $10,000 bonuses per unit to developers building affordable housing in higher-income areas of the city. Another program provides homebuyer assistance for residents of apartment buildings being converted to condominiums. The fund is administered by the San Diego Housing Commission, which functions as both a city housing department and public housing authority.

The fund has two primary sources of revenue—linkage fees levied on commercial and industrial buildings, and in-lieu fees from developers who choose not to build affordable units required under the city's inclusionary housing law. The commercial linkage fee revenue stream was established in the early 1990s and is funneled into the city's original Housing Trust Fund. As of June 30, 2006, the Housing Trust Fund had invested more than $65 million in affordable housing, leveraging an additional $740 million and helping to create 7,755 affordable housing units.[8] The inclusionary housing fees go into a separate sub-fund, the Inclusionary Housing Fund, which had invested $1.7 million to help create 522 affordable housing units as of June 30, 2006.[9] San Diego's fund is notable for its investment in building the capacity of nonprofit housing providers.

Chicago Funds Fill Gaps in Aid to Lowest-Income Renters

Chicago and Illinois have both established trust funds specifically to provide rental assistance to households earning no more than 30 percent of area median income. The funds, which direct half their resources to those earning less than 15 percent of area median income, fill the gap between the number of very low-income people who need rental assistance and the number that can be served through federal subsidy programs.

The Chicago Low Income Housing Trust Fund predates the state rental assistance fund by about 15 years. Until 2006, the Chicago fund was using HOME funds, HUD grants, and City of Chicago funds to subsidize more than 2,000 apartments annually. In 2005, after a bipartisan campaign by real estate, civic, business, and faith-based groups, Illinois lawmakers created the Illinois Rental Housing Support Program.[10] The program is funded by an additional $10 fee on the recording of real estate documents and is administered by the Illinois Housing Development Authority. Program officials expect it to provide $25 million annually in rental subsidies to at least 5,500 households. Beginning in 2006, Chicago's fund began collecting about $10 million annually from the state program.

Washington Fund Expands Statewide Housing Industry

Washington State's Housing Trust Fund (HTF) is considered one of the country's most effective, both for the amount of funds generated and for its expansion of affordable housing development capacity statewide. A bipartisan effort from its inception in the late 1980s, the fund currently receives approximately $100 million every two years from the state's capital budget, thus serving as the state's largest public funding source for affordable housing. From 1989 through 2006, the fund invested $500 million and leveraged a total of about $2 billion to develop, preserve, or rehabilitate more than 32,000 primarily rental housing units for low-income families and individuals.

The trust fund coordinates spending with local jurisdictions and the Housing Finance Commission, which administers the tax-credit and bond programs. Projects that receive HTF awards get extra points on their application for tax credits. The fund supports local nonprofit developers and housing authorities not just with funds for projects, but also with developer fees and technical assistance. This has helped create the statewide affordable housing development industry. About half of the funds go out in low-cost loans, the repayment of which helps to cover operating costs.

The trust is on the leading edge in terms of asset management, ensuring that its investments are protected in the long run. The HTF now requires projects to conduct a capital needs assessment and build long-term reserves into funding. It also works with the Housing Finance Commission, City of Seattle, King County, and some other local jurisdictions on joint inspections and workouts (such as loan restructuring, transfer/ assignment of property, and even sale of properties).

Washington Fund Supports Statewide Effort to Reduce Homelessness

Washington State recently created a separate homeless trust fund from a $10 surcharge on the state's document recording fees. It is expected to raise $20 million annually and support the state goal of cutting homelessness by half by 2015. Some of the funding is allocated by the state through a competitive RFP process. Counties get a substantial portion for implementing their local plans to end homelessness.

2 Federal Home Loan Banks

Created to provide liquidity and stability to the mortgage market, the Federal Home Loan Banks (FHLBanks) offer low-cost financing and other banking services to more than 8,100 member institutions.[11] They also make direct grants, subsidized loans, and subsidized advances to affordable housing projects through the Affordable Housing Program (AHP). The AHP, funded by a congressionally mandated 10 percent set-aside from the FHLBanks annual net earnings, is the largest source of private grants for affordable housing in the US. From inception in 1990 through 2006, the banks have awarded $2.5 billion in AHP subsidies to assist more than 519,000 housing units.[12] Seventy percent of the units receiving AHP subsidies have been for very low-income households.[13]

Designed as a flexible, competitive funding source, the AHP provides grants and below-market-rate loans for projects that target very low- to moderate-income households. AHP funding is intended as gap financing to make a project viable in tandem with other funding sources. AHP funds are often a first or early funding commitment, leveraging other commitments. According to the Federal Housing Finance Board, AHP subsidies have been effective for projects that present underwriting challenges such as housing for homeless people, people with disabilities, and the elderly. AHP funds have also been paired with Low-Income Housing Tax Credits to support rental housing for very low-income households.[14]

AHP funds have also been instrumental in supporting homeownership. For example, one in four Habitat for Humanity homes in the US has had AHP funds in the development financing mix. In addition, all FHLBanks are allowed to set aside up to 35 percent of AHP funding for homebuyer assistance and owner-occupied rehabilitation.[15] Homeownership set-aside funds primarily for downpayment and closing cost assistance are allotted to member financial institutions to make their first mortgage programs accessible to low-income buyers. Between 1990 and 2005, the homeownership set-aside assisted with the purchase of over 47,000 homes.[16]

The AHP funding element of a project is not always apparent to local housing leaders because the funds are channeled through an FHLB member institution, which partners with a project sponsor/developer to apply for AHP funds.[17] How applications are scored depends in part on the criteria set for all AHP programs by the Federal Housing Finance Board (FHFB) and how individual FHLBanks decide to weight the various categories. The scoring system generally gives an advantage to projects led by nonprofit developers, sited on donated public lands, provided for community stability, and offering some form of resident empowerment (whether through on-site supportive services for rental developments or homebuyer education for for-sale housing developments).

To be eligible for AHP funding, a rental project must set aside at least 20 percent of the units for very low-income families. Projects that reserve at least 20 percent of the units for homeless people and provide them with shelter for at least six months are also eligible for points. In general, the lower the income of the households served, the more points the project receives in the targeting category.

Each FHLBank can weight up to 40 percent of the scoring criteria for local priorities. For example, FHLBank Atlanta awards points for projects that are in rural and disaster areas, serve first-time homebuyers, and involve rehabilitation of owner-occupied units. FHLBank Topeka gives priority to rural first-time homebuyers, special needs, member participation, and projects evidencing community support.

This is where local government can make the difference in competing for FHLB funds. If local government steps up with meaningful financial or in-kind contributions, the project will score higher and be more likely to receive funds. While local governments often submit letters of support for projects, this backing does not earn points or improve the project's competitive ranking.

In addition to providing funds, FHLBanks are often a key source of training and technical assistance for member banks and their development partners. FHLBanks and their leaders also serve important roles as sponsors, conveners, and partnership builders. The following are just a few examples of the ways the FHLBanks support local affordable housing initiatives.

▼ CASES IN POINT

Grant Helps Provide Affordable Co-Housing for Seniors in Rural Virginia

The ElderSpirit Community is one of the first mixed-income co-housing communities in the nation for people aged 55 and older. Located in Abingdon, Virginia, the $3.5 million community includes 16 subsidized rental units and 13 single-family homes. Trailview Development Corporation executive director Dene Peterson worked with several community groups and lenders for six years to bring affordable senior housing to this rural community. Funding sources for the two-phase project include the Virginia Housing Development Authority, Virginia Department of Housing and Community Development, Federation of Appalachian Housing Enterprises, Retirement Research Foundation, First Bank & Trust, New Peoples Bank, Commonwealth Community Bank, and First Bank of Virginia. FHLBank Atlanta provided a $178,000 Affordable Housing Program grant through Highlands Union Bank.

Partnership Preserves Affordable Housing for Washington, DC Tenants

Galen Terrace, a federally subsidized 84-unit community in Washington, DC, was in serious disrepair and threatened with sale to the private market. Tenants exercised their right of first refusal and arranged for a "friendly" buyer to work with them in 2004. They succeeded in purchasing their homes in March 2006. The Galen Terrace Tenants Association, Inc., Somerset Development, and National Housing Trust/Enterprise Preservation Corporation. partnered to rehabilitate the complex's six buildings.

The DC Housing Finance Agency provided $5.6 million in tax-exempt bonds and $4.65 million in tax-credit equity toward the acquisition and renovation, and the Department of Housing and Community Development provided $3.25 million in CDBG funds. The Federal Home Loan Bank of Atlanta supported the project with a $100,000 predevelopment loan that helped pay for architectural plans and the upfront studies needed to secure permanent financing. HUD renewed the complex's Section 8 contract for another 20 years. A portion of the development fees and cash flow will support after-school programs and other tenant services. The complex provides homes in a fast-developing section of the city, and is a leading example of green housing projects in the District of Columbia.[18]

Leverage Revitalizes Public Housing in Charlotte

The Charlotte Housing Authority (CHA) and its subsidiary, Horizon Development, have received more than $3.3 million in AHP grants and subsidies from FHLBank Atlanta. The agency and its community partners have leveraged AHP funds to help redevelop five HOPE VI projects throughout the city. In 2005, CHA partnered with FHLBank Atlanta member Bank of America to secure $742,000 in AHP subsidies to help construct Montgomery Gardens, a 76-unit HOPE VI off-site redevelopment of the former Fairview Homes in Charlotte. In addition to AHP funds, the $8.3 million development combined HOPE VI funding, federal and state tax credits, and a City of Charlotte Housing Trust Fund loan. The recently completed project will provide two- and three-bedroom apartments affordable for former Fairview residents.

FHLBank Topeka Partners with Rural Government to Expand Homeownership

Using a $215,000 AHP subsidy from FHLBank Topeka, Commerce Bank and Trust in Emporia, Kansas helped the City of Emporia launch one of its first homeownership initiatives. The AHP subsidy will be combined with conventional financing and other sources to fund construction of 40 new homes and rehabilitation of another 25. With the subsidy, the town will provide downpayment and closing cost assistance to 40 first-time homebuyers. Forty-five of the new and rehabilitated units will be available to people with up to 50 percent of area median income, 10 are for those at 60 percent AMI, and 10 units are for those at 70 percent AMI. Thirteen units will be available for the elderly or people with special needs. Mandatory homebuyer education and credit counseling will be provided.

Colorado Project Preserves Rental Housing for the Homeless

First Bank of Denver and the Colorado Coalition for the Homeless combined efforts to obtain a $450,000 AHP subsidy from FHLBank Topeka to acquire and rehabilitate an apartment complex for homeless people. The Renaissance 88 Apartments, located in Thornton, Colorado, is a Section 8, HUD 236 property that was headed for sale and conversion to market rates. The six buildings in the complex occupy a 9.2-acre site with ample green space and recreation areas. By mid-2007, there will be 180 one- to four-bedroom units with a new multi-purpose community building that contains a computer lab, meeting space, and a kitchen.

The AHP subsidy is being combined with four-percent Low-Income Housing Tax Credits, private activity bonds, a low-interest Housing Opportunities Fund loan, a deferred acquisition loan, deferred developer fees, and state and county HOME funds. Total development costs are more than $20.5 million. Some 120 units will be for residents earning 50 percent of area median income, and 60 units will be for residents earning 60 percent AMI. Sixty of the 180 units will be dedicated specifically to the homeless.

FHLBank Leaders Convene Initiatives Tackling Critical Issues

FHLBanks have provided valuable leadership to local and regional initiatives tackling a range of housing issues. For example, FHLBank Topeka has committed $900,000 since 1998 to homebuyer education in Colorado, Kansas, Nebraska and Oklahoma. Each state is allocated $25,000 a year to help fund efforts to educate and counsel new homebuyers, in part to reduce foreclosures. The money is dispersed through nonprofit housing organizations.

Using research it helped to support at Florida State University, FHLBank Atlanta sponsored a workshop on impact fees for the Florida Housing Coalition, among other educational events. FHLBank Atlanta has also provided training and advice to community banks on setting up or improving their community lending operations. Staff and management are engaged in local and national networks such as the Mixed-Income Communities Initiative, a coalition devoted to tackling the jobs/housing imbalance, and the Georgia State Trade Association of Nonprofit Developers, which works on state policy related to affordable housing development. The bank also helped to form lender consortia that target multifamily tax credit deals in Atlanta and Alabama.

3 Fannie Mae and Freddie Mac

Fannie Mae and Freddie Mac are federally chartered private companies that make mortgage money available to communities across the country, providing lenders with a reliable supply of capital. These government-sponsored enterprises buy home mortgages from lenders, re-supplying capital so that lenders can issue additional loans. Fannie Mae and Freddie Mac also package pools of mortgages into mortgage-backed securities.

To increase the availability of mortgages for low- and moderate-income households and other underserved buyers, both Fannie Mae and Freddie Mac have created mortgage products with low downpayments and flexible underwriting criteria. Fannie Mae's product line is known as MyCommunityMortgage™,[19] while Freddie Mac's is called Home Possible®.[20] Lending partners use the mortgage standards, automated underwriting systems, and servicing guidelines created by these companies to deliver mortgage capital to US consumers. Lenders are more likely to issue such mortgages knowing that they can get them off their books by selling to these secondary mortgage market participants. Both GSEs permit the use of various state and local subsidy programs in conjunction with the first mortgages provided by Home Possible and MyCommunityMortgage.

Through their lender partners, the GSEs also offer multiple products more directly supporting local housing efforts. At Fannie Mae, the company's Community Business Centers are a key conduit for these products. Center staff meet with local government and nonprofit intermediary leaders to help them access the Fannie Mae products they need to fulfill the housing components of their revitalization strategies. At

Freddie Mac, the implementation of affordable homeownership efforts is led by the Expanding Markets staff, working out of regional centers in Atlanta, Chicago, Dallas, Los Angeles, New York, and the corporate offices in Northern Virginia.

Fannie Mae's Housing and Community Development Division (HCD) provides affordable housing developers with debt and/or equity investments. HCD's Community Investment group targets equity and mezzanine investments that increase homeownership and rental opportunities for low-, moderate- and middle-income families and revitalize neighborhoods. On the debt side, the Community Lending group purchases a participation interest in a construction loan or construction letter of credit from lenders. The construction loan participation helps Fannie Mae's lender partners expand relationships with their clients, reduce their exposure, and manage their portfolios.

Fannie Mae is the nation's largest LIHTC investor and the largest private investor in multifamily mortgage lending. To support the construction or rehabilitation of multifamily housing, Fannie Mae invests in projects for which it receives Low-Income Housing Tax Credits, provides loans to purchase or renovate small multifamily rental complexes, and offers credit enhancements for tax-exempt bonds issued to finance, buy, build, refinance, or substantially rehabilitate multifamily housing.[21]

A special group within Fannie Mae serves public entities, including public housing agencies. The group purchases taxable and tax-exempt mortgage revenue bonds issued for single-family and multifamily developments, allowing housing finance agencies to increase funding for their affordable housing programs. The group also makes direct loans to small and mid-size public housing authorities for modernizing their housing stock. The loans, called Modernization Express™, are secured by their federal capital funding streams.

Other Fannie Mae products provide investment capital to community-based financial intermediaries such as LISC, Enterprise, and the Mercy Loan Fund[22] and make grants to nonprofit organizations to support such activities as homeownership counseling and housing development. Community Business Center staff offer technical assistance to city planners, a resource that has been leveraged in efforts to redevelop the Gulf Coast.

For its part, Freddie Mac provides a full range of competitively priced mortgage products for the acquisition, refinance, or moderate rehabilitation of multifamily communities, including independent and assisted-living properties. These include a variety of conventional and adjustable-rate mortgages as well as products targeted for affordable projects, such as credit enhancements for multifamily housing bonds. Under its forward commitment program, Freddie Mac works with housing developers who have received an allocation of tax credits for their projects. Freddie Mac will agree to lock in the rate and establish the terms of a permanent mortgage on the properties prior to construction. The rates and terms, good for 18–36 months, enable the projects to be built and leased. The program also has features allowing developers to use Freddie Mac or bank funds during construction.

Freddie Mac purchases tax credits through tax-credit funds, thereby providing developers with equity to build or rehabilitate tax-credit properties. The company made a record $1.3 billion investment in tax credits in 2004, and met that record again in 2005.

Increasing homeownership opportunity, especially for first-time buyers, is a significant focus. Freddie Mac helps mortgage lenders reach low- and moderate-income and minority homebuyers by creating new outreach and education campaigns, harnessing technology to meet affordable needs, and by strengthening lender linkages to other housing intermediaries. Lenders increasingly look to Freddie Mac to create new lending initiatives with housing intermediaries such as real estate professionals, nonprofit organizations, and employers.

For example, through its Workforce Home Benefit initiative, Freddie Mac assists employers in designing, implementing, and administering homeownership initiatives for their employees. As part of these programs, Freddie Mac often helps employers identify effective approaches, provides links to community organizations that can offer homebuyer education and credit counseling, finds lenders responsive to an employer's needs, and coordinates the initiatives with state and local agencies.

Nonprofit housing agencies need to be empowered with technology to help first-time buyers make informed decisions. Freddie Mac's Loan Prospector Outreach helps housing counselors assess the readiness of their clients to apply for mortgages and helps lenders get more qualified mortgage leads.[23]

Freddie Mac also offers a number of tools that local agencies can use to educate potential and existing homeowners, including Get the Facts!, a bilingual toolkit of instructional videos and other media addressing the common misperceptions that keep people from exploring homeownership; CreditSmart® and CreditSmart® Español, comprehensive financial literacy curricula covering the importance of obtaining and maintaining good credit; and the Don't Borrow Trouble Anti-Predatory Lending Campaign, which combines public education with counseling services to help homeowners avoid scams and resolve financial difficulties. As of 2006, 50 local and statewide campaigns had been launched and more than 100,000 consumers had been assisted through the Don't Borrow Trouble campaigns.

▼ CASES IN POINT

Loans and Investments Support Campaigns to Curb Homelessness

Through strategic partnerships with national organizations, Fannie Mae works to increase private investment in supportive housing. Fannie Mae makes Low-Income Housing Tax Credit equity investments in supportive housing and other projects serving people who are homeless or at risk through two $100 million funds—one with Enterprise Community Investment and the other with National Equity Fund and its network of syndicator partners. For example, in 2005, Fannie Mae invested about $27 million in a 217-unit permanent supportive housing tax-credit project developed by Common Ground Community in Brooklyn, NY, where 160 of the units were set aside for homeless people or residents with special needs. This tax-credit project was part of a more than $109 million investment in 15 homeless housing projects in which Fannie Mae was the sole equity investor.

Fannie Mae has also mobilized other tools to increase production of supportive housing. In one such case, Fannie Mae entered into a $4.5 million master participation agreement with the Corporation for Supportive Housing (CSH) in 2005, providing liquidity by purchasing up to a 50-percent interest in predevelopment and acquisition loans that CSH originates. In 2006, Fannie Mae (and subsequently other investors) joined with Deutsche Bank in a $10 million credit facility to Common Ground Community for acquisition and early predevelopment funds for future supportive housing projects.

Bond Enhancements Preserve Affordable Rental Housing in New York

Both Freddie Mac and Fannie Mae have used bond enhancements to help cities preserve affordable housing units whose original construction was subsidized locally or by a range of federal programs. Using its affordable forward commitment program, Freddie Mac enhanced $39 million worth of tax-exempt bonds, enabling the Wishcamper Group to substantially rehabilitate Parkledge Apartments in Yonkers, NY. The five-building, 311-unit complex, built in the 1970s under HUD's Section 8 program, offered badly needed affordable housing in an area where growing demand was adding to pressures to convert to market rate. Instead, Wishcamper committed to providing units at below-market rates to tenants, the majority of which received housing assistance. The 2003–2004 rehabilitation included improvements to the property's major building components, security, and exterior, along with significant upgrades to tenants' apartments.

A Freddie Mac bond enhancement played a role in preserving a 582-unit Brooklyn complex with expiring tax credits. In 2005, the compliance period for the Low-Income Housing Tax Credits used to finance construction of Spring Creek Gardens expired, leaving the building vulnerable to conversion to market rate. The Arker Companies and the Domain Companies purchased the complex and assembled a financing package to preserve the units' affordability for another 33 years. The New York City Housing Development Corporation provided a $24 million bond-financed construction loan through its Low-Income Affordable Housing Marketplace Program (LAMP). Through this program, tax-exempt bonds are issued to make low-cost loans and qualify developments to receive LIHTCs. CharterMac syndicated the tax credits, yielding $17 million in equity, while Citibank provided the letter of credit necessary to secure the bond financing. Freddie Mac agreed to provide long-term enhancement once construction is completed. This combination reduced development costs, keeping the rents affordable to tenants earning up to 60 percent of area median income.

In 2005, Fannie Mae helped New York City's Housing Development Corporation (HDC) refinance and recapitalize 10 deteriorating apartment complexes that the Progress of Peoples Corporation had developed more than 20 years earlier with HUD 202 subsidies. One of Fannie Mae's multifamily lending partners provided a credit enhancement for HDC's $90 million bond issue, while Fannie Mae itself invested in Low-Income Housing Tax Credits syndicated by the Enterprise Investment Group. With this refinancing, the Progress of Peoples Corporation was able to generate sufficient revenue to bring the buildings up to par and create ongoing funds for more intensive services that would enable residents to age in place.

In another example, Fannie Mae worked with the New York City Department of Housing Preservation and Development to develop a set of incentives for owners of middle-income, rent-regulated properties to stay in the Mitchell-Lama program rather than go market-rate. Fannie Mae provided credit enhancement by approving the Housing Development Corporation as a multifamily seller/servicer, thereby enabling it to refinance these transactions. Through the initiative, property owners were able to reduce their overall debt burden, make needed physical improvements, and maintain affordability requirements for moderate-income residents.

California Initiative Reaches Out to Latino Homebuyers

To improve industry outreach to the fast-growing Latino homebuyer community, Freddie Mac worked with the California Association of Realtors®, the National Association of Hispanic Real Estate Professionals, and key lending institutions to create the California Latino Homeownership Initiative. Started in 2005, the statewide training program uses a curriculum that Freddie Mac developed to educate real estate professionals about how best to reach prospective Hispanic homebuyers through in-culture messaging and responsive products. The course is approved by the state Department of Real Estate for continuing education credit. In the first 18 months of the program, over 2,500 real estate professionals had been trained. Similar statewide education campaigns are either under way or in development in Nevada, Texas, and Washington.

Tools Fund Mixed-Income and Workforce Housing Developments in Atlanta

Fannie Mae has used a variety of tools to fund several mixed-income workforce housing projects spearheaded by the Atlanta Development Authority (ADA). For example, Fannie Mae made a $3.5 million line of credit available through the authority to the developer to transform a severely blighted 900-unit apartment community in southwest Atlanta into four new homeowner neighborhoods. A primary goal of the project, collectively called Cascade Parc, is to enable moderate-income workers to live in the city rather than having to move into the far reaches of the metro area to find affordable housing—a common traffic-producing problem known as "driving to qualify." The development authority retained ownership of the 50-acre site. Developer Sharon McSwain Homes is building 331 condominium town homes and single-family detached homes. A unique arrangement with the development authority allowed the builder to treat the debt as equity, which, along with other features, is helping to keep prices about $20,000 to $40,000 below those for comparable market-rate homes. Fannie Mae's lender partners also offered buyers 40-year mortgages.

Initiatives Dispel Homeownership Myths among Minority Families

In 2006, Freddie Mac launched Get The Facts!, a nationwide outreach and education initiative designed to dispel common misconceptions about buying and owning a home. Recent research by Freddie Mac indicates that many African-American and Hispanic consumers believe owning a home is unattainable, largely because of misunderstandings about credit, downpayment requirements, or length of time in one job. Working through more than 25 participating lenders, the Get The Facts! initiative provides linkages to community-based education providers, distributes collateral materials designed for grassroots outreach, and incorporates a state-of-the-art workshop curriculum that motivates consumers to better understand the homebuying process and take steps toward realizing the possibilities.

Freddie Mac also uses other creative, nontraditional methods to reach underserved families. In response to research indicating that many minority and lower-income families are intimidated by the homebuying process and often do not know which lenders they can trust, five Freddie Mac lender customers were provided with fully retrofitted, high-tech commercial buses that traveled to homeownership centers. The "eBus" goes where people work, live, play, and pray. In 2005–2006, the eBuses reached more than 70,000 individuals in more than 25 states.

Loan Participation Assures New Rental Housing Development

In 2004, Lafayette, Indiana Neighborhood Housing Services borrowed $8 million from National Coop Bank to provide construction financing and bridge Low-Income Housing Tax Credit equity for an adaptive reuse project. The project was to convert the historic Jefferson High School building in downtown Lafayette into a 74-unit complex for seniors with up to 60 percent of area median income. The $8 million loan would be repaid with the pay-in of LIHTC equity from Enterprise Social Investment Corporation, the syndicator of the deal. Because the loan was larger than the bank felt comfortable with, Fannie Mae purchased half the loan. The project budget included $6 million in LIHTC equity, $1.6 million in Historic Tax Credit equity, $500,000 in Affordable Housing Program financing from the Federal Home Loan Bank, and a $242,000 loan from the City of Lafayette, using HOME funds.

Collaboration Makes Home Possible for Military Families

Providing affordable and attractive housing options for military personnel and their families is a challenge in many markets across the nation. At Fort Drum in upstate New York, the return of thousands of soldiers from Iraq and Afghanistan in early 2007 created a housing supply crisis. In anticipation of this need, Freddie Mac worked collaborated with military, community, and lending institutions to create the Fort Drum Homeownership Initiative in late 2006. Special Home Possible mortgage product enhancements help military families qualify for new homes, using free customized homeownership and financial literacy counseling, plus new technology to quickly determine homebuying readiness. Freddie Mac seeks to expand local government involvement in addressing the homebuying needs of military bases experiencing growth.[24]

Line of Credit Generates Workforce Housing in Denver

In 2000, Fannie Mae provided a $10 million line of credit to the City of Denver. Subsequently increased to $17.5 million, the credit line has facilitated efforts to develop new affordable housing and revitalize distressed neighborhoods in the city and county of Denver. According to the city, it has helped to finance seven new developments with 607 units, 527 of which are considered workforce or affordable housing.

Fannie Mae and Freddie Mac Aid Recovery Efforts in the Gulf Coast

After Hurricanes Katrina, Rita, and Wilma battered 90,000 square miles of the Gulf Coast region, Freddie Mac and Fannie Mae stepped in to aid recovery efforts. In the short term, Freddie Mac donated more than $10 million in humanitarian assistance primarily to help displaced families find temporary or permanent housing, provided mortgage payment and other relief to homeowners, and helped mortgage servicers and lenders reestablish operations. Freddie Mac also made a substantial contribution to the long-term recovery of the region by investing $1 billion in state and local mortgage revenue bonds, funding housing for as many as 10,000 families.

On the rental side, Freddie Mac worked with lenders to offer forbearance on 25 loans on apartment buildings located in FEMA-designated disaster areas, to help remediation efforts at those and other complexes, and distribute insurance proceeds for repairs. During the ongoing recovery efforts, Freddie Mac worked with its multifamily lender partners to fund more than $840 million in mortgages on 82 properties, providing a total of 23,494 rental units for Gulf families.

Fannie Mae also brought immediate relief to Katrina evacuees. The company instituted a one-year moratorium on foreclosures, modified thousands of loans to minimize the burden of making up missed payments, instituted new underwriting guidelines that disregard adverse credit caused by the hurricanes, and kept mortgage capital flowing to the region with new single-family products. Fannie Mae was able to support the market by assuring capital flow for workforce housing. Through November 2006, Fannie Mae helped by lending and investing in the multifamily market through $254 million of debt and $110 million in equity, and creating Gulf Opportunity Zone funds to support increased LIHTC investment in the region. Tools used to assist partners in building new housing include an equity fund to support for-sale housing and public entity lines of credit to support redevelopment of critical affordable rental housing.

CENTER FOR COMMUNITY CHANGE
Housing Trust Fund Project (HTFP)
www.communitychange.org/issues/housing/trustfundproject

Operates as a clearinghouse for information on housing trust funds throughout the country and provides technical assistance to organizations and agencies working to create or implement these funds. HTFP publications include "Winning at the Local Level: 5 Housing Trust Fund Campaigns Tell Their Stories," and "Housing Trust Fund Progress Report 2002." The project also publishes a newsletter, *Housing Trust Fund Project News.*

FANNIE MAE
www.fanniemae.com

Provides financial products and services that increase the availability and affordability of housing for low-, moderate- and middle-income families. In 2005, Fannie Mae published "Housing Solutions," a guide to how Fannie Mae's mortgage initiatives, investments, and business strategies are designed to help mortgage lenders and other housing partners expand affordable housing.

FEDERAL HOUSING FINANCE BOARD
www.fhfb.gov

Regulates the 12 Federal Home Loan Banks. The website posts various reports on the Affordable Housing Program and lists information for each of the FHLBanks.

FREDDIE MAC
www.freddiemac.com

Buys mortgages from lenders to keep money flowing in support of homeownership and rental housing, initiates and supports community development projects, and provides consumer education. The website details how Freddie Mac supports the creation and preservation of low-income housing.

MINNESOTA HOUSING PARTNERSHIP
www.mhponline.org

Assists Minnesota communities in creating and preserving housing affordable to low and moderate-income people. The partnership published "Achieving Homes for All: Alternative Revenue Sources for Affordable Housing in Minnesota," analyzing the revenue strategies that several states use to raise funds for affordable housing, the political context of revenue raising in each state, and a ranking of states by per capita affordable housing revenues.

ENDNOTES CHAPTER 10

1. For example, enabling legislation in Pennsylvania allows counties to double their document recording fees. In addition to creating trust funds of their own, states such as Iowa and California provide matching funds for local trust funds, which has a significant impact on new fund creation.

2. According to the Housing Trust Fund Project's "Housing Trust Fund Progress Report 2002," sources include interest from real estate escrow accounts, a state unclaimed property fund, deed recording fees, bond and fee revenues, interest on tenant security deposits, interest on mortgage escrow accounts, eviction court fees, state income taxes, securities act cash fund, unspent TANF reserves, Section 8 reserves, general obligation bond proceeds, interest from the budget stabilization fund, debt reserve funds, penalties on late real estate excise tax payments, unclaimed lottery earnings, loan repayments and interest earnings, surplus funds, and general funds.

3. Under many inclusionary zoning ordinances, developers must either set aside a portion of the units in new projects for affordable housing or pay a fee to the city to be used for affordable housing programs.

4. Florida was an early leader in creating a state housing trust fund that allocates some of its funds directly to local jurisdictions. About a third of the funds received each year go to the state housing trust fund, which supports statewide programs administered by the Florida Housing Finance Corporation. The other two-thirds go to the State Housing Initiative Partnership program (SHIP), which distributes funds to eligible county and entitlement jurisdictions.

5. For more on the campaign to establish the fund, see Center for Community Change, "Philadelphia Wins Housing Trust Fund!," *Housing Trust Fund Project News,* Summer 2005, **www.communitychange.org/shared/publications/downloads/HTFund_Summer_2005.pdf.**

6. The Battery Park City Authority collects revenues (rents and payments in lieu of taxes) from development on city-leased land in the 91-acre Battery Park City.

7. Other fund sources include HOME, a portion of CDBG, and inclusionary zoning revenues, i.e., payments in lieu of building required affordable housing. Revenues go into the Affordable Housing Fund, which also collects some city general fund dollars.

8. The fund has collected $71 million from linkage fees and other revenue sources. About $6 million has been spent on administrative costs. In 2003, the city amended the Housing Trust Fund Ordinance to create a new Affordable Housing Fund consisting of the Housing Trust Fund and the Inclusionary Housing Fund.

9. A citywide inclusionary housing ordinance enacted in 2003 allows developers the option of paying fees in lieu of setting aside 10 percent of the homes in developments for low- and moderate-income families. As of June 30, 2006, developers had built 80 units to comply with the inclusionary ordinance.

10. Center for Community Change, "Illinois Passes Rental Housing Support Program," *Housing Trust Fund Project News,* Summer 2005, **www.communitychange.org/shared/publications/downloads/HTFund_Summer_2005.pdf.**

11. The FHLBanks are the core funding source for community banks. Like Fannie Mae and Freddie Mac, the FHLBanks help banks get mortgage loans off their balance sheets by purchasing those loans. The FHLBanks do not, however, securitize the loans but instead hold them on their own balance sheets. The FHLBanks also make collateralized loans, or advances, to their members and state housing finance agencies.

12. Statement of Ronald A. Rosenfeld, Chairman of the Federal Housing Finance Board to the Committee on House Financial Services Subcommittee on Capital Markets, Insurance and Government Sponsored Enterprises, *CQ Congressional Testimony,* September 7, 2006.

13. Affordable Housing Program Amendments, Federal Housing Finance Board, Final Rule, *Federal Register* 71:194, October 6, 2006, **www.fhfb.gov/GetFile.aspx?FileID=6052**.

14. Under federal law, projects receiving LIHTCs must either set aside 20 percent of the units for households with incomes at or below 50 percent of area median income or set aside 40 percent of the units for households with incomes at or below 60 percent of AMI. Rental projects eligible for AHP funding must set aside at least 20 percent of the units for households with incomes at or below 50 percent of AMI.

15. The new AHP rule published in October 2006 allows but does not require FHLBanks to set aside the greater of $4.5 million or 35 percent of their annual AHP allocation to homeownership set-aside programs. A third must be targeted to first-time homebuyers.

16. Affordable Housing Program Amendments, **www.fhfb.gov/GetFile.aspx?FileID=6052**.

17. The project sponsor/developer applying for AHP funding is usually a nonprofit, for-profit, or quasi-governmental entity, such as a housing authority or community-based housing organization, rather than a public agency.

18. Nikita Stewart, "'Green' Rules for Developers Appear Likely," *The Washington Post,* December 3, 2006, C1, C4.

19. MyCommunityMortgage requires no minimum downpayment or contribution from the borrower and, aided by a reduced mortgage insurance coverage requirement, enables lenders to offer consumers a low monthly payment. It accepts nontraditional forms of credit and provides flexibility on income sources. Recent enhancements include 40-year terms, eligibility for 2-1 temporary interest-rate buy-downs, and several interest-only options. Additional flexibility is available for teachers and other public workers, as well as for borrowers with disabilities.

20. Home Possible mortgages have zero or very low downpayments and offer flexible credit requirements to foster homeownership in underserved communities and among households at or below median income. A broad array of Home Possible product structures is possible, including fixed-rate mortgages up to 40 years and many adjustable-rate options. Home Possible also offers higher loan-to-value ratios, a buy-down feature, and other underwriting criteria to help critical community workers such as teachers, police, firefighters, healthcare workers, and military personnel afford homes in the communities where they work.

21. Tax-exempt bonds issued for housing purposes typically use some sort of credit enhancement that provides a higher rating and therefore a lower interest rate. The purchaser carries a lower risk because another entity rather than the real estate secures its interest. With its AAA rating, Fannie Mae can pass through lower interest rates to the project.

22. Fannie Mae has established lines of credit or made loans to intermediaries that already have a track record of helping developers create housing. The company is expanding upon this model, which leverages existing expertise.

23. The housing counselor inputs the client's financial data into Loan Prospector Outreach, reviews the client's credit history, and considers the various financing and mortgage options. Loan Prospector Outreach conducts a client assessment in minutes, returning either a "Ready to Apply" or "Continue Counseling" outcome. When the client is ready to apply, Loan Prospector Outreach provides an automated way to convey the client's information (with the client's consent) to a participating lender. If a "continue counseling" message is

received, additional feedback is provided to assist the housing counselor in developing an individualized program for the prospective buyer.

24. Local governments can support Home Possible and participating lenders by providing downpayment assistance, closing cost assistance, and funds to temporarily buy down mortgage note rates. Temporary subsidy buy-downs can increase a borrower's buying power by as much as 30 percent. Military families and public safety personnel can benefit from the buy-down features and expanded debt-to-income ratios available through Home Possible Neighborhood Solution mortgages.

Boston Agencies Mobilize for Action, Transcend Institutional Silos

In January 2003, Boston's Department of Neighborhood Development (DND) sold a closed police station in the pricey South End neighborhood to the Boston Redevelopment Authority (BRA) for a dollar. The DND handles state and federal housing funds as well as all city-owned tax foreclosure and surplus property. The BRA is responsible for administering Boston's zoning code and primarily handles all market-rate developments.

The BRA found a private developer who acquired the property for $4 million. This money was then pledged to the Boston Housing Authority (BHA), which manages the city's public housing. The BHA used the $4 million, along with capital funds and other revenues, to gut and rehabilitate a nearby public housing complex that had fallen into disrepair, bringing 160 vacant units back on line. Meanwhile, the developer converted the old police station into 23 luxury and three affordable condos, in accordance with the city's inclusionary zoning program that requires 10 percent affordability on all dispositions of city property.

The public housing tenants returned to their new, safe homes and new neighbors. The city had a high-end residential complex generating additional tax revenues for its coffers. The neighborhood had attractive housing where there once was blight. All this was possible because agencies once operating in their own silos were working closely under the umbrella of the city's comprehensive housing plan.

Creating a Successful Comprehensive Housing Plan

11

A comprehensive approach to housing is a must for communities seeking lasting change. The steps on the housing continuum—supportive housing, public housing, rental housing, and for-sale homes—are parts of a whole, and shortages in one system can flood other systems. It would be fruitless, for example, to attempt to reduce homelessness without also preserving and expanding the supply of lowest-cost rental units, including public housing. Otherwise, every homeless person placed in a low-cost unit would reduce the supply available to other households in precarious circumstances. Similarly, it would be difficult to ease pressures in the rental market if moderate-income renters who want to buy homes cannot do so because they are priced out of homeownership.

Under a comprehensive plan, government functions are also interrelated and require coordination. It is inefficient for zoning to offer incentives for affordable housing development if city building codes are rewritten with new requirements that make construction costlier. Government actions both inside and outside of the housing department can affect housing supply and access.

In addition, a comprehensive strategy leverages resources through partnerships among public and private entities serving similar populations or facing similar needs. Engaging employers in expanding housing opportunities or using trust fund monies to draw in other investments are examples of comprehensiveness. Constructing new complexes with units for both former public housing tenants and homeless families is another.

Among the cities that look at housing comprehensively are Boston, Chicago, and New York. They are profiled below to illustrate how a comprehensive strategy can take different forms. Boston, for example, has a master plan called Leading the Way that encompasses all major housing areas and brings all key stakeholders together weekly for plan monitoring. In Chicago, separate campaigns for affordable housing production, public housing transformation, and ending homelessness operate simultaneously with mechanisms in place to help ensure that the plans work in sync. In New York, the interagency and public-private partnerships fostered by the New Housing Marketplace Plan, a $7.5 billion production plan, enhance all of the city's housing efforts. Success in all three cities is predicated on the personal engagement of the chief executive.

THE FIVE CORE ELEMENTS OF SUCCESS

1 Leadership Commitment to Clear Goals and a Deadline

Mayors Michael Bloomberg, Richard M. Daley, and Thomas M. Menino all made public statements that housing affordability was critical to their cities' futures. By committing to expanding affordable housing options and specifying how they would measure progress, they signaled that their administrations would be judged in part on their success. By publicizing the specific number of housing units that would be built and preserved by a certain date, they also enlisted other city officials, citizens, civic groups and the press in keeping the heat on.

Although the mayor is ultimately accountable for hitting the target, the city's top housing official must develop the strategies and tools to reach goals. This position must be filled by a highly capable manager and innovative thinker equipped to look beyond the rulebook if necessary. The "housing czar" should have cabinet-level or equivalent status.

While the housing czar sees the plan through, the mayor must continue to play a prominent role in bringing lender, philanthropic, and institutional partners on board. For example, Mayor Menino has successfully encouraged academic institutions to create housing (in the form of new student dorms, which open up more rental units to the community) and is now reaching out to engage medical institutions in a similar manner.

2 A Meaningful Game Plan Based on Hard Data and Guided Input

Cities have more success implementing their plans if they go through the tough process of engaging key constituencies. Many of these groups will become crucial resource partners. For example, the New York City Department of Housing and Preservation Development (HPD) designed the New Housing Marketplace Plan with input from key city agencies, and solicited input from a Neighborhood Investment Advisory Panel that included over 60 public, business, financial, and housing leaders.

At the end of 2008, Chicago will wrap up its third successive five-year affordable housing plan. From the very first phase, participants responded to the call to join in the process not solely on behalf of their parochial interests but with broad goals in mind. The planning process for the 2004–2008 strategy engaged about 40 individuals from city departments and the nonprofit and for-profit real estate industries, lenders, faith groups, homeless and housing advocates, and groups serving ethnic constituencies.

To focus the planning group's efforts, cities should provide a detailed description of the city's housing stock and demographic and market trends to identify current and future gaps in meeting needs. Where are the shortages, who is affected, and what are the environmental, economic, regulatory, and social conditions exacerbating the problem? In particular, communities must look at population growth and job generation to ensure that an increase in housing is matched by an increase in jobs, and that there is a supply of land appropriately zoned to meet the housing needs of households in all income categories.

Local academic institutions and civic organizations can help describe the landscape, as the Metropolitan Planning Council and the University of Illinois did in Chicago. Private entities are another resource. There are also numerous national data sources that can inform discussions.[1] Local and national experts can review demographic and policy trends at the local, state, and federal levels, and share what is working in other cities. Finally, by inviting the public to submit data and testimony, planners can shape their efforts and pave the way to securing the necessary political approvals.

3 A Pledge of Reliable Revenue Streams

Comprehensive plans must be supported by a reliable revenue stream or streams. Sources may include bond proceeds, trust funds, general revenues, and other funds. To establish their ambitious but achievable goals, Boston, Chicago, and New York all performed a thorough assessment of resources that could be brought to bear. They outlined in advance how much would be committed to their plans, including new as well as existing funds. In some cases, it may require a leap of faith to pledge funds not yet on hand but producible through partnerships, policy changes, and state advocacy.

At the launch of its second Leading the Way plan, Boston committed $81 million to the plan, including $56 million from ongoing local and entitlement funds, plus another $25 million in new funds to be raised through property sales, enhanced developer contributions, and other sources. In total, Boston expects its investment to leverage another $700 million in other public and private investments.[2]

New York's $7.5 billion New Housing Marketplace Plan target pulls from a range of funding sources and includes leveraged funds. Key, however, is a whopping $4.4 billion from the capital budget.

To reach its target of $1.88 billion in invested and leveraged funds for 2004–2008, Chicago went beyond the usual sources to pledge increased use of tax-exempt bonds (thus generating more tax-credit equity) and tax increment financing (TIF), as well as a $100 million "resource challenge" to come up with new funding without knowing at the outset what the sources would be. In all, $153 million in city resources go into the plan, including corporate funding, TIF funds, general obligation bonds, city land write-downs, and fee waivers.

Often, the pledge of resources sets the policy agenda for the city. For example, Chicago knew that hitting its targets depended in part on successfully lobbying for a state donation tax credit and a state rental subsidy program, both of which were enacted.

---

4 Partners Organized to Act in Concert

Since the beginning of its first five year plan in the mid-1990s, Chicago's housing commissioner and Department of Housing have reported quarterly to the city council and the public. Such high-profile reporting is the quintessential organizing tool because the push toward meeting goals forces partners to bridge administrative divides. With their new interdependence, agency leaders and staff find ways to pull together, often institutionalizing their cooperation with regular meetings of key agency personnel.

Leaders should also consider making someone accountable for coordination. Chicago has appointed a housing coordinator who reports to the mayor and is charged with continually communicating with various city departments.

Within partner agencies, cultures must allow for the flow of money and real estate across agency boundaries. In some cases, restructuring may help. The Boston Department of Neighborhood Development credits greatly enhanced housing production to its control over both state and federal housing funds, as well as over city-owned tax foreclosure and surplus property. Chicago's Department of Neighborhood Development views its oversight of all HUD Continuum of Care programs as a critical tool for coordinating housing policy.

Organizing for action also entails improved coordination with state, nonprofit, and private partners. Boston, for example, restructured its funding rounds to be complete in time for the state's funding rounds, allowing developer partners to line up their financing more easily. The mayor and city leaders have also negotiated multi-year commitments from lender partners to support Leading the Way activities, including a $200 million lending commitment from Bank of America when it took over Boston-based Fleet Bank.

---

5 A Bias for Action and an Eye for Opportunity

Leaders should pursue immediate projects and opportunities rather than labor too long producing the ideal, all-inclusive comprehensive plan. Quick action toward more readily achievable subgoals conveys a sense of urgency, sets a tone of entrepreneurship, and builds confidence by producing visible results. For example, at the outset of the Leading the Way plan, Boston generated confidence in the venture by funding the speedy repair and reopening of 1,000 units of vacant public housing.

The written plan should be a framework for action, specific enough to deploy resources and guide partnerships but leaving room for brainstorming new programs and policies. The Chicago and New York plans identify the broad goal of harnessing the strength of the local real estate market, detail some of the tools that they will use to do that, and then embrace the notion of constantly thinking about new ways to leverage resources. Moderating the level of detail in the plan ensures that agencies do not spend so long drafting sections and balancing constituencies that they have no time or energy left for implementation.

Leaders must be constantly on the lookout for new opportunities. For example, Shaun Donovan, commissioner of the New York City Department of Housing Preservation and Development, has advanced the city's housing efforts by questioning old models. Donovan conceived a $230 million New York Acquisition Fund to help smaller developers compete for land, persuaded HUD to work with the city on getting foreclosed FHA properties to new owners committed to affordability, and successfully lobbied the city to require affordable housing in exchange for rezonings. New York City leaders were also able to spot a small but successful nonprofit-run homeownership rescue program that could grow to scale with city aid, which gave birth to the highly successful PACE program.

Opportunities can also be found by listening to criticism. New York City overhauled a longstanding tax break for housing developers that had been criticized for subsidizing luxury housing, with the new program delivering upwards of $700 million for affordable housing. Chicago has benefited from its relationship with the Chicago Rehab Network (CRN), whose Affordable Housing and Community Jobs campaign led to the first housing plan. CRN monitors Chicago's plan and attends city council meetings, serving as a credible, constructive critic that has the confidence of the advocacy community and a commitment to helping the city succeed. For example, it was CRN and other housing advocates that successfully lobbied the city to improve long-term affordability of assisted housing developments by creating a community land trust.

A WORD OF ENCOURAGEMENT

Comprehensiveness is not easy. It forces an examination of the problem and the setting of priorities, which can lead to conflict.

While praising the city for its progress and its increasing government transparency, the Chicago Rehab Network says the city spends far too little of its own money on housing and relies too heavily on market leverage. Other community advocates say the booming market and gentrification have already chased too many working and middle-class people to Chicago's suburbs, increasing economic segregation in the city.[3] Also on their list of actions they want the city to take is to reuse more vacant land and provide greater property tax relief.

Canvassing stakeholders in other cities would also likely generate recommendations for change. Indeed, these kinds of conversations on policy shortcomings are also happening in New York and Boston. For example, some critics say that leaders in both cities are not paying enough attention to rent control and are losing too many affordable units from the market. Others charge that artists and low-income workers who have made their homes in some of the industrial areas are being pushed out. While difficult, these conversations are better than the alternative—a neglect of affordable housing and the growing number of people who need it.

COMPREHENSIVE STRATEGIES AT WORK

1 Planning Unites Boston Agencies to Address High Housing Costs In a Built-out Environment

Boston takes a comprehensive approach to housing through the complementary activities of key city agencies brought together under the Leading the Way (LTW) plan. This goal-oriented plan addresses the full spectrum of housing needs from homelessness to homeownership. In winter 2007, the city was nearing the launch of its third LTW plan.

An inclusive process spearheaded by Mayor Thomas Menino and led by the city's chief of housing, Charlotte Golar Richie, generated the first Leading the Way plan. Prompted by the need to spend the proceeds from a major property sale, the plan committed the city to building 7,500 new housing units—including 2,100 affordable units—between July 2000 and June 2003. The plan also pledged to preserve 4,300 affordable rental units that were at risk of loss because of expiring use restrictions or financial insolvency.

Success on the three-year plan, together with ongoing housing needs, led to Leading the Way II, a four-year blueprint that committed the city to producing an additional 10,000 housing units (including 2,100 affordable units) between July 2003 and the end of June 2007. As of December 31, 2006, 10,274 new units had been permitted, of which 2,025 were affordable. Another 2,346 affordable rental units had been preserved.

Like the first plan, Leading the Way II's strategies derive from an assessment of market conditions and how actions in one area of housing affect another. With less than 10 percent of apartments affordable to the average Bostonian, Leading the Way seeks to ease some of the market pressures that keep rents high. Strategies focus on stabilizing public housing, increasing the supply of both low-cost and market-rate rental housing, and freeing up more units by helping moderate-income renters—including underserved minorities—become homeowners. Given the dwindling supply of land, the keys to the plan are preservation, increased density, and full use of public assets, including public housing.

Although the production goals get the most press, Leading the Way II also sought to promote neighborhood stability by renovating or reclaiming more than 2,000 distressed or abandoned properties; expanding sustainable homeownership by enhancing home purchase and repair assistance and by preventing foreclosures; retaining workforce housing by preserving at least 3,000 rental units, including privately owned and nonprofit-owned federally subsidized units; and launching a $10 million homelessness prevention and housing campaign.

In addition to setting clear and measurable outcomes, both LTW plans identified the local, state, and federal policy changes, public-private partnerships, and funding sources needed to reach those goals. Under Leading the Way I, Boston combined $33 million from the sale of surplus properties, with ongoing funding sources such as linkage fees[4] and CDBG and HOME monies. The second plan marshaled $56 million from the same funding sources and committed to raising another $25 million through additional property sales, an "in-lieu" fee paid by developers, a change to the linkage formula, and other sources. Ninety percent of the $81 million devoted to the plan is dedicated to programs benefiting households earning less than 80 percent of area median income. City officials expect that investment in affordable units will reach $700 million while investment in all 10,000 new units will total $3.0–3.5 billion.

Key changes made in support of the Leading the Way campaign include an Inclusionary Development Policy (IDP) requiring market-rate housing developments of more than 10 units that need zoning changes to set aside a portion of the units for affordable housing; a policy requiring all assisted rental housing projects with 10 or more units to set aside 10 percent of the units for the homeless; a new downtown overlay-zoning district that increases height limits on residential towers to make housing a more attractive investment; and the identification of about 1,000 vacant, city-owned parcels that could be transferred to affordable housing developers for a nominal fee.

The mayor has ultimate responsibility for the plan, while administrative authority resides with the chief of housing, a new cabinet-level position created in 1999. The chief of housing is the director of the Department of Neighborhood Development, which administers local, state, and federal funds for housing and community development projects and services. Other key agencies involved in executing the plan include the Boston Redevelopment Authority, the Boston Housing Authority, and the Inspection Services Department.

Agency cooperation toward a single goal is a key feature of LTW. The plan largely eliminates the "silo problem" of competing government entities because agencies must work together to meet their targets. All agencies meet every other week in the mayor's office as a means of reinforcing this cooperation. A brief look at each agency's role in Leading the Way illustrates how coordination is critical to attaining plan goals.

Department of Neighborhood Development. The DND oversees development of Leading the Way's new affordable housing units, renovations of distressed or vacant units, preservation of existing affordable units, and conversion of 300 units of unregulated rental housing into new long-term affordable housing.[5] In support of Leading the Way, the department has stepped up the rate of affordable housing production by expediting land disposition and tapping increased resources.

Unlike community development agencies in many other cities, DND manages not only the federal and state financial resources for housing, but also the sale of all city-owned tax-foreclosed and surplus property. The merging of financial and real estate resources into a single agency has been critical to creating the capacity to deliver the city's affordable housing production targets.

In addition to $25 million in LTW funds from city sources (such as municipal asset sales, income from loan funds, inclusionary revenues, and linkage fees), DND is tapping new state programs such as the Affordable Housing Trust Fund and the Transit Oriented Development Fund. Increased production in LTW II also reflects the maturation of the Inclusionary Development Policy and an increase in the on-site affordability requirement from 10 percent to 13 percent of total units.[6]

Increased affordable housing production has required better coordination of governmental and private parties so that money and real estate can easily cross agency boundaries. For example, Boston Redevelopment Authority real estate is used in DND-funded projects. DND real estate is transferred to the BRA to make private deals work. DND funds are used to rehabilitate vacant public housing units. In many cases, both the DND and BRA provide substantial discounts on land prices. Furthermore, inclusionary cash-out funds collected by the BRA are often used by the DND for everything from development subsidies to first-time homebuyer assistance. DND also structures its funding rounds to conclude in time for the state's funding rounds, allowing projects to layer funds more efficiently and preventing the state from funding projects that the city does not consider ready.

In the preservation arena, the DND may arrange and finance tenant/nonprofit buyouts, work with lawyers to enforce old tax agreements that are conditioned on affordability, broker deals with HUD to retain affordability, and provide financing for rehabilitation.

The department also runs the Boston Home Center, a one-stop housing services operation that, among other things, fields calls from homeowners late on their mortgages. In late 2006, the DND and the Home Center established a $100 million lender consortium offering refinance products to homeowners at risk of foreclosure. These "First Choice Lenders"—so designated because they agree not to originate loans that are riskier than the customer can reasonably sustain—have also made financial contributions to a foreclosure prevention fund.

The DND's Neighborhood Housing Division oversees all HUD Continuum of Care programs, helping to ensure Boston takes a housing-centered approach to the city's homelessness crisis.

The Boston Housing Authority. The BHA is the city's largest landlord, owning and managing more than 10,000 units of public housing and more than 11,000 Section 8 vouchers. It is the city's primary provider of housing for people who are homeless or at risk of becoming homeless. In fact, approximately eight out of ten available public housing units go to households in these circumstances, thanks to the BHA's policy of giving priority to people living in shelters or earning below 30 percent of area median income.

Recognizing public housing as the cornerstone of its homelessness efforts, the city contributed about $8.6 million of its own resources to help the BHA repair and reopen 1,000 units of vacant public housing during the first Leading the Way plan. This effort helped the BHA raise its occupancy rate to about 98 percent.

To help sustain that accomplishment, the authority plans to use HUD's Capital Fund Financing program to generate more than $70 million for capital repairs to public housing.[7] Other public housing preservation initiatives include energy upgrades[8] and redeveloping distressed public housing sites into mixed-income communities. To provide additional housing for homeless families, the BHA provides project-based Section 8 vouchers to affordable rental housing projects spearheaded by the Department of Neighborhood Development.

The Boston Redevelopment Authority and the Inspection Services Department.
The BRA uses eminent domain and tax-advantaged bonding capabilities to coordinate redevelopment of city infill lands. Under the Leading the Way plan, the BRA works with other city departments and the private sector to produce market-rate and moderate- to middle-income units through the city's Inclusionary Development Policy. As part of this role, the BRA often assembles land into larger parcels for housing development. The agency has also been working to increase revenues from linkage fees, an important resource for affordable housing.

The Inspection Services Department (ISD), which handles city permitting processes, has streamlined permitting to boost affordable and market-rate housing production. To support LTW's homeownership preservation goal, the department launched a new Residential Assistance and Repair program that helps property owners who want to make repairs but lack the resources to do so, and condemns the distressed properties of owners who do not want to make repairs.

The ISD and BRA administer the zoning code for the city. Operationally, a developer applies for a permit at ISD, which checks for conformance with the zoning code. If in violation, the developer must get approval from the BRA before returning to the ISD, which oversees the Board of Appeal that issues zoning variances.

The Emergency Shelter Commission. The Emergency Shelter Commission works with the Department of Neighborhood Development to ensure that the city's response to homelessness (including the Continuum of Care) coordinates with

Leading the Way and vice versa. The continuum is housing-centered, with a focus on creating or expanding permanent affordable housing over emergency or transitional housing units. LTW partners support the continuum's goal of integrating housing for homeless people into neighborhoods by giving homeless people highest priority for vacant public housing. In addition, when linkage fees, CDBG, HOME, and project-based Section 8 are allocated to developments, units are made available to very low- and extremely low-income households. Nonprofit organizations have become skilled at creating high-quality housing for the homeless that enhances neighborhood revitalization, also in line with LTW.

LTW commits the city to working with the Emergency Shelter Commission and partners on prevention. In 2006, the Boston Homelessness Prevention Center opened with $1 million of city funds matched with $1 million of Fireman Family Foundation funds. The center provides one-stop service to people facing homelessness and matches clients with one of more than 30 homelessness prevention programs operating in Boston. The center also offers emergency funds to clients whose needs are met by existing services.[9]

The city's Rental Housing Resource Center serves as a resource for tenant-landlord mediation and preservation efforts for Boston's dwindling supply of low-income lodging houses.

Mayoral leadership. The mayor plays a valuable role in bringing lender, philanthropic, and institutional partners on board. For example, colleges and universities have created the equivalent of almost 1,000 new apartments through new dormitory construction, returning hundreds of rental units to the market. Efforts are under way to encourage expanded housing efforts by academic and medical institutions. In addition, lenders have entered multi-year partnerships with the city, including a $200 million commitment from Bank of America.

For more information on Boston's plan, see *Leading the Way II: Pre-Completion Report* at **www.cityofboston.gov**.

2 Adverse Beginnings in Chicago Evolve into Synchronized Leadership

Rather than one all-encompassing housing plan, Chicago has three major plans operating in sync through the leadership of the mayor and key agency chiefs. The individual plans focus on affordable housing production and preservation, rehabilitation of public housing, and homelessness prevention.

"Build, Preserve, Lead" is the Chicago Department of Housing's plan of action for 2004–2008. The plan calls for leveraging $153 million in direct city resources into roughly $1.9 billion of public and private investment to create and preserve 48,000 affordable housing units.[10] This is the third of Chicago's five-year plans, which in total had expended about $3.7 billion and assisted about 112,000 units as the end of 2006.

The first plan grew from calls for the city to spend more of its own resources on affordable housing. After advocates won passage of an ordinance allocating city general revenues to housing, the Department of Housing worked with them to craft an implementation plan. Successive housing commissioners—Julia Stasch and then Jack Markowski—have since turned the process into a more positive, cooperative effort by initiating the planning and convening the relevant constituencies.

The Chicago Housing Authority's $1.6 billion, 15-year plan to rebuild or rehabilitate 25,000 public housing units also had its origins in adversity.[11] The CHA emerged from federal receivership in the late 1990s. Having successfully taken over the Chicago public school system in the mid-1990s, Mayor Richard M. Daley pursued similar leadership of public housing. He appointed CHA board members reporting to then-chief of staff Julia Stasch to help convene tenant groups and other public housing stakeholders in developing the CHA's Plan for Transformation.

Chicago's Plan to End Homelessness, which grew out of a national movement and launched in 2003, was developed by the Department of Human Services and the Chicago Continuum of Care. Primary responsibility for the plan has since moved to the Department of Housing, in line with the plan's "housing first" approach to ending homelessness by getting people into permanent, stable housing where their other needs can be met. A closer review of the three plans reveals how closely they interrelate.

The Affordable Housing Plan. The 2004–2008 plan seeks to ensure that working families, young professionals, people with disabilities, senior citizens, and other vulnerable populations are left with housing opportunities amid the city's ongoing renewal. Although the homeownership rate in the city increased from 41 percent to 44 percent in the 1990s, 73,000 Chicago homeowners were paying more than 30 percent of their incomes for housing. More than 225,000 renters faced smilar housing cost burdens.

Inclusionary housing and density bonuses. Since the launch of its five-year planning processes, Chicago has created two inclusionary housing programs. The voluntary Chicago Partnership for Affordable Neighborhoods (CPAN) program, launched in 2002, allows condominium developers in appreciating neighborhoods to build at higher densities and obtain fee waivers and site improvements in exchange for setting aside at least 10 percent of the units affordable to households making up to 100 percent of area median income.

The 2003 Affordable Requirements Ordinance (ARO) requires developers of projects of 10 or more units receiving reduced-priced city land or city financial assistance to set aside 10 percent and 20 percent of the units, respectively, for affordable housing. As of January 2007, the CPAN and ARO programs had created 1,331 affordable units in market-rate developments. Since its inception in 2004, a Downtown Density Bonus program offering additional square footage to downtown residential builders who contribute to the city's Affordable Housing Fund has also generated about $24 million in fees for neighborhood housing development and rental subsidies.

Tax increment financing. Chicago uses tax increment financing (TIF) to capture some of the windfall in property tax revenues from hot markets to support affordable housing projects.[12] Between 1994 and the end of 2006, Chicago had spent more than $200 million in TIF revenues on projects to create or improve nearly 8,000 affordable housing units. TIF funds in the form of grants, loans, upfront financing, and mortgage interest subsidies support new housing construction and rehabilitation, including units built under the city's Affordable Requirements Ordinance.

TIF funds have helped the city make greater use of its tax-exempt bonding authority. Financings using both tax-exempt bonds and four-percent tax credits are generally not subject to the same funding cycles or competitions required for nine-percent credits. Because the credits are worth less, developers face larger funding gaps that TIF funds can help to close.

State legislation. Chicago's five-year plans have always challenged city officials to look for new revenue sources, including from the state. This mindset has produced two major pieces of state legislation that support plan goals. In effect as of 2002, the Illinois Affordable Housing Tax Credit provides donors with a $0.50 state income tax credit for every dollar invested in a qualified housing activity. Of the more than $13 million in credits available statewide each year, $2 million is set aside for employer-assisted housing that serves households earning up to 120 percent of area median income. This law helped to inspire the proposed federal Housing America's Workforce Act.

The Department of Housing and its partners also successfully advocated for a statewide rental subsidy program that has enabled the city to expand its Low Income Housing Trust Fund, which serves households earning up to 30 percent of area median income. The city program, which had relied on city corporate funds, will now receive about $10 million annually from the Illinois Rental Housing Support Program, doubling the number of households served.[13]

Preservation. A range of privately leveraged resources supports a broad array of production and preservation programs. In the preservation arena, programs include the Troubled Buildings Initiative, which acquires and delivers rental complexes to new owners for repairs; the Historic Chicago Bungalow Initiative, which encourages investment in the Chicago bungalow, a defining structure in many of the city's neighborhoods; several home repair and rehabilitation programs; and programs such as Mark-to-Market, which preserve and extend the affordability of project-based Section 8 properties.

To ensure the long-term affordability of new units, the city uses deed restrictions and developer agreements. Going forward, city staff will review all subsidized projects for possible transfer to the Chicago Community Land Trust. Established in 2006, the trust acquires and retains ownership of land under properties, removing land from the cost of housing. Long-term lease agreements cap the resale prices.

In 2003, the city and nonprofit Neighborhood Housing Services launched the Home Ownership Preservation Initiative (HOPI) to work with lenders and servicers to promote best practices, and to offer financial counseling and loan workouts to families at risk of foreclosure. As of July 2006, HOPI had helped about 1,300 families avoid foreclosure. In addition it had reclaimed 330 vacant properties from foreclosure and rehabilitated them for affordable housing.

Key partnerships. The city council, other city and state agencies, nonprofit and for-profit affordable housing developers, and lenders all play important roles. As just one example, the City Department of Planning and Development creates the tax increment financing districts, which the city council must approve. Another example is the multi-agency collaboration arising from code enforcement and subsequent land disposition.

Consider Chicago's takeover and resale of 1,100 units of distressed private housing subsidized by the Section 8 program. Under the Troubled Buildings Initiative, city inspections unearthed 1,800 code violations at 104 apartment buildings in North Lawndale and helped to instigate HUD foreclosure proceedings against the two owners. HUD sold the foreclosed developments to the city for a total of $20. To save the housing, the city distributed the parcels among 23 community-based for-profit, nonprofit, and faith-based developers who agreed to rehabilitate the properties within two years and keep the units affordable for 20 years. HUD provided $33.5 million for renovations. The Community Investment Corporation in Chicago, a pooled-risk mortgage lender, temporarily took title of the properties from HUD and completed the closings with competitively selected buyers. CIC is overseeing the new owners' ongoing compliance with HUD guidelines.

How The Plans Interrelate. Under the Chicago Ten-Year Plan to End Homelessness, public funds are redirected to create a system that quickly moves homeless people and families into appropriate, permanent, and affordable housing. In 2006, more than 6,900 households were able to avoid the shelter system—twice as many as in

2003 when the plan was launched. By the end of 2006, the city had also replaced 1,900 emergency shelter beds with more than 1,500 permanent housing units and more than 1,500 interim housing units.

The Department of Housing's efforts to expand and preserve low-income rental housing and provide rental subsidies for the lowest-income residents support this goal. Significantly, the department is part of an interagency partnership that, at the mayor's behest, has been producing single-room occupancy (SRO) units with support services since 1999. The partnership expanded in 2002 with a $100 million, five-year plan to create or rehabilitate more than 1,600 SRO and 90 family housing units with supportive services.

Housing and homelessness leaders realized they could not rely exclusively on new development to create all the units needed to end homelessness. That prompted the coalition that successfully lobbied state government to create the statewide rental subsidy program mentioned earlier.

The supportive housing initiative also aligns with Chicago Housing Authority's plan to transform severely distressed public housing high-rises into mixed-use, mixed-income neighborhoods. City and CHA staff realized that both homeless people and some CHA residents displaced during renovations share common challenges, such as substance abuse, that make it hard for them to sustain their housing. The city is identifying sites near CHA redevelopment areas. Under the partnerships, DOH works with the Illinois Housing Development Authority (IHDA) to provide construction financing, while the Department of Human Services funds supportive services. The CHA commits project-based Section 8 vouchers to provide an ongoing subsidy for half of the units, with McKinney-Vento funding the rest.

The Department of Housing also plays a key role in the development of communities being built on public housing sites. DOH commits about half of its annual resources for multifamily rental development (primarily tax credits and secondary financing) to those communities. Each year, DOH allocates about $2.7 million in federal Low-Income Housing Tax Credits to help finance affordable rental units at CHA sites and approximately $15–20 million of HOME/CDBG loan funds. The Illinois Housing Development Authority has also provided annual allocations of tax credits of up to $3 million for public housing redevelopment projects. Other sources of funding for the affordable and market-rate units include additional state loan funds from IHDA, the Illinois Affordable Housing Tax Credit (often referred to as the donation tax credit), TIF monies, conventional bank debt, and Federal Home Loan Bank Board Affordable Housing Program funds.

The city provides critical support to public housing transformation by investing more than $500 million in infrastructure in and around the new communities and mobilizing other public agencies to support the plan. For example, the City Department of Planning and Development has created a significant number of tax increment financing districts in areas of public housing. In addition, the Chicago Public Schools are creating charter and magnet schools for the communities. Other supporting entities include the Chicago Park District, Chicago Public Library, Chicago Transit Authority, and water management and environment departments. Counting public agencies, foundations, academic institutions, lenders, and other private entities, the CHA has more than 150 partners supporting the plan. Total investment in the new mixed-income communities should approach $4.5 billion. By the end of 2006, the CHA had rehabilitated or replaced nearly 15,300 units or about 60 percent of its goal. Neighborhoods around CHA construction sites are improving, and developers are investing in residential and commercial projects near the mixed-income communities.

The intense interdepartmental coordination has become institutionalized in the form of monthly meetings among the departments, ensuring that the new communities get critical facilities such as libraries. Coordination also ensures the incorporation of supportive housing and seniors housing, in keeping with a five-year senior housing plan launched by the Department of Housing in 2006. That plan calls for the creation of 4,000 new senior housing units of all types in areas with the greatest need by 2010.

To apply this kind of coordination to the city's broader housing efforts, the mayor's office has created a new position of interagency housing coordinator. The coordinator is charged with ensuring cooperation among the various housing plans and reaching out to other departments to identify how their proposed policy changes might have an impact on housing.

....

For more information on Chicago's plan, see *Build, Preserve, Lead: A Housing Agenda for Chicago's Neighborhoods, Affordable Housing Plan 2004–2008,* **egov.cityofchicago.org.** Commissioner Markowski's presentation of the plan at the National Housing Conference 75th Anniversary Policy Summit in October 2006 is available at **www.nhc.org.**

---

3 In New York, Cooperation Around Nation's Largest-Ever Production Plan Extends to Other City Departments

New York City's $7.5 billion New Housing Marketplace Plan aims to use creative financing from public-private partnerships to produce and preserve 165,000 units of affordable housing between 2004 and 2013. Mayor Michael Bloomberg launched the plan to help ensure that the city remains competitive and enjoys continued growth. Like Chicago's Affordable Housing Plan, the New Housing Marketplace Plan focuses on housing production and is spearheaded by the city housing department. The agency cooperation fostered by this comprehensive production plan enhances coordination of the city's other housing efforts as well.

New Housing Marketplace identifies four key strategies that the city's Department of Housing Preservation and Development (HPD) and its partners must pursue to reach the production goals. As commissioner of HPD, Shaun Donovan helped craft the plan's market-based approach and leads the effort to ensure the plan's success.

Find new land. The first strategy is to find new land for affordable housing through rezonings, interagency partnerships, land banking, and other tools. Rezonings of underutilized manufacturing districts and underbuilt avenues near transportation nodes to allow residential development, and of residential areas to allow greater densities, are in effect creating "new" land for thousands of housing units.

Donovan and the HPD are also collaborating with other city and state agencies to access land for projects expected to create more than 20,000 units of housing by 2013. HPD and the New York City Housing Authority (NYCHA), the city's public housing agency, are planning projects for underutilized NYCHA-owned sites—for example, by moving parking spaces underground to clear land for housing. HPD provides Low-Income Housing Tax Credits to help finance the projects, while construction loans come through the Housing Development Corporation (HDC), which issues bonds for multifamily affordable rental and cooperative housing.

The HPD/NYCHA/HDC partnership alone is expected to produce nearly 6,000 units of low-income affordable housing. As of early 2007, several joint projects involving nearly 1,000 units were under way. HPD is also working with the Housing Partnership Development Corporation[14] to create a land bank that would acquire private parcels for redevelopment into affordable housing.

Encourage new housing affordable to a range of incomes. The second strategy creates incentives to develop housing for households with a range of incomes, including income groups outside the 30–60 percent of area median income traditionally served by HPD programs. Over the course of the New Housing Marketplace Plan, HPD expects to generate 22,000 units of housing for New Yorkers with annual incomes between $50,000 and $100,000. This Middle Class Housing Initiative dovetails with efforts to redevelop New York City Housing Authority sites, adding a middle-income component to some of those projects.

To support the initiative, the New York City Housing Development Corporation updated its New Housing Opportunities program, which finances rental complexes for moderate- and middle-income households in the outer boroughs with taxable bonds and corporate reserves. In addition, HDC launched a mixed-income program that is financing rental housing for low- and middle-income families.

In part to support the city's plan to reduce overall homelessness by two-thirds by 2009, the New Housing Marketplace Plan designates roughly $70 million of Housing Trust Fund monies over three years to subsidize production of about 2,000 units affordable to households below 30 percent of area median income and between 60 percent and 80 percent of area median income. The city's broader homelessness plan, Uniting for Solutions Beyond Shelter, focuses on both prevention and getting homeless people into permanent housing. The $1 billion New York/New York III agreement, also part of the New Housing Marketplace Plan, supports the Uniting for Solutions goal of creating 12,000 new housing units for the homeless. New York/New

York commits the city and state to jointly finance development of 9,000 new units of supportive housing for the chronically homeless and other vulnerable populations.

Harness the private market. Like Chicago, New York City is encouraging the private sector to create housing through property tax incentives, low-cost city-owned land, and density bonuses through inclusionary zonings. Developers benefiting from higher densities through rezoning of formerly industrial lands or from upzoning of residential areas must set aside a portion of the projects for units at varying levels of affordability. By leveraging other supports such as city, state, and federal subsidies and tax benefits, the city is able to increase the percentage of affordable housing required to obtain a density bonus. This program is expected to create 30,000 units, including 8,500 affordable units, in recently rezoned areas alone.

One noteworthy policy change made in support of the program is the revamp of the city's 421-a tax incentive program, which offers tax breaks for residential development. The new rules expand the areas in which a 20-percent affordable housing set-aside is required to obtain the tax break, and grant the longest tax breaks (25 years) only to developments that provide affordable housing. By requiring developers to build affordable units on-site or pay a fee, the program will generate about $300,000 for the New Housing Marketplace Plan. The legislation also established a $400 million Affordable Housing Trust Fund by abolishing a program that allows developers to trade certificates representing affordable housing units. Revenues will be targeted to housing programs in the city's 15 poorest districts.

The new $230 million New York City Acquisition Fund, administered by HPD, bridges the strategies of harnessing private market forces and preserving government-assisted rental housing. The fund provides early-stage acquisition loans to affordable developers through nonprofit and for-profit lenders. To create the fund, the city combined $8 million of its own dollars with $32.6 million in grants and investments from nine foundations to create a $40 million "guarantee pool." The pool is leveraging an additional $192.5 million in loans from 15 institutions.

Many developers accessing the funds are nonprofits that typically have a hard time competing for properties on the open market. These developers are using the low-cost loan funds to acquire and rehabilitate privately owned, government-assisted rental housing and other properties without having permanent financing commitments in place. Officials expect the fund to help create or preserve 30,000 affordable housing units by 2013.

Preserve government-assisted rental housing. The preservation component of the New Housing Marketplace plan includes HPD partnerships with HUD to obtain troubled FHA-insured housing at discounted rates, as well as HPD refinancing products for owners of properties subsidized under the city's Mitchell-Lama program. Owners of the 4,231 tax-credit units reaching the end of their 15-year compliance periods by 2008 are encouraged to preserve their properties with financial restructuring using four-percent tax credits combined with tax-exempt bonds or, when appropriate, other methods such as mortgage rollover or resyndication using nine-percent tax credits.

The Housing Development Corporation also supports rental production and preservation with the Low-Income Affordable Housing Marketplace Program (LAMP), created in 2003 as part of the New Housing Marketplace Plan. Through this program, tax-exempt bonds are issued and combined with HDC reserves to make low-cost loans and qualify developments for Low-Income Housing Tax Credits. As of January 2007, LAMP as well as other HDC programs had financed about 28,000 units under the NHM initiative.

Pulling it all together. New York City's plan allocates about $1.3 million to related efforts such as code enforcement, housing education, and downpayment assistance. Though not specified in the plan, the New York City Department of Buildings is working closely with public and private entities to streamline and modernize the building code. By incorporating new technologies and building practices, the updated code is expected to reduce barriers to housing development.

The city and its agencies are rallying in support of the New York City Housing Authority's aggressive plan to preserve public housing. In New York as elsewhere, the gap between operating expenses and federal reimbursement has widened. Through cost-saving measures and use of its financial reserves, the authority has maintained services, but found itself with budget deficits—$168 million in 2006 alone—that threaten the long-term viability of public housing in the city. The preservation plan, unveiled in April 2006, includes an unprecedented $100 million transitional aid package from the city, management and technological improvements, a limited rent increase for the quarter of tenants with the highest incomes, the designation of 8,400 Section 8 vouchers to previously unsubsidized apartments to preserve the units for low-income New Yorkers, and a $2 billion construction program that is now under way.

HDC helped to fund the $2 billion construction program by issuing $600 million in bonds to make a $600 million loan to the housing authority, which is using its federal capital funding stream to repay the loan. The funds are going toward roofs, boilers, and other essential repairs at complexes most in need. Aiding the preservation plan is an expected $30 million over three years in revenues from ground leases and development fees being paid to the authority for making underused sites available for affordable housing projects.

Efforts to address housing comprehensively are enhanced by having the high-level people charged with making the connections report directly to the mayor. Deputy Mayor Linda Gibbs, former commissioner of the Department of Homeless Services, oversees many social service agencies and the Commission on Economic Opportunity. Deputy Mayor Dan Doctoroff oversees HPD and other city economic development agencies. Progress on the New Housing Marketplace Plan is reported in the annual Mayor's Management Report.

Other efforts operating outside the plan also support NHM goals. For example, New York City's Preserve Assets and Community Equity (PACE) program, launched in October 2005, uses public and private dollars to target intensive education, financial counseling, legal assistance, and loan remediation to first-time homebuyers and homeowners in neighborhoods with high foreclosure rates.

New York City's comprehensive efforts are showing success. A 2006 count found that 13 percent fewer individuals were living on the streets than a year earlier. By early 2007, the city had preserved more than 30,000 housing units and created at least 20,000 new units.

For more information on New York City's plan, see *The New Housing Marketplace: Creating Housing for the Next Generation, 2004–2013,* **nyc.gov**. Commissioner Donovan's presentation on the plan at the National Housing Conference 75th Anniversary Policy Summit in October 2006 is available at **www.nhc.org**.

1. For example, both the National Low Income Housing Coalition and the National Housing Conference publish annual studies comparing local wage levels and housing costs. One central repository for Census and other data is DataPlace™ by KnowledgePlex (**www.dataplace.org**).

2. Boston's funding target is only for city-controlled cash subsidies and doesn't include such resources as tax credits or tax-exempt financing, which the other two cities do include in their resource targets.

3. United Power for Action and Justice, "Creating a City in a Garden: Changing Chicago's Housing Crisis into New Opportunities," October 12, 2006.

4. All nonresidential construction or rehabilitation projects exceeding 100,000 sq. ft. and requiring zoning relief pay a fee that goes either to the city's Neighborhood Housing Trust or the Neighborhood Jobs Trust. Developers may build housing or create job-training programs in lieu of paying the fee. The Boston Redevelopment Authority handles the contracts confirming the linkage payments. Since its inception in 1983, the NHT has committed more than $81 million in linkage funds, helping to create or preserve 6,159 affordable housing units in 115 developments.

5. A Rental Housing Acquisition Pilot helps nonprofit partners acquire and renovate previously unregulated multifamily properties and retain them as long-term affordable properties. Between 2000 and the end of 2006, DND had permitted/completed 407 units in this program.

6. The affordable set-aside must equal 15 percent of the market-rate units, which is the equivalent of 13.04 percent of total units. Other changes implemented since 2003 include a significant increase of the in-lieu fee to encourage on-site development and a significant decrease in the income ranges of households targeted (given that median incomes in the city are much lower than in the metro area).

7. Under the program, an authority or partner issues bond debt to be repaid out of future federal capital subsidies. Boston expects to close its first such transaction in August 2007.

8. As of February 2007, the BHA had completed two energy performance contracts (EPCs) totaling $17 million and will close another roughly $50 million transaction covering 15 sites later in 2007. Under an EPC, an energy services company performs upgrades in exchange for a percentage of the energy savings.

9. Guiding the center's operations is the Boston Homelessness Prevention Steering Committee, made up of advocates, service providers, and resource providers. The committee helps the center develop best-practice homelessness prevention strategies and advocate for policy changes and resources. To enhance coordination, Boston housing chief Charlotte Golar Richie and BHA executive director Sandra B. Henriquez serve on the steering committee and advise the Mayor's Homeless Planning Committee on strategies to prevent and end homelessness.

10. Funding commitments include all of the resources that the city contributes, such as city funds, general obligation bonds, the value of city land provided at low or no cost, the value of tax-credit equity allocated by the city, fee waivers, tax-exempt bond investments, CDBG and HOME dollars used to subsidize development and homebuyer or rental assistance, and tax increment financing revenues. In 1994–1998, the city pledged $750 million and actually committed $928 million. In 1999–2003, it pledged $1.3 billion and committed $1.45 billion.

11. At the plan's inception, 14 public housing complexes administered by the CHA had close to 20,000 units, but just under 9,000 were habitable and occupied. These complexes are being redeveloped and/or rehabilitated into new mixed-income communities that will contain about 8,000 public housing units and more than 14,000 affordable and market-rate rental

and homeownership units. The plan will also rehabilitate more than 17,000 scattered-site, senior, and family housing units. For a breakdown of units before and after transformation, see "Transforming Chicago's Public Housing: FY2007 Moving to Work Annual Plan," **thecha.org/transformplan/files/2006_final_chapter_1.pdf**.

12. Under TIF financing, a city government designates the boundaries of a redevelopment district. New tax revenues generated by rising property values flow to the TIF district. To jump-start redevelopment, the district sometimes issues bonds backed by the future revenue stream to finance projects and infrastructure improvements.

13. The Illinois Rental Housing Support Program is funded by an additional $10 fee on the recording of real estate documents and is administered by the Illinois Housing Development Authority. Enacted in 2005, it is expected to provide approximately $25 million annually in rental subsidies to about 5,500 households statewide.

14. The Housing Partnership Development Corporation is an intermediary providing technical and financial assistance to affordable and workforce housing developers, home maintenance instruction, and homeownership counseling. Since its establishment in 1982, the Housing Partnership has developed more than 30,000 affordable homeownership and rental units throughout the five boroughs and leveraged more than $2.6 billion in private sector financing.

INDEX OF LOCAL PROGRAMS

INDEX OF STATE PROGRAMS

Kimball Hill Homes

Kimball Hill Homes is a recognized leader in the building industry and winner of numerous awards for communities, designs and quality construction. Founded in 1939, integrity in all facets of construction has been the hallmark of each new Kimball Hill home. Based in Rolling Meadow Illinois, the company currently builds in nine states in 14 major markets that include Chicago, Houston, Dallas–Ft. Worth. Austin, Tampa, Sarasota-Bradenton, Naples, Cleveland, Las Vegas, Sacramento, Stockton, Portland, Vancouver, and Milwaukee. Kimball Hill currently ranks as the nation's 25th largest builder.

The National Housing Endowment

The National Housing Endowment was established in 1987 by the National Association of Home Builders to provide a permanent source of funds to address long-term industry concerns. The Endowment seeks to build a better future for housing through its funding of programs that promote industry education and training, support housing research, recognize achievements in residential construction, and encourage industry and community partnerships. To date, the National Housing Endowment has awarded almost $5 million in grants for housing-related initiatives worldwide.

Freddie Mac

Freddie Mac is a stockholder-owned corporation chartered by congress in 1970 to create a continuous flow of funds to mortgage lenders in support of homeownership and rental housing. Freddie Mac purchases mortgages from lenders and packages them into securities that are sold to investors. Over the years, Freddie Mac has made home possible for one in six homebuyers and two million renters across America.

CityView

CityView's mission is to create the highest quality housing for America's working families. CityView provides an attractive project financing alternative for experienced homebuilders and developers who demonstrate a commitment to quality and want a long-term, multiple project relationship.

Federal Home Loan Bank of New York

The mission of the Federal Home Loan Bank of New York is to advance housing opportunity and local community development by maximizing the capacity of community-based member-lenders to serve their markets. The Home Loan Bank helps community lenders in New Jersey, New York, Puerto Rico, and the U.S. Virgin Islands advance housing and community growth and is part of the congressionally chartered, nationwide Federal Home Loan Bank System, which was created in 1932 to provide a flexible credit liquidity source for members engaged in home mortgage and neighborhood lending.

JOINT CENTER FOR HOUSING STUDIES

The Joint Center for Housing Studies is Harvard University's center for information and research on housing in the United States. The Joint Center analyzes the dynamic relationships between housing markets and economic, demographic, and social trends, providing leaders in government, business, and the non-profit sector with the knowledge needed to develop effective policies and strategies. The Center produces the annual *State of the Nation's Housing* report, and is a collaborative unit affiliated with the Harvard Graduate School of Design and the Kennedy School of Government.

ORDERING INFORMATION

To order additional copies please contact:

Angela Flynn
The Joint Center for Housing Studies
Harvard University
1033 Massachusetts Avenue, 5th Floor
Cambridge, MA 02138

phone	617.495.7908
fax	617.496.0911
email	angela_flynn@harvard.edu
web	www.jchs.harvard.edu